# WOMEN, GENDER AND HISTORY IN INDIA

*Women, Gender and History in India* examines Indian history through a thematic lens of women and gender across different contexts.

Through an inter-disciplinary approach, Nita Kumar uses sources from literature, folklore, religion, and art to discuss historical and anthropological ways of interpreting the issues surrounding women and gender in history. As part of the scholarly movement away from a Grand Narrative of South Asian history and culture, this volume places emphasis on the diversity of women and their experiences. It does this by including analyses of many different primary sources together with discussion around a wide variety of theoretical and methodological debates – from the mixed role of colonial law and education to the conundrum of a patriarchy that worships the Goddess while it strives to keep women in subservience.

This textbook is essential reading for those studying Indian history and women and gender studies.

**Nita Kumar** is Professor Emerita, Claremont McKenna College, California, and Honorary Director, NIRMAN, Varanasi. Her research includes the history and anthropology of education, children, women, artisans, and Banaras. Her publications include *The Artisans of Banaras* (1988), *Friends, Brothers, and Informants* (1992), *Lessons from Schools* (2000), and *The Politics of Gender, Communities, and Modernity* (2007).

# Gender History Around the Globe

**Women, Gender and History in India**
*Nita Kumar*

# WOMEN, GENDER AND HISTORY IN INDIA

*Nita Kumar*

LONDON AND NEW YORK

Designed cover image: Two graphics on streetside of the Goddesses
Durga and Kali; a woman worker cycling to work in the front. Photo by
Nita Kumar.

First published 2024
by Routledge
4 Park Square, Milton Park, Abingdon, Oxon OX14 4RN

and by Routledge
605 Third Avenue, New York, NY 10158

*Routledge is an imprint of the Taylor & Francis Group, an informa business*

© 2024 Nita Kumar

The right of Nita Kumar to be identified as author of this work has been
asserted in accordance with sections 77 and 78 of the Copyright, Designs
and Patents Act 1988.

All rights reserved. No part of this book may be reprinted or reproduced
or utilised in any form or by any electronic, mechanical, or other
means, now known or hereafter invented, including photocopying and
recording, or in any information storage or retrieval system, without
permission in writing from the publishers.

*Trademark notice*: Product or corporate names may be trademarks or
registered trademarks, and are used only for identification and explanation
without intent to infringe.

*British Library Cataloguing-in-Publication Data*
A catalogue record for this book is available from the British Library

Library of Congress Cataloging-in-Publication Data
Names: Kumar, Nita, 1951- author.
Title: Women, gender and history in India / Nita Kumar.
Description: Abingdon, Oxon ; New York, NY : Routledge, 2023. | Series:
  Gender history around the globe | Includes bibliographical references
  and index.
Identifiers: LCCN 2022061065 (print) | LCCN 2022061066 (ebook) |
  ISBN 9781138301610 (pbk) | ISBN 9781138301603 (hbk) | ISBN
  9781003393252 (ebk)
Subjects: LCSH: Women—India—History. | Feminism—India—History.
Classification: LCC HQ1742 .K853 2023 (print) | LCC HQ1742
  (ebook) | DDC 305.40954—dc23/eng/20230209
LC record available at https://lccn.loc.gov/2022061065
LC ebook record available at https://lccn.loc.gov/2022061066

ISBN: 978-1-138-30160-3 (hbk)
ISBN: 978-1-138-30161-0 (pbk)
ISBN: 978-1-003-39325-2 (ebk)

DOI: 10.4324/9781003393252

Typeset in Bembo
by Apex CoVantage, LLC

# CONTENTS

*Preface* vii

Introduction 1

1 Gender in South Asia 10
   *Bibliography 21*

2 Ancient India 25
   *Bibliography 42*

3 Buddhism and the Emergence of Hinduism:
   The Maurya and Gupta Periods 46
   *Bibliography 57*

4 The Delhi Sultanate and Mughal Dynasties 59
   *Bibliography 74*

5 The Colonial Period: Changes in Work Roles 75
   *Bibliography 89*

6 The Colonial Period: Changes in Socialisation and Education 92
   *Bibliography 104*

7　The Colonial Period Into the Present: Marriage, Widowhood, Reform　107

*Bibliography 124*

8　Nationalism and Partition　128

*Bibliography 141*

9　Gender, Women, and Hinduism　143

*Bibliography 157*

10　Gender, Women, and Islam　160

*Bibliography 173*

11　Sexuality, Films, and the Arts　176

*Bibliography 190*

*Index*　*194*

# PREFACE

As a privileged daughter of liberal parents getting a top-notch education and left free to roam in her imagination on the basis of her reading and travels, I was uncomfortable to discover in my teenage, not so much that I was not equal to men, but that I was not the "subject" of "history." For myself, I could rant and revolt, but the real challenge was that I could not piece together the larger problem. It was "the problem that has no name" twice over – women seemed to have the problem, starting with my own mother and all my female relatives, with no exceptions; and *then* I seemed to have the problem of not being able to pinpoint *their* problem, which was, by some ironic play of solidarity and empathy, mine as well.

"Women," "gender," "female," "male," and "feminism" – these are all difficult terms because they rely on definitions that they set out to overthrow. "The problem that has no name" just happens to be a phrase I always liked since I encountered it: evocative, elusive, and profoundly accurate, all at the same time. It is not a phrase that sums up women's situation. In its American version, it refers to the sense of inertia and purposelessness felt by American suburban women in the 1960s when they found that, in the middle of a fast-paced world, armed with intelligence, energy, and a fine education, they were not really meant to do anything in life but the bare minimum of childcare and housework which would supposedly exhaust their mental and psychic resources and give them ample rewards to feel fulfilled in life (Friedan, 1963). As Meera Kosambi and others have pointed out, there is a specifically Indian version of this problem, exemplified in many works about many protagonists, for instance, the Marathi film *Umbaratha*. Sulabha, who is

> young, intelligent, and sensitive . . . has been reduced to inactivity within the suffocating atmosphere of her affluent marital family. An array of servants takes care of all the housework; her childless sister-in-law appropriates

> the mothering of her daughter; her husband remains preoccupied with his career, and the mother-in-law immerses herself in the sort of 'charity work' which is culturally mandated for elite women.
>
> *(Kosambi, 2007, p. 3)*

The title translates as "threshold" and is particularly relevant as "the woman's problem" in that it is multiple and invisible and affects all women of a certain class. Numerous critics have pointed out that Friedan's wonderful study ignores and therefore silences working-class women and women of colour. *Umbaratha* too leaves out mention of working-class and lower-caste women. Fortunately, by now, we have insightful and evocative writings on the situation of working-class, Dalit women, as well as men and persons of the third gender, *in* India.

For all the data they have provided through the dignity and rootedness they have displayed that kept me always aware of the intricacies of power, I thank my mother, Suniti; my grandmother, Malti; and my many aunts and great-aunts; and then those of my generation and the next, especially Irfana and Nandini. Many men in the roles of kin, friends, and staff have helped me too, if indirectly, and I simply cannot list them all here. I mention the women because they all strain against any simplistic definitions of themselves as "women" or work within predictable norms of gender, which is one of the themes of this book.

That one could learn as much as I have just from the process of daily living underscores the uncompromising value that feminism places on practice. I cannot emphasise enough how just thinking of the life of one of the senior women above sharpens a hesitant ability to see "women" not as victims, oppressed, or unfortunate, but as immensely multi-layered, complex, bursting with intelligence and energy. To think of my peers or my daughters as "women" is more challenging still. What could it mean?

In that sense, I have been waiting all my scholarly life to write this book. I am probably still as far from naming anything, and making a theoretical contribution is not the scope of this book. But I hope to have presented here glimpses of the convoluted histories of women in South Asia and to have suggested ways of interpreting these that in turn may open up for readers equally diverse ways into more questions and investigations. This book is planned to be introductory and suggestive, rather than conclusive.

I owe thanks to both my professional home, Claremont McKenna College, and my home in India, NIRMAN and Vidyashram – the Southpoint School. In their different ways, they have sustained me and inspired me. My colleagues are too numerous to name and will all, hopefully, recognise their influence on me in the writing.

# INTRODUCTION

"The problem that has no name." There are in fact many problems and they do have names, indeed, many names. Some of the names used in South Asian history are "the Women's Question," "Colonial Constructions," "Orientalism," and "Caste." It is the purpose of this book to discuss some of these as we already know them from the work of scores of scholars and to attempt interpretations of my own from my research and others' over the years, and to also simply tell stories from South Asian history as self-revealing narratives.

There is a rough kind of agreement by those who survey the literature that feminist studies fall into four approaches. We will look at them below. At the same time, the scholars this book relies on do not always argue strictly according to theoretical perspectives that are otherwise more or less recognised as distinct. Therefore, it would be more realistic for our purposes to blur the boundaries between the arguments and narratives that follow in this book. Many scholars prefer to be not categorical in their theorisation; some assert that they are not interested in theorisation. Nor are all of them feminists. However, let us make a simple survey of feminist perspectives.

The first and most common of feminist approaches is liberal feminism. Rooted in the Enlightenment values of reason and individualism, a liberal feminist approach accepts a mind-body dualism based on the presumption that an individual is capable of rational action, and that *that* is the way to achieve ultimate prosperity and happiness. If all this has applied only to men so far, it should, and can, apply to women. Women's struggle, in this perspective, is for a gender parity where women are like men, earning equally, active in the public sphere, with similar autonomy and freedom (in an idealised sense, since men are themselves hardly autonomous or free). In the West, liberal feminism has been about individual rights for women.

In India the rights argument becomes complicated. On the one hand, given the Indian Constitution and other efforts at modernisation, Indian feminists also argue for women's claims to individual rights, as, for instance, in equal pay for equal work (Gandhi & Shah, 1991), liberal education (Chanana, 1988), control over land and property (Agarwal, 1994). On the other hand, anyone who has worked with women is aware that there are other concepts and "rights," rooted in community, religion, and locality, that give other rights and responsibilities. The whole idea of "human" rights is questionable as a particular stream of Western philosophical thought (Tharu, 1995) and further becomes suspect as an idea coming from a West itself guilty of denying human rights. As a result, instead of one dominant approach in South Asia, as liberalism is in the West, there are several different quasi-liberal movements and approaches (Kumar, 1993).

A second popular approach in feminism is one labelled "essentialism." Women are given other definitions than those given to them by patriarchal ideologies, and positive qualities that are uniquely feminine are attributed to them. Certain mythological heroines, such as Sita or Draupadi, may be understood conservatively as docile wives and helpmeets. They are, in this other vision, the essence of earth, fire, and so on, meaning determination, grit, and nurture. Vandana Shiva (1988), an eco-feminist, argues that women have a "natural" closeness to environmental concerns and practices, and their skills and, often, livelihoods, are sacrificed because they are not recognised in developmental modernity. Kakar (1988) and Nandy (1988) are psychologists who believe that women have a specific nature, "womanliness," that may be studied and understood, and, as by Gandhi, be strategically used.

Socialist feminism is a third approach, related, as its name suggests, to Marxism, built on a foundation of Marxist understanding about the primacy of the means and relations of production. Socialist feminists part company with mainstream Marxism when the latter argues that only the division into classes is primary and every other analysis and struggle must follow after the class struggle is over. Socialist feminists want to give primacy to gender as well as class, which means often shifting the focus from the public to the private realm, from paid work to unpaid domestic work. Women are still participants in the labour force (Kalpagam, 1994; Mieis & Shiva, 1993), but they are also housewives, and the distinction of paid and unpaid work by women, often blurred to their detriment, should be clearly recognised.

Radical feminism is an approach that gives primacy to gender as the tool of oppression. It seeks to question the bases of patriarchy and unpack patriarchal discourses, starting with the very definitions of "male" and "female." One could feel tempted to put many of the writings of South Asian feminists within this approach, except that they may not be as comfortable with that as we might imagine. Those who work on religion, for instance, would argue that they were doing a close hermeneutics of their texts and that it is their texts, including rituals and practices, that are themselves free of the stereotypical binaries of (Western) patriarchy. Almost all the scholars of Hinduism and Islam discussed in this book would claim this.

Finally, postmodern feminism seeks to shake the power of the "Centre" or any one dominant narrative or "Grand Narrative." In this approach, diversity is stressed, and multiple locations and points of view are emphasised. The narrative of the colonial state and its legal apparatus is dislodged (Singha, 1998), colonial patriarchy and collusion with Indian patriarchy are deconstructed (Mani, 1990; Sinha, 1997), the constructions of colonial history and nationalist reactions are picked apart (Chakravarti, 1990; Chatterjee, 1990), and the body and experience of the woman are emphasised instead (Pandey, 2001; Sarkar, 2000). The writing by the Subaltern Studies collective of South Asia could also be seen as characterised by this approach. The writers themselves, however, use a variety of nuanced interpretations in their writings, are not strictly a collective, and on the whole are not very interested in gender. Often, other scholars have teased out the implications of their writings (Spivak, 1988), and essays by feminists have been included in their volumes (Visweswaran, 1996). The main critique of postmodernism in general is also applicable in particular to postmodern feminist writings: there is a loss of focus, especially on politics and activism. When many positions are tenable, if not every, then the women's or the feminist one is not privileged. Action is difficult to formulate and problems and issues become multi-layered and contingent. From a feminist perspective, there should be a focus on women's subjectivity and agency, to the extent that, undeterred by missing and ambiguous data, we *presume* that there has been throughout history such a push for subjecthood by women (Anagol, 2005, Kumar, 1994).

With this overall context of intellectual approaches to women and gender, I want to now give a brief introduction to each chapter in this book.

In Chapter 1 we go into a discussion of what is "gender" and what is "history" in South Asia. Almost all feminist scholars agree that gender is a socially constructed definition of what it means to be a woman and a man. It is a fundamental category of analysis in social history. Women and men are divided, however, not only by the theoretical differences that we have surveyed earlier but by their locations, in terms of ethnicity, race, or nationality, including historical experience with colonialism and class. In Chapter 1, we look briefly at what is in common between South Asian and other feminist histories, and then we look in more detail at the differences. These differences are twofold. One has to do with "History": is there a difference in the way South Asians conceptualise history, and how do we access that different kind of history? Answers range from searching for vernacular and oral histories to visualising the home as archive and looking counter-intuitively at sites of powerlessness. The colonial experience complicates the different construction of History in South Asia. The second difference may be put together from the work of anthropologists, and literary and religious history scholars: what are particularly South Asian ideas about sexuality and mothering, agency and individual rights, and power and performance? The chapter ends with a case for an inter-disciplinary approach, such as that used in this book. Insofar as this is a moving away from a Grand Narrative of South Asian history and of South Asian culture, and placing an emphasis on the experience of women, and the diversity of experience, it leans towards – to evoke our "perspectives" discussion above – a postmodern approach.

Chapter 2 deals with three periods in Ancient India: the Indus Valley Civilisations, the Vedic period, and the Vedantic and Epic, or later Vedic period. The Indus Valley period leaves us almost with as many questions unanswered as answered, and many of these concern gender. We simply do not have enough data to say conclusively how gender worked. The Vedic period is a site of contemporary disputes regarding the role of women, but what is certain is the importance of sexuality, the centrality of desire, and the conundrum of asceticism, or celibacy. As we get into the Upanishads, the dilemma of this world being feminine and therefore being shunned by ascetics becomes one in which women seldom have the last word, though sometimes they do. In the epics, *Ramayana* and *Mahabharata*, we look at several kinds of women, the unmarried mother, the virgin, the temptress, the domesticated family member, the ascetic, trying to tease out the implications of "woman."

In Chapter 3, we discuss sources to see what we have and what we wish we had. The picture of the historical periods of this chapter, the Buddhist and the Gupta periods, is one of a slight deterioration in the conditions of women, as some of an earlier flexibility in gender relations is lost. We know tangentially about several kinds of women, including queens, courtesans, nuns, missionaries, city residents, and anonymous women with no written histories. We know about the aggressive patriarchal, paternalistic states. We can worry both about how to expand our data – maybe by using sources such as oral and folklore imaginatively? – and about how to enlarge our interpretations, of possible gender boundaries and meanings.

Chapter 4 surveys the Sultanate and Mughal periods. One of the Sultanate dynasties was a "slave" dynasty, and interesting compendia on the materials from this time have been made to reconstruct its culture of homosociality and homoeroticism. Its emphasis on solidarity between men and the purity of lineages has huge, largely unexplored, gender ramifications. In the Mughal period, there are at least three important issues concerning gender. One is the spread of Islam by the efforts of Sufis. Sufis used a message of love and private effort that appealed to women. We know from songs and texts that women were often the performers as well as the audience for many of these genres. The second issue is the huge burgeoning of the patriarchal model of the state under an Emperor such as Akbar. He was the supreme Father, and, through his harem which was joined by Rajput princesses, also controlled his subjects politically. The third important development is the Bhakti movement. All over India, for about four centuries, male as well as female poet "saints" toured the country singing devotion to uniquely personal, accessible gods, or an abstract spirit. Their message of personal devotion, egalitarianism, and cynicism towards social institutions may have produced a new kind of equality, or potential equality, between the sexes. It certainly posed some challenges.

Our next chronological period, that of colonial rule from the mid-eighteenth to mid-twentieth century, is discussed in four chapters. Chapter 5 focuses on changes in work roles during the colonial period, to see them from a gendered perspective. The coming of the East India Company, for instance, produced a new elite, and in these families women had not only a powerful role but also a curious loss of power. The early control of the Company left Bengal over-taxed and some of its population destitute, in which case, as in the last famine of the 1940s, women were the worst sufferers. The Permanent Settlement produced profound changes in landholding, which percolated down to family relationships and emotions. New professions arose as a result of new education. A middle class arose, and women also entered new professions such as medicine and law. The vast majority, however, either resisted the changes and stayed within older family structures, which sometimes became more rigid, or actively suffered because the loss of old occupations hurt them directly. If we consider industrialisation to be in progress, we see that as a latecomer to that development, Indian women were not able to benefit from it. All over the country, as studies of particularly Haryana, Oudh, Punjab, Tamil Nadu, and Kerala show us, the condition of women changed, and not for the better. Finally, the chapter looks at some specific kinds of neglected work, such as in low-caste occupations, cultural and entertainment services, and mothering.

Chapter 6 is on education and consists of six important themes. Two important themes are class differences and a plural education. When a new education was introduced by the colonial state, women of many upper-class families rejected the colonial plan of change, preferring the status quo to a new prospect of learning and lifestyle. These "conservatives," however, often studied Indian classical languages, their mother tongue, and Indian subject areas with their non-formal curricula. Thus, to do justice to women, we have to recognise this alternative education that they received, particularly women of upper classes, and that they in turn passed on and taught. A third theme is the desire among women to break free. They were "Caged tigers," as an informant from the colonial period puts it. A fourth is the formation of a modern Subject once women do receive a new education, and turn to new professions and lifestyles, again, typically upper-class women in companionate marriages. A fifth important thread is the leadership provided by women in setting up schools and colleges, contrary to our historical record that stresses the leadership by men in all reform efforts. The final theme is the restrictive nature of modern education. Often, it was propagated by female missionaries, who had a narrow view of women's potential and desires. The colonial state could be restrictive as well, as could the nationalist elite.

"Law, marriage, and the family" is the subject of Chapter 7. Marriage is typically the most important experience for the woman. In North India, her experience is of virilocality, where she leaves her natal home for her conjugal, or husband's, home. There are wonderful textual and oral sources that attest to her ambivalence in this, that tell us also that women are not always victims but have voices, subjecthoods, and strategies for fighting oppressive structures of control. In South India, the experience of marriage is different. But in both North and South, the colonial period proved to be one during which patriarchal laws were enforced and strengthened. The "*pativrata*" or loyal-to-the-husband discourse of the Dharmashastras, culminating in *sati daha*, or a widow's immolation on her husband's funeral pyre, was given increased credibility. The important issue of the age of marriage sheds light on the experience of women in marriage. The two cases of Rukhmabai in Bombay and Phulmoni in Calcutta highlight the ways in which colonial law produced dissension among Indian men who sought to preserve their patriarchal control and was non-progressive because it left these controls undisturbed.

There are two important topics in Chapter 8, Nationalism and Partition. Women participated together with men in the Moderate and Extremist phases, as they are called, of the Nationalist Movement. In addition, they added another dimension: a call for freedom from domination by men, just as Indians were fighting to be free of the British. Gandhi's leadership included both a radical call to women to join and a conservative one to play the roles of Hindu mythological figures, such as Sita and Damayanti. We see how "radical" and "conservative" are not polar opposites. These same mythological figures could be re-interpreted as women of determination and independence. Two different positions have to be interrogated. One is of the colonial state, which was patriarchal, and, as argued in the previous chapter, not pro-women when it did not suit its politics. The second is that of the Indian nationalist movement, which had people of many hues, including Netaji Subhash Chandra Bose, who formed a women's regiment in his Indian army, and terrorists who believed in violence as a weapon against the British, and welcomed women's participation. None of the Hindu and Muslim parties that emerged spoke for a community as a whole (there *was* no one unified community to speak of). Then there is the Partition, its beginnings and its aftermath, which has its own historiography. In the history of Partition, women are agents and victims, and also do not have any one fixed identity. They are as diverse and wide-ranging as men are.

The next two chapters, 9 and 10, look at gender and Hinduism, and gender and Islam, respectively. In Chapter 9, we enquire into what it means to be a matriarchal *culture* or discourse, that is to have a world of images, stories, and interconnected narratives that include questioning and reflection, about powerful women. This is what scholars propose the Hindu world view, within all its diversity, may be said to be. We look at the histories and meanings of the goddesses Durga, Radha, Parvati, Sita, Lakshmi, and Kali, and in some detail at village goddesses, to understand if the Goddess, or a goddess, is in any sense a feminist. We also try to understand Saktism, the worship of the Goddess as

Sakti, and the varieties of local rituals that celebrate "when the world becomes a woman."

In Chapter 10, the same exercise is carried on with Islam. As with Hinduism, we are not speaking of a consensual and fixed set of beliefs. In the case of both religions, a profound historical and intellectual diversity of approaches and plurality of beliefs and practices is the norm, not the exception. If there is a "matriarchal culture" produced by the fact of goddesses in Hinduism, there is a "feminine culture" in Islam. This appears in performances, artistic genres, interpersonal relations, and shrines. It is possible because of the immense popularity of Sufism, a different strand of Islamic practice to classical text-based Islam. While few women are famed Sufi saints, there are popular Sufi practitioners at the local level. The history of reform in Islam, revolving around education or modernisation, and Islamicisation or conservatism, is traced in the chapter. Courtesans, working-class women, and specific issues such as divorce and early marriage are touched upon.

In the final chapter on "Sexuality, Films, and the Arts," we have to look at several different things. We touch on the ideas of sexuality in South Asia in Sanskrit sources, and in the Epics. We move on to films, and the dichotomy of the good wife–loose woman. Coming back to Hindu mythology briefly, we note that the role model for both men and women is dichotomous. For men it is the erotic/sexualised householder versus the ascetic, and for women it is the sexualised loose woman versus the virtuous wife/mother. This leads to a discussion of same-sex love and friendship. We look at *devdasis*, and the history of education and reform. Finally, we look closely at the intersection of violence with sexuality and the media, trying to bring the discussion up to the present.

## Bibliography

Agarwal, B. (1988). Neither sustenance nor sustainability: Agricultural strategies, ecologic degradation and Indian women in poverty. In B. Agarwal (Ed.), *Structures of patriarchy: State, community and household in modernising Asia* (pp. 83–120). New Delhi: Kali for Women.

Agarwal, B. (1994). *A field of one's own: Gender and land rights in South Asia*. New Delhi: Cambridge University Press.

Anagol, P. (2005). *The emergence of feminism in India 1850–1920*. Hampshire and Burlington: Ashgate.

Anderson, M., & Guha, S. (1998). Introduction. In M. Anderson & S. Guha (Eds.), *Changing concepts of rights and justice in South Asia*. Delhi: Oxford University Press.

Carroll, L. (1989). Law, custom, and statutory social reform: The Hindu widows' remarriage act of 1856. In J. Krishnamurthy (Ed.), *Women in colonial India: Essays on survival, work, and the state* (pp. 1–26). Delhi: Oxford University Press.

Chakravarti, U. (1990). Whatever happened to the Vedic *Dasi*? Orientalism, nationalism and a script for the past. In K. Sangari & S. Vaid (Eds.), *Recasting women: Essays in Indian colonial history* (pp. 27–87). New Brunswick, NJ: Rutgers University Press.

Chanana, K. (Ed.). (1988). *Socialization, education and women: Explorations in gender identity*. New Delhi: Orient Longman.

Chatterjee, P. (1990). The nationalist resolution of the women's question. In K. Sangari & S. Vaid (Eds.), *Recasting women: Essays in Indian colonial history* (pp. 233–253). New Brunswick, NJ: Rutgers University Press.

Friedan, B. (1963). *The feminine mystique*. New York: W. W. Norton.

Gandhi, N., & Shah, N. (1991). *The issues at stake: Theory and practice in the contemporary women's movement in India*. New Delhi: Kali for Women.

Kachuck, B. (1995). Feminist social theories: Theme and variations. *Sociological Bulletin, 44*(2), 169–193.

Kakar, S. (1988). Feminine identity in India. In R. Ghadially (Ed.), *Women in Indian society: A reader* (pp. 44–68). New Delhi: Sage Publications.

Kalpagam, U. (1994). *Labor and gender: Survival in urban India*. New Delhi: Sage Publications.

Karlekar, M. (1988). Women's nature and education. In K. Chanana (Ed.), *Socialization education and women: Explorations in gender identity* (pp. 129–165). New Delhi: Nehru Memorial Museum and Library.

Kishwar, M. (1990). Why 1 do not call myself a feminist. *Manushi*, 2–8.

Kumar, N. (Ed.). (1994). *Women as subjects: South Asian histories*. London and Charlottesville, VA: University Press of Virginia.

Kumar, R. (1993). *The history of doing: An illustrated account of movements for women's rights and feminism in India, 1800–1990*. New Delhi: Kali for Women.

Mani, L. M. (1990). Contentious traditions: The debate on Sati in colonial India. In K. Sangari & S. Vaid (Eds.), *Recasting women: Essays in Indian colonial history* (pp. 88–126). New Brunswick, NJ: Rutgers University Press.

Mieis, M. (1986). *Patriarchy and accumulation on a world scale: Women in the international division of labor*. London: Zed.

Mieis, M., & Shiva, V. (1993). *Ecofeminism*. New Delhi: Kali for Women.

Mohanty, C., Russo, A., & Torres, L. (Eds). (1991). *Third world women and the politics of feminism*. Bloomington, IN: Indiana University Press.

Nandy, A. (1988). Woman versus womanliness in India: An essay in social and political psychology. In R. Ghadially (Ed.), *Women in Indian society: A reader* (pp. 69–80). New Delhi: Sage Publications.

Pande, I. (2012). "Coming of age" law, sex, and childhood in late colonial India. *Gender & History, 24*(1), 205–230.

Pandey, G. (2001). *Remembering partition*. Cambridge: Cambridge University Press.

Panigrahi, L. (1972). *British social policy and female infanticide in India*. New Delhi: Munshiram Manoharlal.

Sangari, K. (1993). The "amenities" of domestic life: Questions on labor. *Social Scientist, 21*(9–11), 3–46.

Sangari, K., & Vaid, S. (1990). Recasting women: An introduction. In K. Sangari and S. Vaid (Eds.), *Recasting women: Essays in Indian colonial history* (pp. 1–26). New Brunswick, NJ: Rutgers University Press.

Sarkar, T. (2000). A prehistory of rights: The age of consent debate in colonial Bengal (Points of departure: India and South Asian diaspora). *Feminist Studies, 26*(3), 601–622.

Shiva, V. (1988). *Staying alive: Women, ecology and development*. New Delhi: Kali for Women.

Singh, R. (1990). *The womb of mind: A sociological exploration of the status-experience of women in Delhi*. New Delhi: Vikas.

Singha, R. (1998). *A despotism of law: Crime and justice in early colonial India* (pp. 123–124). Delhi: Oxford University Press.

Sinha, M. (1997). *Colonial masculinity: The "manly Englishman" and the "effeminate Bengali" in the nineteenth century*. New Delhi: Kali for Women.

Spivak, G. (1988). Can the subaltern speak? In C. Nelson & L. Grossberg (Eds.), *Marxism and the interpretation of culture* (pp. 271–313). Urbana, IL: University of Illinois Press.

Tharu, S. (1995). Slow pan left: Feminism and the problematic of rights. In J. Bagchi (Ed.), *Indian women: Myth and reality* (pp. 44–57). Hyderabad: Sangam.

Tharu, S., & Lalita, K. (Eds.). (1993). *Women writing in India*. New York: Feminist Press.

Visweswaran, K. (1996). Small speeches, subaltern gender: Nationalist ideology and its historiography. In S. Amin & D. Chakrabarty (Eds.), *Subaltern studies IX: Writings on South Asian history and society* (pp. 83–125). New Delhi: Oxford University Press.

Willis, E. (1984). Radical feminism and feminist radicalism (The 60's without apology). *Social Text*, (9/10), 91–118.

# 1
# GENDER IN SOUTH ASIA

When I was in school in the 1960s, I studied a history of India authored by Vincent Smith (perhaps Smith, 1919/1958). He specialised in the history of pre-Muslim India. For him the "Hindu" period reached its peak under the benevolent despots Chandragupta and Ashoka Maurya (3rd–4th century BCE), the Gupta emperors (4th–5th century CE), and Harsha (7th century CE) – after which Indian civilisation declined.

> Compared with the other civilisations of Europe, China, and the Near East, India appeared to be singularly lacking in political unity and therefore, in history. Writing seventy years earlier, Hegel, whose world history was the global narrative, of which orientalism was a part, provided the reason for this. . . . India was a land dominated by imagination rather than reason. Still earlier, commentators like James Mill had argued that in India an exotic institution, caste, prevented political unity.
>
> *(Inden, 1990, p. 8)*

Smith was influential as a historian. Not only did my generation, decades after his book was first published, imbibe his messages, other historians unreflectingly repeated his theses about the lack of cohesion among "Hindu" rulers, the absence of any progress or advance, and the overall weakness of India as a nation. India was denigrated for being under the thrall of religion and caste, the two defining institutions of India. The chaos produced was the opposite of the serene rationality of European nations; India was jungle-like instead of being machine-like. The vision was a perfect justification for imperial rule. This *discourse*, or holistic set of attitudes about Indian civilisation, permeated the consciousness of Western people and South Asians alike. Edward Said wrote a powerful expose of this attitude, calling it an *ism* in an influential book, *Orientalism* (Said, 1978).

While Said's book primarily deals with the Middle East and the Far East, it was taken from the very outset to apply to South Asia as well, although South Asians identify other Asians, and not themselves, as Orientals. Indeed, the book provided a tool of analysis that became more sharpened and more widely applicable with time. We could comfortably replace "the Orient" with "South Asia" in the following extract. Orientalism, for Said, is

> a way of coming to terms with the Orient that is based on the Orient's special place in European Western Experience. The Orient is not only adjacent to Europe; it is also the place of Europe's greatest and richest and oldest colonies, the source of its civilizations and languages, its cultural contestant, and one of its deepest and most recurring images of the Other. In addition, the Orient has helped to define Europe (or the West) as its contrasting image, idea, personality, experience. Yet none of this Orient is merely imaginative. The Orient is an integral part of European material civilization and culture. Orientalism expresses and represents that part culturally and even ideologically as a mode of discourse with supporting institutions, vocabulary, scholarship, imagery, doctrines, even colonial bureaucracies and colonial styles.
>
> *(Said, 1978, pp. 1–2)*

The "Orient" was created by rendering certain nations exotic and inferior. They were also characterised as effeminate, since they were inferior by virtue of sporting supposedly "feminine" qualities, such as passivity, sentimentalism, and irrationality. Moreover, while women in these countries had always been diverse and complex, in the Orientalist gaze, they became either victims of oriental male oppression or objects of eroticism who displayed a fascinating perverse nature. To see women as imbued with certain essential qualities made it easier to see the whole Asian country in question as over-sensual and over-sexual, or simply barbaric and closer to nature than to civilisation. Thus, Orientalism has always been a gendered discourse. The history of India as first written by the colonialists was oriental and gendered in manifold ways.

One of the most interesting turns in South Asian history occurred when in the nineteenth century, missionary, colonial, and other orientalist commentaries on women in India aroused Indian men and women, but especially men, to take overt sides. Some claimed that women's conditions were fine and worth conserving and responded by defending their values, as they saw them. Others insisted they had to change and attempted to reform the conditions of women. Both views were based on articulated or unarticulated notions about women and gender. In the twentieth century, this history of reform and conservatism evolved into yet more conscious thinking and debating about the roles of women. Present-day academic work especially probes this preoccupation. An important contribution to the history of women in South Asia is evocatively titled "Recasting Women" as a comment on the nineteenth- to twentieth-century movements to re-define, reconstruct, and *recast* women in a new image, in the interest of progress and refinement (Sangari & Vaid, 1989). Women were required to *play* a new role whether it was of conservation or change, and almost always it was a combination of the two. We have *stages, directors, producers, props, scripts, actors* and *roles to play*. In this book, we will often use the metaphor of performance to understand women's actions and experiences from their own points of view. This is one way to retrieve women's own consciousness of what was happening to them. Another linked way is to always ask if they indeed *accepted* subjugation to the roles prescribed for them. Did they not resist? Did they actively protest?

The modern enquiry into gender in South Asia has not been an abstract subject of study, but one that has been tied up with practical considerations of the conditions of women. To some extent, this is true everywhere since feminism is by definition rooted in activism. "By feminism," say two scholars, "we indicate the critical examination of gender relations from the position of protest against women's unequal status" (Lancaster & di Leonardo, 1997, p. 2). However, when scholars did wish to enquire into South Asian women's pasts because of their interest in present-day women, it turned out that there was not only a conceptual or data-related problem, such as "Where are the women in the historical record?" or "How should women's roles in a particular historical period be understood?" there came to appear many interpretive problems associated with the recovery of these histories. For instance, gender divisions were gradually discovered in every society in the world to be inextricably tied to class, ethnicity, racial, and national divisions, but in South Asia all this appeared immediately and with intensity as soon as the historical enquiry into gender began.

Janaki Nair argues that in India there has been less tension between academic and activist or political feminism, and some of the most influential scholarship has been driven by critical events, such as state-instigated conflict between communities, including the protests against caste-based reservations, the state-tolerated demolition of the Babri Masjid, and the Partition of 1947 itself. As Nair (2008) points out, fruitful advance was made in questioning the relationships between caste and gender, and religion and gender, in ways inspired by current protests that went beyond the questioning of caste and religion in previous feminist studies. As a result, studies of feminism and women's history in India have been less influenced by Western feminist theorising but also relatively lacking in their own theorisation. As Atwal and Flessenkamper (2020) emphasise, however, this supposedly lower level of theorising in India is a function of conflating Western with universal theorisation. There are modes of theorising and analysis that are pertinent to Indian history but are invisible because of the domination of the Western academy (Anagol, 2005; Kumar, 1994).

An activist-oriented interest in gender is attested to by most scholars and applies across the board, sometimes to topics that do not, at first sight, seem compatible with an interest in women's contemporary situation. An example is the subject of women in the ancient Vedic period. There are several ways in which activists could worry about the ancient period. One, if the overall historical vision of students, scholars, and the general population is bereft of discussions of the importance of women's work and productivity, and is confined to celebrating them as mothers or noble women, it will prove detrimental to any project of empowering women qua women (and not, for instance, as symbols of Indian civilisation). Great women will be presented as historical exceptions and distorted to emphasise their emotional and dependent selves, rather than their power-seeking and competitive selves. This is the simplest level of the problem. History as a discipline will also, of course, suffer if its expanding interest in cultures, marginalised groups, and power relationships leaves out questioning of the meaning of gender. Even the occasional great woman cannot be properly explained in the absence of context.

Second, women who are *not* celebrated as great or noble are treated stereotypically. The idea that there was a special group of people called the "Aryans" from whom descend self-identified Indians is referred to as the "Aryan myth," and depends on a myth of the "non-Aryan" or "*dasa/dasyu*," a person who was inferior in most ways. These myths of essentialist qualities based on class and lineage then become entrenched and influence contemporary thinking. Meanwhile, politicians and the media exploit the missing gaps in research or ignore the subtler research, to perpetuate dangerous hierarchical ideologies. Thus, almost all scholars who work on gender in South Asia in any way are interested in doing so because of their concern with contemporary conditions of gender inequality and violence, based partly on misperception and mis-representation of the past.

Another narrative to examine is how the modern system of education was introduced into India by the state in the middle of the nineteenth century. This gave the state a control over textbooks and examinations, percolating down to the local from metropolitan universities through colleges and schools. This did two related things. One, a new consciousness about History was developed. As South Asians studied the histories of European nations, they were aware of the need for a similar teleological history of their own. A debate arose regarding whether Indians had ever in the past a "historical" consciousness and, indeed, a "history" – partly as part of an Orientalist vision of India as profoundly different, including in its concepts of space and time. Romila Thapar in a 1974 lecture argued that the people of ancient India had a special kind of historical tradition. This was one in which "the past was not recorded as a succession of political events, for the legitimation of political authority was more important, and it was to this that the historical tradition gave precedence" via the transmission of genealogical lists. Since she also views many genealogies as fabrications, it is clear her definition of "historical" is more complex than many historians', and this enables her to find "history" in Sanskrit texts where others may not (Guha, 2004, p. 1088). This lecture was only the beginning of a discussion in various books, articles, and interviews by Thapar, of the thesis that there could be many different understandings of "history," and that Indians *did* have their own unique sense of history. She has been joined in this approach by several scholars such as Rao, Shulman, and Subrahmanyam, who claim that India had sophisticated traditions of historiography (Rao et al., 2003). There are also some critics who feel that the idea of "an Indian mode of history" is achieved at the cost of blurring, if not obliterating, the distinction between historical *evidence* and historical *narrative, cult* and *chronicle*. Meanwhile, largely ignored by the Anglophone academy, Indian scholars have worked on recovering and editing their respective literary and historical legacies in institutions in different language areas, such as Bengal, Maharashtra, and Rajasthan.

The many ways of keeping and transmitting the historical record in its various states, regions and communities were seen by the nineteenth-century colonials as not really "history" and the Indians therefore lacking in a historical consciousness. Europe had meanwhile developed such a consciousness and as the political masters of India, they could apply it and bring it to India. Indians themselves were split into a new division on the basis of their education. Those who received colonial schooling regarded Western trajectories of history as normal and accepted a European version of India's past and present. Those not thus schooled but alternatively educated continued to approach history in other ways. Subject to colonial domination, they also began to give history an explicitly anti-colonial twist. They were joined by nationalists who, albeit colonised in their schooling, strove to see beyond it and strained to find alternative interpretations to the European ones. Moreover, there has been, from the nineteenth century, an interest in questioning the monopoly of a nationalist history, which is always also evolutionary and patriarchal. This has been done in practical ways, by searching for "indigenous" histories, "people's" histories, and "alternate histories."

This is all very relevant for women's history. Almost all women were in the category of the unschooled in the colonial regimen. They were legatees and transmitters of a historical consciousness that was expressed in local narratives, poetry, and mythology. The few who had received the masculine education of the colonial school were of course much like men in their consciousness. But without doubt there is the possibility of multiple kinds of histories in India based on region, community, and, in our case, gender.

A fascinating historiographical issue is raised by Indrani Chatterjee (2013) as "the genealogy of postcolonial amnesia," dating from the early nineteenth century. A combination of the East India Company's need for taxation money and an evangelical outlook of reform of Indian (Hindu-Buddhist-Sufi) custom worked to erase the economies and status of meritorious acts of charity and service performed by women as disciples, teachers, widows, daughters, and wives of monastic men. We thus misread the history of reform from the nineteenth century onwards, and of women's roles in the knowledge and social economy in the centuries before, which Chatterjee claims extended from the second century CE. If she is correct, then a new and different subjecthood must be ascribed to women, otherwise typically seen as passive and dominated by men.

Another historian, Antoinette Burton in her 2003 book, *Dwelling in the Archive: Women Writing House, Home and History in Late Colonial India*, pleads for a different perspective on the historical *archive*. She says that women write oftener of domesticity, of spaces, of memories of architecture – the house, the home. Not only does each account serve as evidence of individual lives, "the memories of home that each woman enshrined in narrative act – for us – as an archive from which a variety of counter histories of colonial modernity can be discerned" (Burton, 2003, p. 5). The home is a material archive and "a very real political figure in an extended moment of historical crisis" (Burton, 2003, p. 5). This "cult of domesticity" is defined by the larger culture and the political economies of race, nation, sexuality, and empire. The zenana, or the woman's secluded space, is a problem to be reformed – yes. But it is also a product of British colonial gender ideology that provoked Indian nationalists to define conjugality and gender relations in spatial terms that separated the feminine and domestic as spiritual as opposed to the masculine, public and material (Burton, 2003, p. 8).

Yet a third historian, Dipesh Chakrabarty, makes a critique of "historicism." Historians are unable, according to him, to escape keeping every community and person within a phased structure of history where their trajectories in life are already ordained and predetermined. The failure in the case of South Asian history-writing lies in not being able to take "difference" seriously, either by reducing it to a consumerist foible or by disenchanting the world. He also critiques the marginalisation of India by Europe and the West. When Chakrabarty argues that India has unjustly been treated as unequal to the West, and that history presents the wrong model of judging the "development" of a society, we realise that from our feminist perspective, the inequalities *within* Indian society are even more important to worry about. If "the abstract human of the Enlightenment" (Chakrabarty, 2000, p. 47) did not appear in South Asia, we may quibble and say that *she* certainly did not. The introduction of modern education into India in the nineteenth century gave birth to a new desire to be a modern Indian that could be the best possible synthesis of the East and West. This impacted men and women in different ways and produced new gender configurations. Through education, professional work, and role in public life, men were more socialised into liberal autonomous subjecthood than women were, but both also remained "non-subjects" to different extents, a topic that will be explored in following chapters.

Given the present trajectory into neo-liberalism, we have to ask how capitalism and colonialism have worked for women – and men – in a specifically gendered way. There are various critiques of modernity that seek to overcome Eurocentrism, including a world system analysis that goes beyond the macro narratives of

Western enlightenment and capitalism. Mignolo (2002) puts it in the most useable form for us when he says that "difference" has to be understood as "the production of difference." In the case of South Asia, along with other colonies, this would be "colonial difference." It lies in the *making* of difference through power. During, and especially after, the process of difference-making,

> the world became unthinkable beyond European (and, later, North Atlantic) epistemology. The colonial difference marked the limits of thinking and theorizing, unless modern epistemology (philosophy, social sciences, natural sciences) was exported/imported to those places where thinking was impossible (because it was folklore, magic, wisdom, and the like).
> *(Mignolo, 2002, pp. 90–91)*

In this book, I wish to present a history that is partly still "enchanted," in which folklore, magic, wisdom, and the like are all viable systems of thought. This reveals a world where Enlightenment reason has not won a victory and the subject does not consider herself a "Subject" fulfilling, or on the way to fulfilling, a world-destined modernity that is global and capitalistic. As I discuss elsewhere (Kumar, 2001, 2007), the modern Indian subject has been produced by a dual education, one site of which is the mother and the home. Typically, the woman has had a different consciousness to the man, arising from the relative absence of formal education for women after its introduction in the 1850s. She has transmitted this different possible identity in every generation through the "mother tongue," childhood socialisation, and a complex of stories, local histories, and mythology. We may call this "a narrative of the self." Its perpetuators are not literally all women, rather those who play the role of mothering.

This book adopts the perspectives that (a) the history of gender and women in India needs to be thoroughly inter-disciplinary and (b) we need to interrogate even the familiar disciplinary boundaries in order to write a gendered history at all. The two points overlap if we scrutinise the fluctuating dimensions of two sets of terms, structure/patriarchy and subjecthood/agency. In inspecting patriarchal structures historically, we need to look first at the role of the state in different historical periods: the tribe; the kingdom; the empire; the self-declaredly Buddhist, Islamic, or Saivite state; the British colonial; and the Indian secular or Hindutva-dominated state. We need to understand the particular economic-ritual structures of caste and their base in patriarchy. Cultural definitions of marriage, widowhood, public and private, and other rubrics of the social and everyday that seem geographically and historically peculiar to India must be understood in all their specificities but also as produced by global contexts of production, trade, law, and governance. In looking for subjecthood and agency, we need to give attention to women's actual lives, in all the diverse roles they play, the belief and practice systems that give them power, the styles of resistance and conformity to larger structures that they employ, and their voices; in short, whatever forms the voices may take (including seeming silence). It is not that the woman is an autonomous actor but rather that she derives and produces meaning in all kinds of complex ways, and her meaning-making and meaning-experiencing processes must be an equally important focus alongside the deconstruction of the larger political contexts.

The vast oeuvre of one scholar of Religious Studies, Wendy Doniger/O'Flaherty, gives us an idea of the implications of this. Doniger studies Indian literature, chiefly the Vedas, and Indian mythology in a comparative perspective. She finds that there are many universal patterns in the ways that women are conceptualised and depicted but that there are also many important concepts regarding gender that are different in India to what they are elsewhere, though there may be common origins even to these in a period lost to us, and the difference may have appeared in a later period and that is all we have access to. In *Women, Androgynes and Other Mythical Beasts*, she looks at sexual metaphors and animal symbols to interpret gender in India. While giving exciting interpretations of androgyny in Indian mythology – having the characteristics of both male and female simultaneously or interchangeably – she still finds a basic gender imbalance. Men may double as both sexes, reproducing by themselves or refraining from interacting with the other sex, but women may not, or do not. If they do, they are condemned and shunned (Doniger, 1980). However, what is also important to note is that there are Indian systems of thought regarding "fluids" – milk, semen, blood – and how their flowing, channelling or obstruction, may create or control power. Doniger is careful to emphasise that both seemingly contrary things are true: that gender is differently delineated in South Asia between men and women, and masculinity and femininity, than in the modern West or Judeo-Christian traditions, and that both Indian myths and women's lived-in experiences in India reflect a patriarchy, no matter how different. She is interested in the difference, however, and she, and other scholars, have contributed richly to our understanding of sexuality, androgynity, crossover, and power *in India*.

As we will see in greater detail in Chapter 9, some scholars have pursued the question of "Shakti" or the Mother Goddess as literally meaning and standing for power. Others look at daily lives and rituals to interpret how structures and processes that give women power lie behind the seemingly monolithic power of patriarchy. They point out that, often, when explaining the dominance of men, we are reflecting our own inability as scholars to access the worlds of women that are made invisible in a universe where the "public" has more credibility than the "private," when even scholarly disciplines emphasise the importance of the political and social over the domestic and internal.

Nancy Auer Falk, for example, in her co-edited volume on women's religious lives, shows how women have separate, parallel practices to men's that give them a different power to that of men (Falk & Gross, 1980). Kathleen Erndl, in her co-edited volume, evocatively entitled *Is the Goddess a Feminist?* brings together the two strands of scholarship, on the goddess, and on feminist questioning of religious theology and practice. She argues that the goddess shows us how India's is not simply a hierarchical society, the opposite of a Western one, as is often argued. Instead, it places a different valence on power and equality, such as in the concept of Shakti or Kali. This is a creative power primarily associated with women, one that establishes a "profoundly non-hierarchical axis of value" which cuts across caste and other social divisions based on seemingly more entrenched oppositions of power (Hiltebeitel & Erndl, 2000).

Tracy Pintchman in another edited volume (Pintchman, 1994), this time on Mahadevi, or the Great Goddess, shows how Indian philosophical and devotional traditions *also* employ different strategies to deconstruct the Goddess, just as scholars do. Thus, there are arguments about the amalgamation of local within pan-Indian goddesses, about personal experience versus theology, and about the *real* power and the *enduring* status of the Goddess. These debates all refer to the seeming conflict between high and low, between a classical practice and local ones. Scholars are divided into two camps: one places value on texts, the opinion of upper castes, and on theory; the other, on ethnographic data, on lived culture and on everyday practices and the views of ordinary people. "Classical" is often contrasted by them to "folk" or "popular," and "textual" to "contextual" or "ethnographic."

In a study of rivers in Maharashtra, Anne Feldhaus, while taking into account textual traditions, describes people's beliefs and practices on the ground. Rivers in Hinduism are always feminine and are always deified. Feldhaus shows how their power resides in both their fertility and mothering – this domesticity accompanied by the fact that no male deity has control over them – and their ability to wash off sin. There is apparently no conflict here between the textual and the contextual tradition (Feldhaus, 1995). Similarly, Kathleen Erndl, in her study of Vaisno Devi, the goddess of Northern mountain India, gives an ethnographic account with a wealth of important detail and successfully argues against a dichotomisation of the goddess into "domesticated/auspicious" and "independent/dangerous" (Erndl, 1993). For her devotees, she is both the opposing sides at the same time, without conflict. Here, and elsewhere, the goddess overcomes another potential conflict: between the material and the spiritual. She can be a mother who reflects material mothering practices and also an embodiment of more abstract power, often fierce, which is up for more theoretical exegesis.

The other conflict that scholars discuss is between *purusa*, the male principle, and *prakriti*, the female principle. The former is passive and abstract, the latter active and material. In one of the most intriguing pieces on the subject, Nicholas Geir argues that the yogi, or Titan as he calls him, embodies the male principle of self-sufficiency, distancing from the earthly and rejecting the feminine (Geir, 1997). The Goddess has been important throughout history as the Supreme Principle and Supreme Knowledge. However, she has been treated variously. The *Samkhya* philosophical tradition devalues her as *prakriti* or matter, even while recognising matter as the active power of the cosmos, and teaches how she may be ignored and thereby rendered inert and ineffectual. The *Sakta* tradition, on the other hand, claims that no one escapes nature or the cosmic web of relations and that this, indeed, is the source of all power (Geir, 1997 [sic. Also Geir], p. 272). Siva is the ultimate *yogi*, who turns his back on nature. Parvati rebukes him by saying,

> You should consider who you are, and what nature is. . . . How could you transcend Nature? What you hear, what you eat, what you see – it's all Nature. How could you be beyond Nature? You are enveloped in Nature, even though you don't know it.
> *(Skanda Purana 1.1.21.18–22; Doniger's translation quoted in Geir, 1997, p. 278)*

If women are being equated with nature, the question is whether nature is normative and powerful, or marginal and inferior – or is neither one nor the other.

The *Devi Mahatmaya*, the premier text of *Sakta* philosophy, sings the praise of Devi: "[You are] the cause of all the worlds . . . the supreme, original, untransformed Prakrti (4.6)" (quoted in Geir, 1997, p. 273). The gods in the *Puranas* are impotent without their *saktis*. While each god has his own consort, Indra with Saci, Visnu with Lakshmi, and Siva with Sati or Parvati, these latter are not just wives of the gods. They are aspects of Devi's *sakti*. When Durga is created to fight the demon that the gods themselves cannot fight, it is a coming together and equipping for battle of a power that already exists and is immanent everywhere.

The tension between the ascetic *purusa* and the material, earthly *sakti* is exemplified by a quote in Doniger, 1973 (150):

> Love and anger both are states
> hostile to self-control
> What then did Siva hope to gain
> by slaying Love in anger?

The penance of the Goddess succeeds in persuading the great *yogi*, Siva, to a union, an interdependence, and an androgyny – the *Ardhanrisvara* (half man-half woman). All this provides evidence as well as a complex interpretation of the power of femininity in Hindu epistemology. However, the debate continues regarding how far this is reflected in the actual conditions of women.

First, as Geir himself admits, after his powerful case for the Devi (Geir, 1997), Goddess worship itself is controlled and administered by men. Devi is a leader not of women but of men going to battle, or going to rule. To use the Goddess as a feminist resource, women in India have worked to interpret or re-interpret her selectively. One could argue that the discursive spaces for feminist action are greater in India because of the presence of the Goddess. As Geir says, Sakta is the principle of power as embodied in the Goddess, and "the worship of the Goddess appears to require that we view matter, as did the ancients and Hindus today, as dynamic, organic, interrelated, and alive" (285). More powerful, however, is to look at the actual conditions of women, historically (as in the next chapter), anthropologically (as by several scholars discussed in Chapter 7), and artistically (Singh, 1993 on Ray's "Devi"). We could feel persuaded by such materials to see that there may indeed be an inverse relationship between the power of Devi and the power of actual women. Hindu Goddess discourse presents femininity as a metaphor, removing from actual women their freedom to realise their humanity. The burden of present or potential divinity could be said to weigh them down and entrap them. In this it resembles colonial and nationalist discourse.

This is true mostly for middle-class women. What about the gendered patterns of worship for lower-class and village women? We have evidence for the preponderance of rituals for the Goddess in their belief systems as well. There is evidence of this from pre-historic times, that is, the Indus Valley Civilisation and earlier (Elgood, 2004), and we will look at some of this evidence later. There is plenty of evidence of the worship and propitiation of *yakshas, yakshninis* (male and female nature spirits), and nature-related supra-human beings of many kinds. Then, in literary sources, from the Vedic period onwards, while we have the absence of certain classic female deities that become important in Hinduism later, such as Lakshmi, Parvati, and the Matrakas, there is a recognition of non-Vedic practices that include rituals for local goddesses, including ambivalent ones. Some of these practices, symbols, and iconography were comfortably adopted into Brahmanic and Vedanta Hinduism, in variously changed forms. Some continuities may still be discerned, such as the categorisation of goddesses into two kinds, albeit overlapping: the hot goddesses who must be calmed and the cool goddesses that bring fertility and auspiciousness. In general, scholars call village Hinduism "an amalgam of local superstitions, non-Vedic cultic practice and orthodox Puranic Hinduism, which is itself an assimilation of many of these elements" (Elgood, 2004, p. 340). The goddess Sitala, for instance, who brings smallpox and also its prevention and cure, was "gentrified" when she was raised from her local, low-class status to be known as the daughter of Brahma, recognised by Siva and Visnu, and mentioned as a Devi in the *Skanda Purana*.

From a Hindu-Shakta perspective, such as Patel (1994) adopts, there is no modifying the approach that religious activity has meaning if all relationships are seen as part of the feminine principle of the universe; indeed, when the female body is seen to represent the divine. Scholars such as Vandana Siva feel that a complex of environmental, social, and even economic problems arise when this is forgotten. Maldevelopment in India

> ruptures the cooperative unity of masculine and feminine, and places man, shorn of the feminine principle, above nature and women, and separated from both. . . . Nature and women are turned into passive objects, to be used and exploited for the uncontrolled and uncontrollable desires of alienated man.
>
> *(Shiva, 1988, p. 6)*

The paradox remains that "the oldest and richest living tradition of female divinity cannot prevent the patriarchal subordination of women in social praxis" (Henn, 2004, p. 107). That may well be, however, because of a more limited understanding of "woman," "female," and "gender" than actually possible. The *Mahabharata* scholar Alf Hiltebeitel examines a famous episode in the epic that narrates how the oldest Pandava, Yudhishthira, loses his wife Draupadi in a dice game in which he first bets all his wealth, then his brothers and himself, and then her. We are prepared for the culmination of Draupadi's helplessness as she is lost to the enemies, but she turns the tables and asks, "Whom did you lose first, yourself or me?" Draupadi's question, according to Hiltebeitel, is more than simply a challenge of the patriarchal claim of ownership over women, which it also is. By referring to a deeper level of Samkhya philosophy (one of the six major schools of Hindu philosophy), it illustrates that *purusha*, the sovereign male self, stands in an ambivalent relationship to *prakriti*, the female world or matter that makes it "highly dangerous to claim to be a self" (Henn, 2004, p. 108).

A discussion of a gendered history of South Asia must play a balancing act between politics and meaning, structure and agency, and context and subjecthood. A gendered history of South Asia must be multi-disciplinary, utilising the methodologies of folk lore, religious studies, and literary criticism, along with the more familiar ones of sociology, economics, and political science. But it must also go out of the boundaries of these conventional disciplines to look for the unformulated, a possible feminist theorising that is uniquely South Asian. History in South Asia is already very exciting, bristling as it is with multiple narratives, ontological levels, political conflicts, and sociological sites of learning and transmission. Sometimes it is difficult to fit the different discussions on to a chronological chart, but that is not necessarily the only important exercise to engage in. Sometimes there seems to be a peculiar absence of communication between scholars of diverse fields such as history and religion, but that can be bridged. In effect, scholars and scholarship already talk to each other albeit without always addressing each other.

## Bibliography

Ali, D. (1999). Introduction. In D. Ali (Ed.), *Invoking the past*. New Delhi: Oxford University Press.

Anagol, P. (2005). *The emergence of feminism in India 1850–1920*. Hampshire and Burlington: Ashgate.

Atwal, J., & Flessenkamper, I. (Eds.). (2020). Nature of violence against Dalit women. In *Gender and violence in historical and contemporary perspectives*. London: Routledge.

Bagchi, J. (1985). Positivism and nationalism: Womanhood and crisis in nationalist fiction – Bankimchandra's *Anandamth*. *Economic and Political Weekly*, 20(43), 58–62.

Bagchi, J. (1990). Representing nationalism: Ideology of motherhood in colonial Bengal. *Economic and Political Weekly*, 25(43), 65–71.

Basu, A., & Ray, B. (Eds.). (1990). *Women's struggle: A history of the all-India women's movement 1927–1990*. New Delhi: Manohar.

Burton, A. (2003). *Dwelling in the archive: Women writing house, home and history in late colonial India*. New York: Oxford University Press.
Butalia, U., & Sarkar, T. (Eds.). (1995). *Women and right-wing movements, Indian experiences*. London: Zed Books.
Chakrabarty, D. (1992). Postcoloniality and the artifice of history: Who speaks for Indian pasts? *Representations, 37*, 1–26.
Chakrabarty, D. (2000). *Habitations of modernity*. Chicago, IL: University of Chicago Press.
Chakravarty, U. (1990). Whatever happened to the Vedic Dasi? Orientalism, nationalism and a script for the past. In K. Sangari & S. Vaid (Eds.), *Recasting women: Essays in Indian colonial history* (pp. 27–87). New Brunswick, NJ: Rutgers University Press.
Chatterjee, I. (2013). Monastic governmentality, colonial misogyny, and postcolonial amnesia in South Asia. *History of the Present, 3*(1), 57–98.
Chatterjee, P. (1989). The nationalist resolution of the woman question. In K. Sangari & S. Vaid (Eds.), *Recasting women: Essays in colonial history* (pp. 233–353). Delhi: Kali for Women.
Cohn, B. (1996). *Colonialism and its forms of knowledge: The British in India*. Princeton, NJ: Princeton University Press.
Dirks, N. B. (2000). *The hollow crown: The ethnohistory of an Indian Kingdom*. Cambridge: Cambridge University Press. (Original work published 1987)
Doniger, W. (1973). *Asceticism and eroticism in the mythology of Siva*. Oxford: Oxford University Press.
Doniger, W. (1980). *Women, androgynes, and other mythical beasts*. Chicago, IL: University of Chicago Press.
Doniger, W. (1999). *Splitting the difference: Gender and myth in ancient Greece and India*. Chicago, IL: University of Chicago Press.
Elgood, H. (2004). Exploring the roots of village Hinduism in South Asia ("The archaeology of Hinduism"). *World Archaeology, 36*(3), 326–342.
Erndl, K. M. (1993). *Victory to the mother: The Hindu goddess of northwest India in myth, ritual, and symbol*. New York: Oxford University Press.
Falk, N. A., & Gross, R. M. (1980). *Unspoken worlds: Women's religious lives in non-western cultures*. San Francisco, CA: Harper & Row Publishers.
Feldhaus, A. (1995). *Water and womanhood: Religious meanings of rivers in Maharashtra*. New York: Oxford University Press.
Gedalof, I. (1999). *Against purity: Rethinking identity with Indian and western feminisms*. London: Routledge.
Geir, N. F. (1997). The yogi and the goddess. *International Journal of Hindu Studies, 1*(2), 265–287.
Geir, N. F. See Geir, N. F.
Guha, R. (1982). On some aspects of the historiography of colonial India. In *Introduction to subaltern studies I* (pp. 1–8). Delhi: Oxford University Press.
Guha, R. (1987). *An Indian historiography of India: A nineteenth-century agenda and its implications*. Calcutta.
Guha, R., & Spivak, G. C. (Eds.). (1988). *Selected subaltern studies*. Delhi: Oxford University Press.
Guha, S. (2004). Speaking historically: The changing voices of historical narration in western India, 1600–1900. *American Historical Review*, 1084–1103.
Henn, A. (2004). Review of *Is the goddess a feminist? The Politics of South Asian goddesses* by Alf Hiltebeitel and Kathleen M. Erndl. *Sociological Bulletin, 53*(1), 106–109.

Hiltebeitel, A., & Erndl, K. M. (Eds.). (2000). *Is the goddess a feminist? The politics of south Asian goddesses.* New York: NYU Press.
Inden, R. (1986). Orientalist constructions of India. *Modern Asian Studies, 20*(3), 401–446.
Inden, R. (1990). *Imagining India.* Oxford: Blackwell Publishers.
Kumar, N. (2001). *Lessons from schools: The history of education in Banaras.* New Delhi: Sage Publications.
Kumar, N. (2007). *The politics of gender, community and modernity: Essays on education in India.* Delhi: Oxford University Press.
Kumar, R. (1993). *The history of doing: An illustrated account of movements for women's rights and feminism in India 1800–1990.* Delhi: Kali for Women.
Lancaster, R. N., & di Leonardo, M. (Eds.). (1997). *The gender sexuality reader.* New York: Routledge University Press.
Mignolo, W. D. (2002). The geopolitics of knowledge and the colonial difference. *The South Atlantic Quarterly, 101*(1), 57–96.
Mohanty, C. T. (1991). Under western eyes. In C. T. Mohanty, A. Russo, & L. Torres (Eds.), *Third world women and the politics of feminism.* Bloomington, IN: Indiana University Press.
Nair, J. (2008). The troubled relationship of feminism to history. *Economic and Political Weekly, 43*(43), 57–65.
O'Flaherty, W. D. (1980). *Women, androgynes, and other mythical beasts.* Chicago, IL: University of Chicago Press.
O'Hanlon, R. (1988). Recovering the subject: Subaltern studies and histories of resistance in colonial South Asia. *Modern Asian Studies, 22*(1), 189–224.
Patel, K. C. (1994). Women, earth, and the goddess: A shakta-Hindu interpretation of embodied religion (Feminist philosophy of religion). *Hypatia, 9*(4), 69–87.
Pintchman, T. (1994). *The rise of the goddess in the Hindu tradition.* Albany, NY: State University of New York Press.
Rao, V. N., Shulman, D., & Subrahmanyam, S. (2003). *Textures of time: Writing history in south India 1600–1800.* New York: Other Press.
Said, E. (1978). *Orientalism.* New York: Pantheon.
Sangari, K., & Vaid, S. (Eds.). (1989). *Recasting women.* New Delhi: Kali for Women.
Sarkar, M. (2004). Looking for feminism. *Gender and History, 16*(2), 318–333.
Sarkar, M. (2008). *Visible histories, disappearing women: Producing Muslim womanhood in late colonial Bengal.* Durham, NC: Duke University Press.
Sarkar, M. (2012). Between craft and method: Meaning and inter-subjectivity in oral history analysis. *Journal of Historical Sociology, 25*(4), 578–600.
Sarkar, S. (1999). The many worlds of Indian history. In *Writing social history.* Delhi: Oxford University Press.
Sarkar, T., & Butalia, U. (Eds.), (1995). *Women and right-wing movements: Indian experiences.* London: Zed Books.
Shiva, V. (1988). *Staying alive: Women, ecology, and development.* London: Zed Books.
Singh, N.-G. K. (1993). From flesh to stone: The divine metamorphosis in Satyajit Ray's "Devi". *Journal of South Asian Literature, 28*(1/2), 227–250.
Sinha, M. (2006). *Specters of mother India: The global restructuring of an empire.* Durham, NC: Duke University Press.
Smith, V. A. (1958). *Oxford history of India.* Oxford: Oxford University Press. (Original work published 1919)
Spivak, G. C. (1987). Subaltern studies: Deconstructing historiography. In *In other worlds: Essays in colonial politics.* New York: Methuen.

Spivak, G. C. (1988). Can the subaltern speak? In C. Nelson & L. Grossberg (Eds.), *Marxism and the interpretation of culture* (pp. 271–313). Urbana, IL: University of Illinois Press.

Subrahmanyam, S. (1999). Recovering Babel: Polyglot histories from the eighteenth-century Tamil country. In D. Ali (Ed.), *Invoking the past* (pp. 280–321). New Delhi: Oxford University Press.

Sunderrajan, R. (1993). *Real and imagined women: Gender, culture and postcolonization*. New York: Routledge.

Thapar, R. (1974). Ideology and the interpretation of early Indian history. In *Interpreting early India*. New York: Oxford University Press.

Thapar, R. (1989). Imagined religious communities? Ancient history and the modern search for Hindu identity. *Modern Asian Studies*, *23*(2), 209–231.

Visweswaran, K. (1988). Defining feminist ethnography. *Inscriptions*, 3/4, 27–44.

# 2
# ANCIENT INDIA

> In the first age of the gods, existence was born from non-existence. After this the quarters of the sky were born from her who crouched with legs spread.
> – *(Doniger, 1981, p. 38)*

> Among rude people, the women are generally degraded; among civilized people they are exalted. . . . Nothing can exceed the habitual contempt which Hindus entertain for their women. . . . Hardly are they ever mentioned in their laws, or other books, but as wretches of the most base and vicious inclinations on whose nature no virtuous or useful qualities can be engrafted.
> – *(Mill, 1972, pp. 279, 281)*

These quotes direct us to two different ways to pursue an interest in women and gender in History. To reconstruct women's social and cultural position in the past by searching among extant material and interpret it in a light favourable to women is one way. The first quote is from an early hymn of the *Rig Veda* (composed c. 1500–900 BCE). It leaves us with the vision of probably an entrenched patriarchal society but one that has a nuanced view of women and in which women's experiences are also understood and represented.

Another way is to critique the steps taken by dominant groups, typically of men, to do this same work of searching in the past to reconstruct history. The critique would centre on their politics that produce certain distortions of the past. The second quote is from James Mill (1773–1836), who, together with other Orientalists, tried to justify British presence in India in the late eighteenth and early nineteenth centuries through a scholarly interpretation of Hindu backwardness. The colonial period of mid-eighteenth to mid-twentieth century is one in which much intellectual work was done, but the priorities of colonial rule,

DOI: 10.4324/9781003393252-3

with its ideologies, shaped the work. The study and translation by Europeans of Sanskrit texts into English and other European languages were done in the early period of the East India Company's rule in India by some of the Orientalists in its employ. Famous among them are William Jones (1746–1794), Henry Thomas Colebrook (1765–1837), Horace Hyman Wilson (1786–1860), actual servants of the Company, followed by scholars such as Max Muller (1823–1900), a great scholar, but one who never visited India. Through their language studies, these Orientalists, Indologists, or Sanskritists, as they may variously be called, traced the philological base of the Sanskrit language to a proto-Indo-European that was also the fount of most European languages. Their translation of Sanskrit texts led them to the "discovery" of a glorious Indian past that had touched remarkable heights of philosophical and literary achievement. As partners in colonialism and citizens of the colonising nation state of Britain, they also had to explain the degraded state of Indian society of their time, on which there were no two opinions. The higher the pinnacles of the past, then, the more the condemnation of the present and the need for an explanation for the decline.

Of the two quotes above, the poem recovers the woman's experience, which was constructed in words and image by a poet of perhaps 1200 BCE, who seems cognisant of a woman's birthing experience even while placed in the middle of many other activities that are both earthly and cosmological. Much can be, and indeed has been, said about James Mill and other colonial scholars, but their most important characteristic is the judgementalism that is predisposed to prove both the glory in the Indian past and the fall from that time to the present. Many of the scholars share Mill's gendered view, and all would have agreed that history proved that Indians were advanced in the past because their women were advanced and that Indians are behind in the present because their women are behind. While deconstructing this perspective of two centuries ago, we still have to retrieve information from the ancient period itself, being careful to acknowledge that all analysis would reveal a political bias – in one case of colonial politics, in another of feminist politics. Accordingly, we will look at the "facts" below in the light of the debates and controversies that accompany them.

In an article published in 1988 in the popular journal *Economic and Political Weekly*, the scholars Chakravarti and Roy describe early writers on the subject. Looking at their argument allows us to gather together some of the topics that will be explored later in this book. The first is that to understand women or gender, we should be careful about an over-dependence on textual sources, especially when there is a dearth of other data. At least we must be equipped with difficult questions to put to those sources in order to interpret some of their silences. For instance, the woman of the Vedic period is eulogised in Vedic sources. That is partly the nature of the Vedas, a fairly celebratory account of the universe if read literally. But the same evidence could lead us to ask: if the woman *attends* the rituals, why is she not a subject in her own right? Why may she not perform rituals? Why may she not utter mantras? If the woman is allowed into the arenas of studying or debating, why is she stopped from asking more questions? Chakravarti and Roy discuss how early pioneers in the study of a new subject were partly romantics, products of their times, constrained by their views of social change. Clearly, the study of women and gender in South Asia has been shaped by an over-dependence on texts, thanks to both the availability and richness of these texts, and the need to respond with classical texts as evidence to the challenges of Christian missionary and British colonialist activity. As Chakravarti and Roy say, "The deciding factor in the debate was the relative antiquity of the sources utilised, the underlying assumption being that the older the source, the more authoritative and authentic it was" (1988, p. WS-3).

Other historians such as Altekar (1959) make generalisations about noble qualities exhibited by Aryan women and inferior qualities that characterise non-Aryan women. His approach was common, to exalt Brahmans as a class and the Aryans as a race. This left many other classes and communities out of the picture (in a doubly prejudiced way, since the Aryans were not a race). It also produced a warped picture of women in history, making the lower caste/class woman and the non-Aryan woman characterisable by many inferior traits.

> The introduction of the non-Aryan wife into the Aryan household is the key to the general deterioration of the position of women that began imperceptibly about 1000 BC and became quite marked in about 500 years. The non-Aryan wife with her ignorance of Sanskrit language and Hindu (sic) religion could not obviously enjoy the same religious privileges as the Aryan consort. Association with her must have tended to affect the purity of the Aryan co-wife as well.
>
> *(Altekar, 1959, pp. 345–346)*

If we look at other early historians, such as Chaudhuri (1956), Das (1962) and Jayal (1966), we find again that the stereotype of the Vedic woman as on a pedestal within an exalted Vedic society is already in place and not challenged. The restrictions placed on women, such as their inability to own property, or to perform rites for dead ancestors, are presented as almost biological characteristics of women, their essential qualities being passivity, timidity, conservatism, and so on. Underlying almost all these assumptions about the low status of women are two common beliefs. One is a racist or quasi-racist one in which the downfall in the status of women is ascribable to the intermarriage of upper with lower classes, attended by lower status for women, lower educational standards, a more diluted culture, and so on. The second is the trivialising of women's work, in agriculture, manufacture, and the house. The work is either ignored or treated as secondary and insignificant. An exception is the importance given to courtesans, as by Moti Chandra (1973), but his work also bears the underlying racist assumptions of others.

Chakravarti and Roy move on to looking at the work of Marxist and liberal historians, such as Kosambi (1962, 1975a, 1975b), Thapar (1978) and Sharma

(1983). The advance these historians make is in analysing the economic structure of society more rigorously, thus moving away from some prevalent stereotypes, but their failure lies in their blindness to the importance of searching directly for women's roles and gendered structures in society. The understanding of women and gender remains limited to a search for the occasional great woman, and even she is presented as a historical exception, and distorted to emphasise an emotional and dependent self, rather than a power-seeking and competitive self. Chakravarti and Roy call for a gendered history that would, from simply marshalling more data, take into account the issues of sexuality, production, as well as social reproduction.

Axel Michaels, in his *Hinduism: Past and Present* (2004), discusses how difficult it is to define Hinduism and attempts a definition which stresses the historical and geographical variations. Like many other scholars, most prominently Romila Thapar and Wendy Doniger (but see also Fuller, 1992; Hawley, 1991; Dalmia & von Stietencron, 1995), he finds it more precise to speak of a cluster of religions collectively given the name "Hinduism," which for convenience most of us prefer to call by one name, even if it is difficult, for Hindus and others, to find a common bottom line for what constitutes a Hindu. This is an ongoing debate, insofar that other scholars, such as Lorenzen (1999), do wish to use the name "Hinduism" as an appropriate term for the religion and feel that the questioning is overdone (and for different nuances of this, see Babb, 1986; Hiltebeitel, 2000; Talbot, 1995; Trautmann, 2005). In the schema of historical epochs that Michaels, Thapar, and other scholars draw up, the first four epochs concern us in this chapter, and we will explore their women and gender dimensions here.

The first period is that of the Indus Valley Civilisation (c. 3000–1800 BCE). Two findings are consensually agreed upon. The first is the probable worship of some form of a superior being or concept possible to identify as a Mother Goddess. Clay statues of a female form with an exaggerated womb and vagina point to the importance of reproduction and the possibility of cults and rituals revolving around fertility. At the same time, the reliance of the society on farming implied a participation by women in economic activity, alongside probable domination by men in other economic activities such as trade and construction.

The other information we have is of pleasure in beautification of the body at an everyday level, through the remains of accessories such as beads, bangles, and necklaces. While these must have been worn by both men and women, a little statue of a girl with an arm full of bangles, looking as if she were an ordinary, everyday person, with no hint of seclusion, indicates a certain equality of the sexes. However, the evidence is scarcer than we would have liked, and many of these ideas are not conclusions as much as speculations. Trade was intense and widespread and surely there were women as well as men traders. We simply do not know the gender of the engineers who were responsible for the uniform and precise cities of the Indus Valley, their drainage systems, and their impressive baths. Nor do we know the genders of those who administered and led the cities, nor of the many varieties of traders and manufacturers, craftspeople and labourers.

In some recent popular fiction that strives to base itself partially on history, authors such as Amish Tripathi try to fantasise from available evidence (Tripathi, 2010). Amish has created a civilisation called Meluha, another name of the Indus Valley Civilisation. Meluha's emperor is male, but many of its scientists are female. Women are trained warriors as men are. They choose on their own who to marry. The strictures of Meluha society fall equally on men and women, oppressively against those with birth defects, giving the name "Naga," for instance, to people with malformed limbs. One of these Nagas is a woman called Kali, the author's spin on a complex goddess in the Hindu pantheon who sometimes puzzles us by her non-conformism (to be discussed in Chapter 9), and another is a young man called Ganesh, a god in the Hindu pantheon who has an elephant head. The lesson from these contemporary writings is not only that we know very little about Meluha or the pre-Vedic civilisations but also that it is possible to imagine it one way or the other, which is the privilege of fiction, and that continuing questions and interpretations of the past are only natural.

All speculation is imbued with politics, however, which is important to take into account. Amish favours a scientism. His ancient India has made impressive scientific and technological advances, in city building, naval engineering, agriculture, manufacture, commerce, communication, philosophy, and even splitting the atom to make a nuclear bomb. Based on the uneven historical data that we actually have, this is clearly a position favoured by some educated Indians who would like to claim an advanced and glorious past. "Advanced" means an equality of the sexes and power to women, as well as technological advances. When this period of 2500 BCE to about 1200 BCE is celebrated as "advanced," there is a clear statement about gender. If an ancient civilisation was so advanced and present-day India or Pakistan is not, the idea is casually introduced and internalised that something went wrong with South Asian history in the middle period. The actual important debates about the denizens of the Indus Valley Civilisation are side-tracked in the implied questions of who should get the credit for their advanced level of life and who should be blamed for the fall after that. We should emphasise that while we have impressive archaeological evidence, especially the ruins of cities and a range of handicrafts, we do not have access to the script of the Indus Valley Civilisation. We know far more about the trade of the people (Kenoyer, 1991a) than about their consciousness, including gender consciousness. Historians and archaeologists interpret their data to tell us, for instance, that kin networks must have sustained such a large array of cities, and kin and lineage networks, we can safely say, indicate the role of women as both agents and pawns. The same is true of the distributed, but standardised, production of crafts and seals (Kenoyer, 1991a; Thapar, 1984).

The Vedic period (c. 1500 BCE–400 CE) follows after apparently a break in the historical record. The Indus Valley Civilisation came to an end, and the

Vedic people, also called the *Aryas* (English, Aryans), arrived in India from central Russia. There is no documented contact between the two and no carryover of Indus Valley achievements in urbanism and manufacture, or mutual influence of language or religion. For the Vedic period, we have a richer assortment of information, though it remains hugely controversial. The most important information comes from texts datable from circa 1200 BCE to 400 CE, all written in Sanskrit and include the Vedas, a corpus of hymns and poems; the Brahmans and Upanishads, books of teaching and reflection; and the two epics *Ramayana* and *Mahabharata*, with complicated multi-plotted stories of powerful families and ordinary people. The study and interpretation of all these texts are actively carried on by scholars, including for their gender implications.

In the Vedas, apart from esoteric and ritual meanings, we have sociological, political, and cultural information about Vedic society. The Aryans were patriarchal tribes of cattle herders who came to Northwestern India in search of pastures. They spoke an archaic Sanskrit, itself derived from an Indo-European mother tongue. They composed thousands of hymns which describe their social, political, religious, and philosophical concerns. Some of the hymns refer to battles in which those defeated are labelled "*dasas*" or "*dasyus*," that is "slaves." Some scholars, such as Thomas Trautmann and Romila Thapar, have tackled the controversial "Aryan debate" and "the racial theory of Indian civilisation," on which we can only touch briefly. The racial theory which in the colonial period itself became an accepted fact, states that

> the constitutive event for Indian civilisation . . . was the clash between invading, fair skinned, civilised Sanskrit-speaking Aryans and dark-skinned, barbarous aborigines. It was a local application of the double binary that guided all nineteenth-century European ethnologies, the double binary of the fair and the dark, the civilised and the savage.
>
> (*Trautmann, 1997, p. 194*)

"It was the work of Sanskritists, and British Sanskritists were at the forefront in its construction" (206). What the actual facts are, as Trautmann describes them, deserve to be quoted in full:

> The evidentiary base of the racial theory of Indian civilisation was never very firm, and subsequent developments have only served to weaken it further. Its great appeal for Europeans has been that it attributed the civilising of India to peoples related to themselves. But by the 1920 . . . [t]he discovery of the Indus Civilisation should have put paid to the racial theory of Indian civilisation. Coordinating the evidence of archaeology and textual study is never easy and what successors to the Indus Civilisation may have meant by the Vedic expressions "Dasa" and "Dasyu" is uncertain, but it is clear enough from the texts themselves that these peoples were in some ways more economically advanced . . . .

> What we know of the human resources out of which Indian civilization was built includes the following: We know that Sanskrit was brought to India from without and was spoken by people calling themselves Arya. We know that in India Sanskrit speakers encountered the speakers of distinct language families, including the Dravidian and the Austro-Asiatic. We know that there is a variety of complexions and physical features in the population of the Subcontinent today. . . . But, as has been argued since the 1850s, there is no necessary connection between race and language, or between race and civilization, so of what value is "race" as a biological concept for history?
>
> For Britons and Americans it is different. "Race" and "race relations" are meaningful terms with which they talk about the socially constructed "races" in their populations. But when they go to India, Britons and Americans cannot help being struck that these expressions disappear and their functional equivalents in Indian discourse are "communities" and "communalism." The markers of such communities are language, religions, and caste, but not complexion. Why then project an alien discourse onto the distant Indian past?
>
> *(Trautmann, 1997, pp. 215–216)*

The significant turn of historical events was the adoption of this racial theory of Indian civilisation by Indian nationalists and others. Almost from the time it was constructed by Western Orientalists, it came into favour among the new colonial-educated Indians. They were almost all upper caste and upper class themselves, and they needed a tool by which to prove their superiority against their colonial masters. To be armed with a theory that made them higher than the "rest" of Indians was empowering, even if the definitions of "us" and "them" within India remained imprecise.

These imprecise divisions continue to exist in the minds of Indians today, producing a grievous hierarchy. It is not uncommon for a college-educated young woman from North India to claim online that according to the history she knows she is descended from "the Aryans" and people in the South from "the Dravidians," implying, without her consciously bearing any fellow-Indians any ill-will, that her forefathers and present community are the true or superior bearers of Indian civilisation. This has a huge gender implication. Our college informant is female, thanks to the expansion of modern education, but even she is speaking only as her father's daughter. For the majority of Indians, identity is constructed by males along their descent lines, regardless of whom they marry. Male, upper-caste North Indians may typically carry a certain swagger of superiority that derives from nothing else but a vague knowledge of this racial theory of Indian civilisation. Women carry it because they identify with the male members of their families, even when there are many other dimensions to their identity, and a vague belief in "race," or "upper class-ness" comprises only *one* of the dimensions.

The racial theory of Indian civilisation, explains Romila Thapar (2005), was then given two interpretations, a Dalit one, pioneered by Jyotirao Phule (1827–1890), and a Hindutva one, pioneered by Veer Savarkar (1883–1966). According to the Dalit interpretation, the Aryans did invade and assert their superiority over indigenous peoples, who had already reached heights of civilisation unknown to the Aryans. For the Hindutva version, the Aryans did not come from outside but were already an indigenous people and are the same as the Indus people. The crux lies in that the Dalit interpretation divides a "Hindu" population into at least two, and the Hindutva interpretation seeks to emphasise a putative Hindu unity, with the only enemies the "outsiders," Muslims and Christians. The debate over the racial theory, explains Thapar,

> provides an insight into the political agendas of the groups who used it. These groups were involved in seeking identities from the past and in countering each other's claims to these identities as well as choosing a homeland and working out a national culture. The interpretation therefore hinged on specific ideological needs. . . . The primary concern in establishing an Indian identity was the need to define the rightful inheritors of the land, all within the context of a gradually growing nationalism where the question of origins and affirmation of common descent were central to nation-building. Such a concern required legitimation from history.
> *(Thapar, 2005, pp. 109–110)*

The history of this period is used in the present all the time. The Dalit interpretation of Jyotirao Phule was an incentive for reform. Phule, his wife Savitri, and his supporters set up schools for men and women. They regarded, as many have done since and do now, that the best way to remove the stigma of backwardness, produced by oppression and denial of opportunities over centuries, is to provide equal opportunities now. In this perspective, Dalits were and are targeted for reform, and similarly, women are regarded as an oppressed group in a way that cuts across caste and class.

"Hindutva" was a term that was coined in 1923 by Vinayak Damodar Savarkar, loosely translated as "Hindu-ness" or "Hindu identity." For the Hindutva interpretation, the project was the creation of a nationalism based on a "Hindu" identity. There were other kinds of nationalists as well but those who opposed the British on the basis of a certain reading of the Vedas and worked for a homeland that was "Hindu" came to join or sympathise with the BJP (Bharatiya Janata Party), the RSS (Rashtriya Swayamsewak Sangh), or the VHP (Vishwa Hindu Parishad). For this project, all differences in the past were erased. Whether low class or high, Dalit or Brahman, woman or man, everyone had been united in the past and had been at a pinnacle of achievement, and that was what they had to be brought about to become again. Indeed, women were celebrated even more than men for having been great in the past, since they had clearly fallen so low in the present. The main problems of women in the nineteenth century – their seclusion, lack of education, early marriage, enforced rules upon widowhood, and ban on remarriage – were labelled as later rules, having arisen from the influence of outsiders in Indian history. There had been a time somewhere in the Vedic age when women had not had these problems and were splendid torchbearers of an exemplary civilisation.

We can see the clear lines that lead from the Orientalist scholarship of Jones, Wilson, Mills, and Muller to Hindu nationalism, with the irony being that the nationalists thought that they were setting out to repudiate British intellectual control. The initial impact of British "discovery" of India's glorious past made a profound impact on Indian nationalists, both directly from their colonial education that included Indian history written from colonial perspectives and indirectly from a growing dissemination of images and narratives celebrating the Golden Age of Vedic society. That the British followed far more racial and imperialist policies in their rule in the next century, leading to no further celebration of any part of India's past, did little to weaken this initial impact. The story shifted from being one told by Europeans about India to one told by Indians about themselves. Historians such as Uma Chakravarti who have traced the intellectual history of the idea of Vedic greatness, have this to say:

> What was gradually and carefully constituted, brick by brick, in the interaction between colonialism and nationalism is now so deeply imbedded in the consciousness of the middle classes that ideas about the past have assumed the status of revealed truths. . . . But for women in particular this heritage, this perception of the past, of the 'lost glory', is almost a burden. It has led to a narrow and limiting circle in which the image of Indian womanhood has become both a shackle and a rhetorical device that nevertheless functions as a historical truth.
>
> *(Chakravarti, 1989, p. 28)*

Other scholars such as Wendy Doniger (1980) have focused on the other side of the question – how gender divisions in the Vedas may be understood from another, also partisan, feminist viewpoint that wishes to be more accurate about women's experiences, and to keep the body and sexuality at the centre. From Doniger's work, we know that pre-Vedic Indians tended to view the processes of sexual intercourse and birth in terms of the interaction of various bodily fluids. Fluids can substitute for each other, thus milk, rain, butter or honey for semen, and vice versa. All fluids are female, so women are important in the Vedas. The Vedic ritual is a model for sexual creation, but this is a chicken or egg question, for "the rituals are created and accepted because of their resonances with the basic processes of human physiology" (Doniger, 1980, p. 31). The rituals are described with sexual metaphors, sexual activity, and birth itself, with ritual metaphors. Male and female are mixed-up categories, though they are precise as grammatical categories. Woman is more complicated than man – she has two sites of sexual fluids to his one. She is also ambiguous – positive and negative, life-giving and life-draining. Her milk is ambiguous too. These body-sex ideas move from folk to classical as commonly as from classical to folk.

The Vedic pantheon personified nature, moral principles, and human and natural forces. Of these the majority were male, some were female, and there was scope for androgyny. The most important female deity was Aditi, the Un-bound or Free, the mother of all creation, the sky and air, all the celestial bodies, and all principles. Others included natural phenomena such as Ushas, the Dawn, and abstractions such as Vac, or Speech, also Breath. While the Vedic civilisation seems to originally have had a less developed patriliny – the father's name is not always adopted, nor are there separate names for paternal and maternal grandfathers – the movement was in the direction of greater evolution of father-centredness.

There are numerous references to the child, both son and daughter, in the Vedas. There was inequality between girls and boys for instrumental reasons – only sons performed the post-cremation rituals for males in the family – and, alongside that, ideological reasons. One could argue in rather a literal vein that, being a patriarchy, Vedic society gave no importance to daughters and that even though there is affection and attention given to the daughter, this is for mythological figures such as Ushas and Surya. In social terms, there would be no desire for a daughter, and most of all for a daughter without a son (Chakravarty, 2000). Other scholars, such as Stephanie Jamison (1996, 2011), make a case for dynamism and change. She argues that the language of the Veda can be read "against the grain" to find out about the social lives of the people, especially those not represented, such as women, and by extension, girls. If the sacrificer's wife becomes important in the yajna ritual, this indicates a change in Vedic society at a certain point to give more space to women. The yajna ritual was at the centre of the Vedic universe and permitted control over all kinds of yardsticks of success, including the begetting of sons (Patton, 2002). Almost all birth rites are for male children, but, surprisingly, there is the occasional one for females. The *Ashvalayana Grihya Sutra* (1.7.4–6) has a rite that allows a couple to choose whether they want only male children or female children or both (Patton, 2004). Maybe patriarchy is simply too broad a term, and we need to refine distinctions within it. Vedic society had a concept of gender that called for the participation of women, not only as producers of children but also as a complement to men – allowing us to complicate "rights" as well as "patriarchy," both very modern terms (Schmidt, 1987).

Then there is the interesting question of androgynes. Androgynes were usually males who become endowed with the properties of women, such as men who can have babies. Prajapati is suddenly endowed with a womb and breasts. No goddess gets endowed with a phallus. The "thigh" of the male is "churned" (*manthna*) – as butter is churned from milk or fire made by rubbing two sticks. The woman is the "field" in which the seed is sown and is not an active partner: "the child resembles the father in all socially significant qualities. . . . The early expressions of this idea are often coupled with aggressive and competitive feelings, not only toward the woman but toward the rival seed-sower" (Doniger, 1980, p. 29). But both men and women can create separately without each other. Semen and milk are both fertile, but semen more so; thus, it is the man who is typically androgynous.

In the *Brhadaranayaka Upanishad* also, we have the beginning of the idea of the importance of semen. It can be lost to one's body and carried to a rival or a woman. This exemplifies Geertz's idea that culture, or religion, is both a "model of" and a "model for" – ascetics are respected for retaining semen, but in everyday life, procreation is desirable and performed (Doniger, 1980, p. 47) – again in both classical and folk belief. In other Upanishads, the quest for knowledge conducted between teachers and students occasionally concerns girl students, but typically only males. Teachers are always male, though their wives are given respect alongside. Students are typically male, and the rare girl students, Maitreyi, Gargi, and Leelavati, are exceptions – and a pleasure – to read about.

A few more social descriptions of Vedic society would include an emphasis on the importance of cattle, as wealth, for their products, and as objects of rivalry and possible conflict. Men were almost certainly the raiders and fighters here, and women economically active, as those who milked and cared for the cows. The clans comprised by the Aryans originally had no kings and conducted their affairs in meetings from which women were not excluded, though they did not have an equal voice. As kingdoms emerged, and kings were male, some of the earlier fluidity disappeared. Rituals such as the *ashwamedh*, or horse sacrifice, tell us how power was conceived. The ritual included a mock copulation between the king and his senior queen, and between the queen and the sacrificed horse, which had been made to roam the extent of the king's territory to mark it. Land, power, sexual activity, and the magic produced by ritual come together to mark the horse sacrifice as one of the dominant sacrifices of the later Vedic period.

While Indra and other male gods of the Vedic pantheon have typical patriarchal marriages, many other forms of marriage are described. These include marrying outside one's clan or group, choosing one's spouse oneself, polygamy, polyandry, and even instances of brother-sister and mother-son incest. One myth describes Yama, the first mortal and then the ruler of the deceased, being seduced by his sister Yami, and rejecting her, which seems to mark the labelling of incest as forbidden – but not without a fight, as different powerful figures are shown to support Yama and Yami, respectively. Marriage is almost always depicted as based on love or desire, and emotionally equal for men and women. Sexual union and the corresponding relationship between husband and wife is a common metaphor for longing, clinging, intimacy, and fulfilment. We could end this discussion of the earlier and middle Vedic period with this comment about desire: desire is a great equaliser, and for a society to ascribe it to both sexes gives the questions of equality and inequality a continuing value.

Moving on to the later Vedic period, we come to the epics, *Ramayana* and *Mahabharata*, both composed in Sanskrit verse (c. 500 BCE–400 CE) and transmitted orally until they were put down in writing in the medieval period. With these epics, we are now truly in a land of multiple discourses. They reflect the movement of the Vedic peoples down the Gangetic Valley to Central India and the South, and the rise of kingdoms and possibly empires that sought to hold control over diverse communities in South Asia. The story of Prince Ram, in the epic *Ramayana*, is equally the story of Sita, his queen. If he is an *avatar* of Vishnu, she is of Lakshmi, and the daughter of Mother Earth, appearing in *sit*, a furrow. Ram's decisions and actions are important, but Sita's provide, equally, the turning points in the story. When Ram is banished for 14 years to the forest, Sita insists on accompanying him and braving all hardships. She continues to show the dignity of a queen and an ascetic, while also quite openly in love with her husband and affectionate towards his younger brother, Lakshman. Left alone in the forest, in one instance, she decides to respond to an ascetic's cries for alms. The ascetic is Ravana in disguise who abducts her. While she is Ravana's prisoner, she is adamant about holding aloof from him, although threatened by cannibalistic demonesses. She resists Ravana's advances through the sheer strength of her virtue and determination. When Ravana is defeated by Rama, however, and Rama and Sita are back in their home in Ayodhya, doubt is cast on Sita's chastity and she is exiled once again to a forest hermitage. Thus, Sita is repeatedly mistreated by men and stands proud and independent while that happens. At the same time, we must note the incident that leads to her abduction. It consists of a double folly, and one that seems peculiarly a feminine folly. She cannot resist the attractiveness of a doe that runs past and insists that Ram chase it and bring her its skin. The doe is a magical creature and both causes and symbolises her fall. She could have still remained safe because Lakshman drew a magic boundary line, or *rekha*, to protect her while he chased after Ram and the doe. Sita, unfortunately, crosses the line, again befuddled by the call of a magically disguised sage. Her "feminine" virtues of love for the beautiful and service of ascetics prove to be her undoing, and the fulcrum on which the whole story of the Ram-Ravana battle unfolds. Other readings of the story provide many nuances. What is Sita's *dharma*, both *stridharma*, or women's code of conduct, and *svadharma*, or her personal code? At more than one place, she successfully argues in favour of her own preferences by invoking the very concepts that seem to go against her. Hiltebeitel (2010) calls this a narrative crack or a counter-narrative that belies more solemn talk about laws and rules.

Other female characters in the *Ramayana* are important as well. Kaikeyi, the youngest of the three queens of Dashrath, is beautiful but impressionable and is persuaded by a scheming maid, Manthra, to demand her own son Bharat's succession as king in place of Ram, and Ram's exile. This demand sets the first portion of the story in motion. Dashrath is both a slave to her and an honourable man who has given her a promise to fulfil any two vows because of her prowess in an earlier battle. She had saved his life in the battle – a feat not remarked upon in the story as being exceptional. There are also queens in Lanka, Ravana's kingdom, who are bored with their degenerate luxury and doubtful about their lord's ethics. They have beauty and also intelligence, particularly Ravana's chief queen, Mandodari, who provokes his anger by reasoning with him about his poor choices. There are the demonesses throughout the land, who seem to be one-dimensionally evil, as do the demons, but have prior histories that often explain their being trapped in hideous bodies. Then, there are the less interesting characters such as Ahalya and Shabri. Ahalya proves that adultery does not pay. She made love once to a disguised Indra while her husband was away and was cursed to become a stone who could be brought back to life only upon Ram's advent. He comes and her imprisonment is over. Shabri is a low-caste woman bursting with love for Ram. He visits her and she greets him with berries that she has personally tasted to ensure their sweetness. He is not, of course, contaminated by the touch of this underclass person's mouth. Men can be unjust and fierce, and also be charitable and sensitive. Women are also different things: whimsical, conspiratorial, self-sacrificing, determined, and also weak, misled, and waiting for a saviour. The core story is arguably not told from a woman's point of view. But it has thousands of re-tellings, as scholars tell us (Richman, 1991, 2001), and some of them are pro-women. In one version, the maid Manthra is simply an oppressed lower-class citizen of Ayodhya, speaking out against the injustice of the dictatorial regime of Dashratha. All in all, the *Ramayana*, precisely because it is a story open to interpretation and one that legitimately has hundreds of versions, is both anti-women and has complex gender messages about women's strength.

The *Mahabharata*, if anything, has even more complex gender messages. It features two related families, the Pandavas and the Kauravas, sons of two brothers Pandu and Dhritarashtra. The five Pandavas are more or less true to their identity of being male warriors of the Kshatriya caste. The hundred Kaurava brothers, and their eldest, Duryodhana, are not, and get swayed by greed, jealousy, and ambition. There are interesting elders of great power and teachers of secret knowledge, martial and spiritual. All these roles are strictly restricted to males. Not only are the Pandavas and the seniors all male bearers of *dharma*, that is, personal law and the law of the land, *Dharma* itself is personified as a male god.

There are at least four women who are interesting as embodiments of different aspects of gender relations. The first is Kunti, the mother of the Pandavas and of an earlier son born out of wedlock. She exemplifies the honour given to mothers as grown sons throughout seek her blessings and support. They are proud of their appellations as "sons of Kunti." To her son who was born when she was unmarried, she apologises some 20 years later, and when he expresses his anger at being abandoned, she explains, humbly (as if the composer of that part of the epic was a woman), "I was young and insecure." This son has been born of the Sun, and her other sons are born of other Gods. Her co-wife and she are both obliged to choose such fathers for their offspring because a curse disables their husband Pandu from sleeping with them. So, women feel strongly that they must be mothers of sons, but they could have them with their husbands *or* other lovers, and abandon them *or* bring them up.

Gandhari, the mother of the Kauravs, does not apparently pay any attention to her sons' upbringing, and they are unethical and treacherous. But she is a fine wife, choosing to voluntarily act blind with a blindfold on her eyes to keep her blind husband company. Hers is not a major role, and my second interesting character is Amba, a princess who swears revenge on her stepbrother Bhishma, because he initially has her abducted together with her sisters and then abandoned because she does not accept the proposed marriage. Her vow is that the invulnerable Bhishma, who has the boon of invincibility against man or woman, *will* meet death at her hands. Through unmatched penance, she is re-born as a woman-man, a woman who changes into a man, and is thus both man and woman, or neither. Shikhandi, as they are now called, kills Bhishma. Bhishma wills it, in that he announces, "I will not use my arrows against a woman, one who was once a woman, one whose name is like a woman's, or one who resembles a woman. For this reason, I will not kill Sikhandi" (Vanita & Kidwai, 2008, p. 36). It is the biggest death, perhaps, of the Mahabharata, and there are many to choose from, as the epic's grand heroes fall left and right. Bhishma's character points to one of the subversive themes of the seemingly normative epic. It is not really enthusiastic about heterosexual couples, and not simply because of any misogynous ways but as a conceptual universe that sees procreation as the justification of marriage, and friendship between man and man, or woman and woman, and more rarely, man and woman, as more liberating and satisfying. Asceticism, as Bhishma's, is of course the most-empowering state of being. Even within marriage, however, as in the case of the Pandavas, a man could partner with his wife only minimally and remain for many purposes an ascetic. That was partly the secret of the Pandavas' power. The patriarchal compulsion of marrying and producing male heirs, although seemingly the preoccupation of Hindu society, is precisely what leads to trouble and tragedy (Vanita & Kidwai, 2008).

The third woman is Satyavati, the stepmother of the aforementioned Bhishma. She is brought up as a lowly fisherman's daughter who first has an illegitimate son, Vyasa, on negotiation with her lover that he should restore her virginity and make her fragrant (instead of smelling of fish). Vyas is left on an island. Then, she marries King Shantanu on condition that Bhishma, his son, or his progenies will not succeed to the throne and her sons will. When her sons die childless, she persuades Vyasa, her oldest son, to sleep with her daughters-in-law, in turn, which acts give her the grandsons Pandu and Dhritarashtra. Her calculations and confidence at every turn are responsible to a large extent for the plot of the Mahabharata; her greed or ambition, her articulation of events as they unfold, and her clear choices and decisiveness are all as admirable as any man's in the epic. More interestingly, we have an instance, repeated elsewhere, that virginity meant, as it were, freedom, and that some women, reflected in their virginity being restored after sex, were constantly free.

Finally, we have Draupadi, the wife of the five Pandava brothers. Draupadi is not developed as elaborately in the Mahabharata as elsewhere, except to say that she was dedicated to her husbands and furious at being gambled away by them and then disgraced in public. She is of a fiery nature, being born of fire, and this and other similar associations have led her to be celebrated in many parts of India, North and South, as a goddess, indeed, the supreme protector of the Pandavas, a persona for whom anything is possible (Hiltebeitel, 1988). Draupadi is in fact correlated with powerful, emerging goddesses, Durga and Kali. Draupadi is an epic goddess, and also a wife, mother and virgin. She is the *Sakti* of the five Pandavas who guards and protects them. She delivers them after the battle from their sins of Brahminicide and the killing of all the Kauravs and making their wives widows.

Apart from the Vedas, Upanishads, Epics, and the multiple strands in the reading and understanding of each, there is something called "folk religion."

> [U]nlike other religious traditions, such as, the *bhakti* of the saints; the brahmanical approach to deities who, according to the *Puranas*, mostly reside in heaven; or such ascetic, yogic or Saivite movements as the Naths, folk religion does not describe or explain itself.
>
> *(Sontheimer, 1995, p. 389)*

This religion consists of deities, rituals, and observances concerned with fertility and reproduction, with leading a good life and well-being and prosperity to the family, and with renewal of life and immortality through children. These concerns are expressed through performance, competition, playacting, dance, narration, possession, sacrifice, and ribaldry. Nothing is "sacred" as gods themselves fall madly in love, act foolishly, and are chided. Social groups are temporarily abolished and the impure is regarded as a source of auspiciousness. This "instinctive, periodical re-alignment with the power of nature" comes in modern times to often be condemned as superstition and to be de-linked with religion.

Insofar as that fertility, seasonality, reproduction, and the good life are all gender-neutral values and are more attuned to the female, this modern "loss" of folk, tribal, and popular religion has marked a shift of balance between the male and the female. Organised and urbanised, middle-class religion is more patriarchal and masculine. Examples of the folk, such as the *jatra* in Maharashtra and the *Chho* dance in Purulia, West Bengal, are polyvalent practices and not best understood under generalising constructs such as "folk" or "tribal," just as "Hindu" itself is not a homogeneous construct. Moreover, any folk practices today are reconstructions in modern times, datable variously over a hundred to two hundred years. They have become objectified and strive towards an authenticity, even while the practitioners themselves remain fluid, recognising the need to perform for an audience and for scholars (Chatterji, 1995, p. 440).

We can look for the influence of the Vedic period on today's India, or more precisely, look at the influence of the *ideas* about the Vedic period, in two contrasting roles of women today. One is that of ascetics, and the larger practice of asceticism. The other is that of the worldly woman, one who gratifies her senses and presents herself for the consumption of others. Let us begin our discussion of asceticism by looking at the four life stages, or *ashrams*. These are *brahmacharya*, or celibate studenthood, entered upon by performance of the thread ceremony; *grihastin*, or householding, entered upon by marriage; *vanaprastha*, or retirement, entered upon (informally) by becoming a grandparent; and *sanyasa*, or renunciation, a stage rarely entered and needing a guru's initiation. There is some evidence that in the Vedic period girls, together with boys, had the sacred thread ceremony and could become students who learnt the Vedas and to perform Vedic rituals (Denton, 2004, p. 27). By around 500 BCE, this sacred thread ceremony "had become for girls a symbolic rite performed just before marriage" (Denton, 2004, p. 27). Still later, say about 300 CE, girls had lost the right to student status altogether. Their initiation consisted of the ritual of marriage and their guru consisted of their husband. "As the Manusmrti (II.67) succinctly puts it:

> The nuptial ceremony is stated to be the Vedic sacrament for women (and to be equal to the initiation), serving the husband (equivalent to) the residence in (the house of the teacher, and the household duties (the same) as the (daily) worship of the sacred fire.
>
> *(quoted in Denton, 2004, pp. 27–28)*

This is far from the whole story, however. From ancient times, the textual authority of the *shastras*, or classical texts, is balanced by the authority of *laukik*, or popular practices. Some of these are indirectly referred to in the texts, some are directly incorporated, and some are simply observed as legitimate by people ("the fifth Veda"). If the classical strictures, such as in Manu, are *stridharma*, or the duties of women, women's everyday practices are *striacar*, or the traditions of women. Moreover, there is ambiguity about the actual nature of women. On the one hand is their dependence on, and inferiority to, men. On the other hand is their *ardhangini* (half-body) status with men, that is, their need at every household ritual; their *manglic*, or auspicious status; and their *shakti*, or power in procreation. Because of all these dimensions of a woman, consensually reported in oral discourse and practised every day but also acknowledged in the texts, the possibility of becoming ascetics is open to women as well. Asceticism is the highest status possible in the Hindu world view.

On the opposite side is the worldly woman or the seeker after beauty and charm. Much will be said about her later, but in this chapter, we want to see the prevalence of a discourse for women that claims descent from the Vedas. These claims are intangible but they include a preference for a fair skin since descent from fair ancestors is being claimed. Such claims have been mined for huge market profit by multinational and national companies such as Pond's, L'Oreal, and Fair and Lovely to present fairness as "natural," and if elusive, as something hiding under the surface that will be teased out by creams and appropriate treatments. At the same time, in a research I conducted on ideas about beauty, almost every woman interviewed claimed that her preference as beauty treatment was for "natural" products – flours, herbs, vegetables, milk, honey, and so on – rather than chemical products. The companies marketing their lab-based products then have to play a really interesting game of words and images to project what they are proposing as "natural" at two levels – part of the nature of the people addressed, and the products as being not in conflict with the natural world. They prove beyond any doubt how the "natural" is the most constructed of all.

The later Vedic period came to be called "Vedanta," or "the end/culmination of the Vedas." Vedanta has come to be the name of the philosophy enshrined in the Upanishads, over two hundred texts composed between 600 BCE and 200 CE, of which about a dozen are considered the most important ones. Women figure in the Upanishads more than they do in the Vedas, though women such as Apala Atreyl, Ghosa Kaksivati, and Lopamudra are said to have authored whole or parts of Rig Vedic hymns (Haddad & Findly, 1985) The two fundamental concepts of the Upanishads, namely Brahma and Atman, or the Universal Essence and the Personal Soul or Life, respectively, are a-gendered or un-gendered nature. Thus, when the teacher asks the student to bring a seed or a pot and asks searching questions regarding it, the actual student described may be male, but the conclusion of the conversation is not restricted in any sense to male beings. The second related way in which women are seen is as actual people engaged in learning and questioning. The most famous of these are Gargi and Maitreyi.

Yajnavalkya, one of the learned Brahmans of the Brhadaranyaka Upanishad, who claimed to be the most learned, was set questions in turn by a host of learned Brahmans. He patiently answered them all, in doing which he covered a large territory of the philosophy of the Upanishads. Then a woman, Gargi, begins to question him. She proceeds exactly like the others, in a style where the answer to a question leads logically to the next question, and Yajnavalkya is answering her with the same mixture of patience and confidence that he shows the others. Except at the end, when he seems nonplussed.

> "On what, then, are the worlds of Prajapati woven back and forth?"
> "On the worlds of *brahman*, Gargi."
> "On what, then, are the worlds of *brahman* woven back and forth?"
> At this point Yajnavalkya tells her: "Don't ask too many questions, Gargi, or your head will shatter apart! You are asking too many questions."
> 
> (Olivelle, 1996, p. 40)

A while later, Gargi questions the eminent sage again, saying, "Distinguished Brahmins! I am going to ask this man two questions. If he can give me the answers to them, none of you will be able to defeat him in a theological debate." She proceeds with her two questions and is satisfied with the answers: "Distinguished Brahmins! You should consider yourself lucky if you escape from this man by merely paying him your respects. None of you will ever defeat him in a theological debate" (Olivelle, 1996, pp. 45–46).

It was the same Yajnavalkya who was making a settlement of his wealth and property between his two wives when he was challenged by one of them, Maitreyi, with the central Upanishadic question about reality, "If I were to possess the entire world filled with wealth, sir, would it make me immortal?" She then spurns his wealth and says, "Tell me instead, sir, all that you know." Yajnavalkya obliges with a long discourse that includes the Upanishad's conundrum, "By what means can one perceive him by means of whom one perceives this whole world? Look – by what means can one perceive the perceiver?" (Olivelle, 1996, pp. 28–30).

Whether this was a question for both women and men, or just men, we do not know. There is no reason to believe that men monopolised learning and thought. However, our own knowledge is limited and our tools for finding out more about this period.

Those who were not part of the Upanishadic scholastic tradition nevertheless were knowledgeable in other ways. There were craftsmen, farmers, merchants, and assorted professional groups, each with their own knowledge systems and structures of transmission. Women definitely participated in these. Additionally, they had their own "women's knowledge" since they were the primary child bearers and caregivers in the family. All the historical details of these are still to be uncovered.

## Bibliography

Altekar, A. S. (1959). *The position of women in Hindu civilisation*. Delhi: Motilal Banarasidass. (Original work published 1938)

Babb, L. A. (1986). *Redemptive encounters: Three modern styles in the tradition*. Berkeley, CA: University of California Press.

Basham, A. L. (1975). *The wonder that was India* (Based revised edition of 1967). Calcutta: Rupa and Co.

Chakravarti, U. (1989). Whatever happened to the vedic *Dasi*? Orientalism, nationalism and a script for the past. In K. Sangari & S. Vaid (Eds.), *Recasting women: Essays in colonial history* (pp. 27–87). Delhi: Kali for Women.

Chakravarti, U., & Roy, K. (1988). In search of our past: A review of the limitations and possibilities of the historiography of women in early India. *Economic and Political Weekly, 23*(18), 2–10.

Chakravarty, U. (2000). Vedic daughter. *Annals of the Bhandarkar Oriental Research Institute, 81*(1/4), 179–189.

Chandra, M. (1973). *The world of courtesans*. New Delhi: Vikas.

Chandra, V. (2010). *Gender relations in early India*. Jaipur: Rawat Publications.

Chatterji, R. (1995). Authenticity and tradition: Reappraising a 'folk' form. In V. Dalmia & H. von Stietencron (Eds.), *Representing Hinduism: The construction of religious traditions and national identity* (pp. 420–441). New Delhi: Sage Publications.
Chaudhuri, J. B. (1956). *Position of women in the Vedic ritual.* Calcutta: The Author.
Dalmia, V. (1995). 'The only real religion of the Hindus': Vaisnava self-representation in the late nineteenth century. In V. Dalmia & H. von Stietencron (Eds.), *Representing Hinduism the construction of religious traditions and national identity* (pp. 176–210). New Delhi: Sage Publications.
Dalmia, V., & von Stietencron, H. (Eds.). (1995). *Representing Hinduism: The construction of religious traditions and national identity* (pp. 420–441). New Delhi: Sage Publications.
Das, R. M. (1962). *Women in Manu and his seven commentators.* Varanasi: Kanchana Publications.
Denton, L. T. (2004). *Female ascetics in Hinduism.* Albany, NY: State University of New York.
Dirks, N. (1989). The invention of caste: Civil society in colonial India. *Social Analysis, 5.*
Dirks, N. (1992). *Colonialism and culture.* Ann Arbor, MI: University of Michigan Press.
Doniger, W. (1973). *Asceticism and eroticism in the mythology of Siva.* Oxford: Oxford University Press.
Doniger, W. (1980). *Women, androgynes, and other mythical beasts.* Chicago, IL: University of Chicago Press.
Doniger, W. (1991). Hinduism by any other name. *Wilson Quarterly,* 35–34.
Doniger, W. (1999). *Splitting the difference: Gender and myth in ancient Greece and India.* Delhi: Oxford University Press.
Frykenberg, R. (1989). The emergence of modern 'Hinduism' as a concept and as an institution: A reappraisal with special reference to South India. In G. D. Sontheimer and H. Kulke (Eds.), *Hinduism reconsidered.* Delhi: Manohar.
Fuller, C. J. (1992). *The camphor flame: Popular Hinduism and society in India.* Princeton, NJ: Princeton University Press.
Haddad, Y. Y., & Findly, E. B. (Eds.). (1985). *Women, religion, and social change.* Albany, NY: State University of New York Press.
Hawley, J. S. (1991). Naming Hinduism. *Wilson Quarterly,* 20–34.
Hiltebeitel, A. (1980). Draupadi's garment. *Indo-Iranian Journal, 22,* 198–212.
Hiltebeitel, A. (1981). Draupadi's hair. *Purusartha, 5,* 179–214.
Hiltebeitel, A. (1988). *The cult of Draupadi: Mythologies: From Gingee to Kuruksetra* (Vol. 1). Chicago, IL: University of Chicago Press.
Hiltebeitel, A. (1991). Of camphor and coconuts. *Wilson Quarterly,* 26–28.
Hiltebeitel, A. (2000). Draupadi's questions. In A. Hiltebeitel & K. M. Erndl (Eds.), *Is the goddess a feminist? The politics of south Asian goddesses* (pp. 113–122). Washington Square, NY: New York University Press.
Hiltebeitel, A. (2010). *Dharma.* Honolulu, HI: The University of Hawai'i Press.
Hopkins, T. J. (1971). *The Hindu religious tradition.* Encino, CA: Dickenson Publishing Co.
Jamison, S. W. (1996). *Sacrificed wife/sacrificer's wife: Women, ritual, and hospitality in ancient India.* New York: Oxford University Press.
Jamison, S. W. (2011). The sacred lives of texts. *Journal of the American Oriental Society, 131*(1), 1–7.
Jayal, S. (1966). *The status of women in the epics.* Delhi: Motilal Banarasidass.
Kenoyer, J. M. (1991a). The Indus valley tradition of Pakistan and Western India. *Journal of World Prehistory, 5*(4), 331–385.

Kenoyer, J. M. (1991b). Urban process in the Indus tradition: A preliminary model from Harappa. In R. H. Meadow (Ed.), *Harappa excavations 1986–1990: A multidisciplinary approach to third millennium urbanism*. Madison, WI: Prehistory Press.

Kosambi, D. D. (1962). *Myth and reality*. Bombay: Popular Prakashan.

Kosambi, D. D. (1975a). *An introduction to the study of Indian history*. Bombay: Popular Prakashan.

Kosambi, D. D. (1975b). *The culture and civilisation of ancient India in historical outline*. New Delhi: Vikas.

Lorenzen, D. N. (1999). Who invented Hinduism? *Comparative Studies in Society and History*, *41*(4), 630–659.

Lutgendorf, P. (1997). Imagining Ayodhya: Utopia and its shadows in a Hindu landscape. *International Journal of Hindu Studies*, *1*(1), 19–54.

Marshall, P. J. (1970). *The British discovery of Hinduism in the eighteenth century*. Cambridge: Cambridge University Press.

Michaels, A. (2004). *Hinduism: Past and present* (Trans. B. Harshav). Hyderabad: Orient Longman.

Mill, J. (1972). *The history of British India, with notes by H. H. Wilson* (5th ed.). London: James Madden. (Original work published 1840)

Mueller, M. (1880). *Lectures on the origin and growth of religion, as illustrated by the religions of India*. London: Longmans, Green.

O'Flaherty, W. D. (1981). *The Rig Veda: An anthology*. Harmondsworth: Penguin.

Olivelle, P. (Trans.). (1996). *Upanisads*. Oxford: Oxford University Press.

Pargiter, F. E. (1972). *Ancient Indian historical tradition* (p. 69). Delhi: Motilal Banarsidass.

Patel, K. C. (1994). Women, earth, and the goddess: A Shakta-Hindu interpretation of embodied religion (Feminist philosophy of religion). *Hypatia*, *9*(4), 69–87.

Patton, L. (2002). Mantras and miscarriage: Controlling birth in the late Vedic period. In *Jewels of authority: Women and textual tradition in Hindu India*. New York: Oxford University Press.

Patton, L. (2004). If the fire goes out, the wife shall fast: Notes on women's agency in the *Ashvalayana Grihya Sutra*. In *Problems in Vedic literature: Essays in honor of G. U. Thite* (pp. 294–305). New Delhi: New Bharatiya.

Pollock, S. (1993). Ramayana and political imagination in India. *Journal of Asian Studies*, *52*(2), 261–297.

Ramaswamy, S. (2001). Maps and mother goddesses in modern India. *Imago Mundi*, *53*, 97–114.

Richman, P. (1991). *Many Ramayanas: The diversity of a narrative tradition in South Asia*. Berkeley, CA: University of California Press.

Richman, P. (2001). *Questioning Ramayanas: A south Asian tradition*. Berkeley, CA: University of California Press.

Roy, R. (1978). *The English works of Raja Rammohun Roy with an English translation of 'Tuhfatul Muwahhidin'* (This is a reprint of the 1906 edition). New York: AMS Press.

Schmidt, H. P. (1987). *Some women's rites and rights in the Veda*. Pune: Bhandarkar Oriental Research Institute.

Sharma, R. S. (1983). *Perspectives on the economic and social history of early India*. New Delhi: Munshiram Manoharlal.

Smith, W. C. (1989). *The meaning and end of religion*. Minneapolis: Fortress Press (First published in Sontheimer, G. D. and Kulke, H. (Eds.). (1989). *Hinduism reconsidered*. Delhi: Manohar).

Sontheimer, G. D. (1995). The erosion of folk religion in modern India: Some points for deliberation. In V. Dalmia & H. von Stietencron (Eds.), *Representing Hinduism: The construction of religious traditions and national identity* (pp. 389–398). New Delhi: Sage Publications.

Talbot, C. (1995). Inscribing the other, inscribing the self: Hindu-Muslim identities in pre-colonial India. *Comparative Studies in Society and History, 37*(4), 692–722.

Thapar, R. (1978). *Ancient Indian social history.* Delhi: Orient Longmans.

Thapar, R. (1984). *From lineage to state: Social formations in the mid-first millennium B.C. in the Ganga valley.* Bombay: Oxford University Press.

Thapar, R. (1985). Syndicated Moksha? *Seminar,* 14–22.

Thapar, R. (1989). Imagined religious communities? Ancient history and the modern search for a Hindu identity. *Modern Asian Studies, 23,* 209–231.

Thapar, R. (1996). *"The tyranny of labels," IX Zakir Husain memorial lecture.* New Delhi: Zakir Husain College.

Thapar, R. (2005). Some appropriations of the theory of Aryan race relating to the beginnings of Indian history. In T. Trautmann (Ed.), *The Aryan debate* (pp. 106–128). New Delhi: Oxford University Press.

Trautmann, T. R. (1997). *Aryans and British India.* New Delhi: Vistaar Publications.

Trautmann, T. R. (Ed.). (2005). *The Aryan debate.* New Delhi: Oxford University Press.

Tripathi, A. (2010). *The immortals of Meluha.* Delhi: Westland Press.

Vanita, R., & Kidwai, S. (Eds.). (2008). *Same-sex love in India: A literary history.* New Delhi: Penguin Books.

Wilson, H. H. (1850–1888). *Rig Veda-Samhita: A collection of ancient Hindu hymns* (6 volumes). London.

Wilson, H. H. (1972). *Religious sects of the Hindus.* Varanasi: Indological Book House. (Original work published 1846)

Witzel, M. (2009). Female rishis and philosophers in the Veda? *Journal of South Asian Women's Studies, 11*(1).

# 3
# BUDDHISM AND THE EMERGENCE OF HINDUISM

## The Maurya and Gupta Periods

In this chapter, we are going to look at the period roughly seventh century BCE to seventh century CE, comprising three historical eras: the Mauryan Empire and Buddhism; Preclassical Hinduism; and Classical Hinduism or the Golden Age of the Gupta Empire. The starting dates overlap with the period discussed in Chapter 2, and similarly we will not be hard and fast about the ending date. The historiographical issues are three inter-related ones: the question of periodisation, the implications of "equality," and the meaning of "Classical."

Indian history has tended to be periodised as divisible into the Ancient, Medieval, and Modern periods, and also as the Hindu, Muslim, and British periods. The Hindu-Muslim periodisation is based on a colonial prejudice that preferred to see historical developments in India as dependent on religion, with the "British" standing for a rationality that overcame religion. The Ancient-Medieval-Modern is based on a division used in European history that has limited our understanding of the actual historical changes in India that might more fruitfully be periodised in completely different ways. For instance, the dominance of Buddhism with both elite and masses should lead to a Buddhist period, or that of Ascetic Reformism, including the Mauryan Empire. Only if we make the correct chronological divisions could we ask the important questions for this book: was this period substantially different from the earlier Vedic period with regard to the conditions of life for women and with regard to the constructions of masculinity and femininity?

The second challenge is to be sensitive to our modern ideas about equality and egalitarianism, according to which one important aim is to erase the difference between women and men. As many feminists argue, while such equality is desirable, it should still be complicated by the internal differentiation between women and men. Women are divided among themselves, and the issues of class

DOI: 10.4324/9781003393252-4

and power *within* the category "woman" must be given as much consideration as an overall separation of the categories "women" and "men." So should the differentiation of men along class and status lines always be recognised? When we look at a historical period two thousand years ago as in the present chapter, we must be sensitive to context as we pass judgement on "equality," specifically the period's own divisions of people according to gender, and equally, class, caste, and power.

The third issue, then, is for whom precisely is the "Classical" period to be considered that height of Indian or Hindu civilisation, as several historians, such as the venerable A. L. Basham, present the Gupta period to be? Other historians, such as Romila Thapar, explain how cities were less advanced in this period compared to other times, class divisions were greater, poverty worse, and caste emergent. It seems fair to say that this top-down version of history that makes this period seem like a Golden Age of India is definitely one of the impressive achievements *for the upper classes*. In a gendered version such as ours, we would discover right away that masculinity became more aggressive and pronounced in this period. The true "Golden Age" from a feminist perspective still has to be researched and discovered, if we hold that one indeed might have existed.

In the late Vedic period (c. 850–500 BCE), there was continuity from the past in that the sacrifice, or *yajna*, remained the main ritual to make the gods perform according to the laws that were understood to underlie the functioning of the universe. The knowledge about rituals was in the hands of priests who had by then become all-powerful "gods on earth." These were male Brahmans of a certain age. At the same time, monks and ascetics continued their quest for knowledge and control outside the Vedic ritual system as well, and they increasingly became critics of the Brahman way of life. They were called *Shramans*, a term that may be used for a large variety of practitioners of non-Brahmanic belief systems, such as Naths, Yogis, Saivites, and Bhaktas. The term came to include Buddhist monks as well.

Scholars call the sixth century BCE a watershed in Indian history, marked by profound economic, political, and ideological changes. Economic changes took place as iron-based technology developed, and iron tools and weapons were used to clear the lower Ganges valley for agriculture. With the emergence of an agricultural surplus, there came to be kingdoms and cities, tax collection, bookkeeping, and writing. There was a clearer division of labour and an association of labourers and merchants, each on professional grounds, even as hereditary divisions of work gradually got more entrenched. The appearance of cities and a new urban elite in turn produced rationalisation in thought and religious philosophy. The two main rationalist philosophies of South Asia, Buddhism and Jainism, have been described as products "of the time of urban development, or urban kingship and the city nobles" (Max Weber, quoted in Michaels, 2004, p. 36). This is perhaps surprising in that the new monastic movements of Buddhism and Jainism, just as in Upanishadic thought, seem to see life as suffering and the task of knowledge to propound a doctrine of salvation from it. Apparently, improved technological and ecological conditions were also accompanied by famine, poverty, and oppression. The new urban cultures, the use of writing, and the patronage of elites also made possible more in-depth philosophical debates.

The Maurya dynasty (c. 327–187 BCE) was of a low varna, perhaps *Sudras*. Its founder Chandragupta was mentored into starting an empire by the Brahman Chanakya, called Kautilya (c. 321 BCE) (all the dates of this period are somewhat tentative). He is typically called "clever" or "wily," and authored the important treatise, the *Arthashastra*, a book on political economy (or it might have been attributed to him by several different authors compiling it over a period of time). After territorial conquest and diplomatic negotiation, the largest empire known in South Asian history was founded, famous as the Maurya Empire. The third king of this dynasty, Ashoka, who called himself Piyadassi, the beloved of the gods, both made history and left us wonderful historical records. He dotted the landscape with edicts on rock surfaces and polished sandstone pillars. In c. 260 BCE, Ashoka campaigned against Kalinga in Orissa, to control or re-control the last remaining territory outside his empire. According to the way history has been pieced together regarding this event, the violence in this particular battle led Ashoka to adopt Buddhism and forswear violence both for himself and for his whole population. His rock edict states

> On conquering Kalinga the Beloved of the Gods felt remorse, for when an independent country is conquered the slaughter, death and deportation of the people is extremely grievous to the Beloved of the Gods and weighs heavily on his mind.
>
> *(Thapar, 2002, p. 181)*

A second important source for the period are Buddhist chronicles that record the spread of Buddhism. According to them, Ashoka's conversion to non-violence and other Buddhist principles was at least partly related to his marriage to Devi, of a Shakya family with perhaps kinship to the Buddha's own Shakya family. She was a Buddhist, and her children with Ashoka, Mahindra and Sanghamitra, were ordained as young adults as Buddhist monk and nun.

Buddhism was an egalitarian preaching with regard to class and caste and, to some degree, gender. Women were converted independently to Buddhism – when Ashoka supposedly fell in love with Devi, a merchant's daughter, *she was already a Buddhist* who influenced him to take the Buddha's teaching seriously. Devi's influence on Ashoka is perhaps more important in history than is recorded in our three sources. The princess Sanghamitra is somewhat better documented. Together with her brother Mahindra, she was an ambassador of Buddhism who travelled far and wide. She was the first of many ambassadors, but arguably the most important, who brought Buddhism to Sri Lanka, China, and East and Southeast Asia.

There were Buddhist women ascetics, even if we cannot say how many. At the same time, the love of life, apart from withdrawal from it, continued unabated.

The sources for the period, Ashoka's inscriptions, and Kautilya's *Arthashastra*, a manual of advice and description as to how an ideal kingdom should be administered, bear witness to this love of life. The carvings and images, as well as the literature, tell us that there were women archers and guards, prostitutes, musicians, and dancers. The prostitutes were regarded as independently wealthy and were taxed. There were women artisans and farmers and of course ordinary townswomen and peasant women. In certain communities, women and men shared equally in work: "fishermen, fowlers, cowherds, vintners and others" (Habib & Jha, 2004, p. 136). Perhaps the "individualism" that characterised the period, if that is the right term, infected both women and men. However, one of the differences that marked higher classes as different from lower ones was, even then, the seclusion of women. Those who were bonded and enslaved were not only women but both men and women. Women had rights to *stridhana*, literally, women's property, but these could be forfeited, and if there were sons, then a daughter could end up inheriting nothing.

Another important source, the Greek ambassador Megasthenes' *Indica* (not itself extant but partly available to us from extracts and quotations in other places) also gives us odd bits of information on women. Together from all the sources, we know that Chandragupta was guarded by female slaves. They must have been trained specially and trained well. They must have been trusted. We also know that domestic slavery was common, and women slaves could be harshly treated. While only a few temples are mentioned, they seem to have had "slaves" or dedicated women, *devadasis*. Then, there was a marriage alliance between Seleucus and Chandragupta of which the details are unknown; obviously, an established procedure was to exchange a woman for solidarity. Megasthenes also records an instance of *sati daha*, or the immolation of a widow on her husband's funeral pyre.

From Kautilya's *Arthashastra* we know that the King had to attend to people in a certain order. In this order of 11 categories, the bottom-most consisted of "the helpless and women" (Chap. III.iii, Rangarajan, 1992, p. 148). Property was inherited only along the male line, with the rights to maintenance by widows. However, "rich widows" are mentioned in several places, and exceptions to rights, at least until they re-married. The age of puberty was defined as 12 for girls (and 16 for boys), with an emphasis on virginity. If a father did not settle a marriage for his daughter within three years of puberty, she could choose her own marriage partner, even outside her *varna*. The rationale for marriage was procreation of sons, so after that was fulfilled, a woman could leave her husband or beg off sex with him. Different punishments are prescribed for adultery and rape, depending on the circumstances, and interestingly, for misbehaviour with women. Many types of consideration are shown to women who are pregnant. On the whole, women had a range of rights. Many of them, however, arose from the previous definition of a subservient position for women and the intersection of this definition with the state's ideology of caring for its subjects, including the weakest ones.

What is equally interesting is the masculinity that characterises the men, as we can tell from the sources. The *Arthashastra* considers the battlefield and statecraft the legitimate field of activity of men. The newly-converted-to-non-violence emperor Ashoka is incredibly condescending to his citizens, to whom he is the lord and master, lawmaker and patriarch. Nowhere is there a hint of self-consciousness or questioning regarding the rights of men, to conquer, rule, legislate, trade, negotiate, and resolve. In none of these important matters are women remotely acknowledged, nor is there a suggestion of a possible mix or overlap of gender attributes or roles.

Who was the Buddha? The written records of Siddhartha Gautam, called the Buddha, or the Enlightened or Awakened One, were composed several centuries after his death, and in the interim oral records were composed and transmitted. Historians dispute some facts, but all agree on the historicity of his birth, learning and meditation experiences, teaching, building up followers, and death. Born into a small oligarchic state in the clan of Shakyas, hence also called Shakyamuni or the Sage of the Shakyas, the little Siddhartha was brought up as a Prince. His mother having died a few days after his birth, he was brought up by his aunt, Maha Pajapati, and protected, in the manner of a spoilt Prince, from all suffering or knowledge of suffering. He was married at 16 to his same-age cousin, Yashodhara. They became parents to a son, Rahul, at the age of 29. Following excursions outside the palace in which he encountered various forms of suffering such as disease, old age, and death, and glimpsing asceticism as a possible solution, Siddhartha left his sleeping wife and son soon after his birth to discover the answer to the newly perceived riddles of existence. At first, he followed the usual ascetic paths to enlightenment. Then, he left several teachers in turn and followed his own style of meditation and asceticism. He attained his goal before too long and, around the age of 35, became a Buddha, or Enlightened One (soon to be known as *the* Buddha). He visited his wife, son, and home six years after having left them. In that time, Yashodhara has led a simple existence, and though initially heartbroken at his departure, made terms with it, admired Siddharth's progress, and, in her own dignified way, sought to participate in it by also becoming a nun. It took some time. Gautam Buddha spent the rest of his life until his death at 80 travelling and teaching, and built up what was initially and centrally, even when nuns came to be admitted, a male *sangha* or community of followers. Judging by the geographical and numerical spread of Buddhism, the Buddha was spectacularly successful.

However, most of these stories about his life are apocryphal. He was an ordinary human being, to begin with, but soon came to be deified to different degrees. It is interesting to note, before leaving the biographical narrative, what a tangential role any woman plays in it. His mother had a blessed vision of an immaculate conception, bore him in a glade on a journey, and died almost immediately. His wife was apparently a spirited young woman of his age but was never seen as an equal, or even a partner. No woman was influential in his life except very indirectly as a giver of alms or an instigator of a lesson in philosophy. When he visited home, apart from various male relatives, his stepmother and his wife wanted to join his sangha. But he did not allow them, until later, and with qualifications. We cannot know whether the quasi-misogynist account of his life is a by-product of the rich, erratic, streams of recording; whether the Buddha simply could not pierce the veil that transformed real human beings into essentialised "women;" or whether we are simply putting questions to the period that are products of our own consciousness and not of Buddha's times.

Buddhism overall appears to be a more egalitarian religion than the Vedism that prevailed in the time of its emergence or the Hinduism that followed. Many suppose it to be egalitarian in its support of gender equality as well. Laywomen as well as nuns are visible in extending the new religion. However, the main historical sources that we have are penned by the educated religious elite and these do not reflect sexual egalitarianism. As Diana Paul says,

> Like Judaism and Christianity, Buddhism is an overwhelmingly male-created institution dominated by a patriarchal power structure. As a consequence of this male dominance, the feminine is frequently associated with the secular, profane, and imperfect. Male Buddhists, like male religious leaders in other cultures, established normative behavior for women by creating certain ideals of femininity. At the same time, men's opportunities for interaction with women were minimised by the restrictions of devout practice.
>
> *(Paul, 1979, pp. xix–xx)*

This polarisation between men and women in social life as well as representation is a theme that is found cross-culturally. As Sherry Ortner discusses in an influential structuralist essay, "Is female to male as nature is to culture?" (Ortner, 1974), the polarisation may be explained by the equating of women with nature.

In Buddhism, too, the feminine is closer to nature in several ways. Women are vindictive and destructive but also mysterious and therefore threatening. This force, that is, women, must be controlled and disciplined in order for society, its religion and culture, to thrive. The other theme is that the kind of nature the feminine is close to is nature as creative, productive, motherly, nurturing, and gentle. This kind of an emotional, abstract realm is important for the male to interact with for his own sublimation in this life to an afterlife. In these two themes, we see how women's sexuality may be either transcended, as when she is a virgin or a nun, or controlled as when she is a mother. The Buddha's own mother, Maya, or Mahamaya, is respected and even worshipped, for her ability to procreate and give birth to the ultimate son. But overall, Buddhism prefers the nun who abstains from sex and procreation. The two images of women, as destructive and maternal, are not combined in Buddhism as they are in the goddess Kali (see Chapter 9) although Buddhism took over some of the mythological structure of existing religions in India.

A dialogue between the Buddha and his favourite disciple Ananda displays the importance of the avoidance of this natural, threatening female by the disciplined, evolving male.

| | |
|---|---|
| *[Ananda:]* | "How are we to conduct ourselves, Lord, with regard to womankind?" |
| *[The Buddha:]* | "As not seeing them, Ananda." |
| *[Ananda:]* | "But if we should see them, what are we to do?" |
| *[The Buddha:]* | "Not talking, Ananda." |
| *[Ananda:]* | "But if they should speak to us, Lord, what are we to do?" |
| *[The Buddha:]* | "Keep wide awake, Ananda." |

(Paul, 1979, pp. 7–8)

The position of the mother in Buddhism is interesting. Whereas in Vedism and in Hinduism, value was ascribed to motherhood and a mother's role was sanctified, in Buddhism it is the woman's preoccupation with reproduction and mothering that does not permit renunciation and therefore ultimate freedom for her. Thus, powerful characters are not mothers but nuns, virgins, childless women, and prostitutes. Motherhood was valued in an ordinary, secular context and to bear great sons was a life-path that even the Buddha pronounced as venerable for a woman (Paul, 1979, pp. 62–63).

The history of how a nun's order was established is the same in Buddhism as in Jainism: the Buddha's aunt, and Mahavira's aunt, requests that an order for nuns be established. When, after the Buddha's initial refusal, an order does come to be established, the nuns, at least in India, were under the monks and not independent. Buddhist texts have no pointers about an intellectual life for the nun, and she was not one of the student body of the great Buddhist universities, as the monks were "productive of extraordinary thought and art" (Paul, 1979, p. 82). Or perhaps the majority of monks were *not* thus productive, as were not the majority of nuns. If liberation of the self was the issue, we have a collection of poems by *theri*s, or nuns, called *Therigatha*, that dates from the sixth century BCE, making it perhaps the oldest extant women's literature. The compositions typically describe an epiphanic experience of freedom as the tensions of worldly life are replaced by the peace of a Buddha-led life of renunciation. As Tharu and Lalita, in their wonderful anthology of women's writings, say:

> even though the structural focus is on the message of the Buddha, that message itself depends for its texture and quality on the actual lives it transforms, and acquires fresh currency in each lyric. If one reads the songs of the theris only for the resolution they offer – as one would if one read them in the context provided by the Buddhist canons – the structural design of testimony dominates the experience. . . . We can focus instead on the way women used the spaces Buddhism opened up, individually and collectively, to contest the powers that determined their lives. We can ask how women

inflected the concerns of Buddhism, extending its scope and infusing its schemes with their aspirations. But we must then also ask how and why these gestures were contained as they were annexed into its architecture.
*(Tharu & Lalita, 1991, p. 67)*

Many of the theris' poems are beautifully evocative. Here is Sumangalamata, or Sumangala's mother, a daughter and wife to workers in the rushes:

> A woman well set free! How free I am,
> How wonderfully free, from kitchen drudgery.
> Free from the harsh grip of hunger,
> And from empty cooking pots,
> Free too of that unscrupulous man,
> The weaver of sunshades.
> Calm now, and serene I am.
> All lust and hatred purged.
> To the shade of the spreading trees I go
> And contemplate my happiness.
> (Tharu & Lalita, 1991, p. 69)

Were the Buddhist and Jain social-epistemological worlds at least more gender-equal than the previous and prevalent Vedism? In most ways, yes. Sanskrit was the language of Vedic sacrifice and learning and was learnt mostly by Brahmans and as far as we can tell, mostly by males. There is mention of assorted female scholars in the later Vedic literature, such as Gargi and Lilavati, which tell us that if there were a few names that have come down to us, there must have been more. But in secular literature, such as plays, when a female or low-class character speaks it is in *prakrit*, or one of the non-Sanskrit languages. Sanskrit is a male language, and, by contrast, Pali, the language of Buddha's discourse, is one of the languages shared by females.

At the same time, what Buddhism replaced Vedic ritual with was meditation and reflection, culminating in asceticism. Now, whereas asceticism is a feature of most religions, *sanyasa*, or renunciation in the Indian sense, is the most radical form of asceticism. To remain in the world is to engage in various actions, related to family, work, society, and so on. These are precisely the actions that have to be torn away from in order to focus on liberation. In the Vedic ritual, a wife had been essential. A wife was supposed to be "one-half" of the husband and was considered essential to Vedic life. As Olivelle puts it, "The ideal religious person within the Vedic theology was a married householder devoted to study and ritual activities and intent on fathering children, especially sons, to continue his line" (Olivelle, 2002, p. 124).

In the masculinist discourse of twentieth-century India, leaders such as V. D. Savarkar claimed the Buddhist teaching of non-violence as a putatively feminine characteristic that taught Indians passivity and an inability to resist aggressive foreigners such as Huns, Turks, and Afghans. In his vision, there had been manly values in the times of Chandragupta and Kautilya that were lost when Ashoka converted to Buddhism. Buddhism was responsible for the loss of masculinity, and masculinity was a core component of Hinduism. At the time of his teaching in the twentieth century, Savarkar linked non-violence to Gandhi's leadership as a continuation of the retreat from the essence of Hinduism that waited to be restored.

Preclassical Hinduism (c. 200 BCE–300 CE) is the period between the Maurya and Gupta dynasties. Classical Hinduism is roughly the Gupta period (end of the 3rd to the end of the 6th century) and a little beyond. Hinduism emerges from a synthesis of the ascetic reform movements and the revival of interest in Brahmanism. When discussing these periods, one must remember the caveats: the entirety of India did not conform to a single set of norms regarding "culture," just as it did not conform economically or technologically. Different regions had their classical periods at different times. "Classical" also refers to norms of excellence that explicitly rely on written, upper-class, privileged products of culture and leave out the popular, folk and tribal, as well as women's and lower-class culture that co-exists with upper-class, male culture. However, insofar that we do need to talk of the subcontinent as a whole, Sanskrit needs to be recognised as the language and the idiom of various intellectual and social-ritual activities and while these may have been restricted to sites of power and knowledge, they affected society on the whole. We must just remain cognisant of the basic fact that while the classicism of the Gupta period refers to urban upper classes, ordinary people simply did not enjoy the same standards of living. Women should be classified with lower classes and castes, from the evidence of Sanskrit, as we shall see.

The Guptas were probably of a *Vaishya* caste, although it is tempting to think of them as a mystery (Hindi, *gupta* = secret). There are interesting roles played by princesses in this dynasty. The founder Chandra Gupta I married a princess from the Lichchavis, an old, established *gana-sangha*. This conferred a legitimacy on the new ruler that he pushed forward in his coins with an image of his queen on their reverse sides. The most important king of the dynasty, Chandra Gupta II, married Dhruvadevi, supposedly his brother's wife, an incident variously reported in the texts. More than strategic alliances, however, we encounter in almost all the historical records the presence of women as alms-givers when ordinary people, and granters of villages, lands, and property, when royal.

As we saw earlier, in its quest for a European-style narrative, Indian history-writing found a "Golden Age" in the Mauryan and Gupta dynasties, especially the latter. Some key texts of the turn of the millennium, however, such as the *Manusmriti*, talk about women as comparable to lower castes in their inferiority, and others such as the Kamasutra ascribe equal agency to the woman as to the man, but still treat the man as the subject and reader of the book. In contrast, art and sculpture from the same period show women to be as publicly active as men, including in their dress and body language. When historical characters such as the Emperor Ashok, the teacher Gautam Buddha, the King Chandragupta Maurya, the Court adviser Kautilya, and the author Kalidas are presented and represented by us in history, it is with no problematisation, as if the whole functioning of society was exhausted by the multi-layered nature of male activity, and there was no room, indeed no need, for women's contributions at all. At the same time, the images in both text and media, from textbooks to comic books to TV serials and Bollywood movies, are of these leading figures as unutterably *male*, with a set of male characteristics that already fashions what "a man is."

The text *Kamasutra*, composed sometime in third century CE, demonstrates some of the problems with the historiography of the period. The text is celebrated in two ways. In the 1882 translation by the Orientalist Richard Burton, and the many other versions that it spawned, as well as popularisations of the book in the West through other translations (and now the internet), the *Kamasutra* is recognised as an emancipatory document that could provide the key to a fulfilled sexual life, for women as well as men. Getting this role makes it a compliment, albeit indirect, to India. However, it belongs squarely to a lost golden age of India, in an ancient period when India was apparently a different place. No Western articulation on the subject from Burton's time to the present would consider India advanced in its sexual tolerance and clarity today. Thus, the celebration is a-historical, and racialises and exoticises India.

The second way it is celebrated is as a scientific product, part of the many scientific achievements of ancient Indians, and the Aryans in particular. This is the stated or implied approach in Indian translations and discussions. It arises from a nationalist urge to prove equality, and even superiority, in the face of colonial practices, and it has stayed with Indians in the post-colonial era. In this approach, the whole idea is to maximise sexual consummation through an objective, scientific, even taxonomic, set of approaches, all of which is a tribute to the Indian mind. In both approaches, the subject experiencing the emancipation or the scientifically derived pleasure remains a male subject. Although the *Kamasutra*, being in fact an impressively imagined, researched, and written book, gives space to women as subject and their experience of pleasure and desire, all this is underplayed and variously elided in both approaches.

The historical truth is that the subject of such a treatise was exclusively the elite man. A few women did have an education but they would not be considered part of the readers for such a book, which pointedly addresses the urban, aristocratic young man. Women were marginalised in law, work, and family life. The practice of *sati daha*, or self-immolation on a husband's cremation pyre, was beginning to proliferate. Divisions were hardening, not only overall according to caste and class but within the category "woman" of the sexually available, promiscuous, therefore free but "low," woman and the domesticated, controlled, and respected woman. This dichotomy led to further control of the proper, normative woman, leading to further reduction in economic and legal rights. The association with caste was a close one. Caste purity depended on women's virginity, and the control of their sexuality, accompanied by an overall subordination to caste norms. Given the historical record of the period, we cannot consider the *Kamasutra* to be a liberating testament of women's sexuality.

This was also the time in which more caste distinctions are noted, caste identities are depicted, and a more rigid division on the way to becoming a "system" is described. Caste is based on bloodlines and the purity of lineages. Caste is, therefore, almost totally about control over women's sexuality so as to guarantee the authenticity of offspring, even though it is given a patriarchal twist and descent is traced through males. Caste reduces women often to property in that they have to be selected and approved, and often bartered and sold, along with considerations of what is to the advantage of the caste community. For kings we hear, as with both the Mauryas and the Guptas, that their lineage was questionable because of marriages "outside their caste." The Buddha himself, in an interview with a young Brahman named Ambattha, points out that the rather rude young man's ancestry is from one of the slave girls of the Shakyas' own ancestors. "In another discourse . . . the Buddha lampoons Brahmanical ideas of upper class purity, saying that Brahmans 'are in fact born from vaginas'" (Hiltebeitel, 2010, p. 39).

Another less systemic discourse that was emerging was that of *Purusartha*, or the ends of life, as the values of *dharma, artha, kama,* and *moksha*. The first value, that of dharma, or duty/religion/one's nature, has proved flexible and multivocal. Hiltebeitel (2010) gives an interesting account of dharma by talking of a dissonance between a strictness associated with it in legal books such as that by Manu, and the narrative traditions of the epics and folklore. Manu, the hypothetical author of the *Manavdharmashastra*, says

> Even in their own homes, a female – whether she is a child, a young woman, or an old lady – should never carry out any task independently. As a child, she must remain under her father's control; as a young woman, under her husband's; and when her husband is dead, under her sons' (Hiltebeitel, 2010, p. 89).

Then Hiltebeitel tellingly adds, "Such a norm will have narrative subversions" (2010, p. 89). He specifically discusses women's dharma as not only *stridharma*, or the duty of women in society and vis-a-vis men, but also as *svadharma*, or women's own duty to themselves. There may be a clash and the need for manoeuvring, and a narrative resolution (in favour of the woman) that goes unacknowledged in the law books. *Stridharma* is limiting along the lines of Manu's proposition above. It also characterises women as conniving and selfish. *Svadharma* respects women's personality and temperament, as well as caste and community dignity – very much as men's *svadharma* does for them. Hiltebeitel discusses the case of the epic heroines Sita and Draupadi. One of the interesting points he makes is that both these heroines have occasion to chide their spouses, Rama and Yudhistir, respectively, of a possible human approach to the single-minded pursuit of dharma that they favour, which is often detrimental to their, the women's, interests.

With regard to *artha*, we have the *Arthashastra*, a masculinist tract that along with all other treatises on politics in the world creates a public world of men acting and a dependent, largely private world of women receiving, and men as well. As we have noted earlier, women *were* producers and wage workers. That is not, however, the identity they are mostly associated with. *Kama*, on the other hand, is mostly associated with women and is a value of equal import to others. The conflict that arises with both *kama* and *artha* is that it is the place of householders to practise them. Householders, in both the Brahman and the Buddha's schemes, are inferior to ascetics. Ascetics can retain their semen, being celibate, and thus harness tremendous power. Householders can be happy and are valuable because of their progeny, but finally theirs is not the highest pursuit. The Buddha warned off his monks and nuns from sex, indulgence in which would lead to prompt expulsion from the sangha.

We can hardly be conclusive in this chapter since there are so many open-ended issues and questions begging answers, but we *can* end with yet another conundrum. Asceticism is not simply a denial of sex, and therefore an otherwise wonderful dimension of life. It is a replacement of the usual model of sex and partnering with a new solidarity based in brotherhoods and sisterhoods, sometimes teachers and disciples. This is all about friendship. It turns out that friendship is a state of being that is celebrated in the epics, the Buddha's teachings, and the Classical texts, seemingly as an antidote to the circumscribed world of the householder, but in fact as a rich and valued situation in its own right. In another way, this new eroticism, if we may call it that, comes to be channelled, beginning in this very period, to a devotionalism, in which God is the supreme friend – and lover.

## Bibliography

Gross, R. M. (1991). Buddhism after patriarchy? In P. M. Cooey et al. (Eds.), *After patriarchy: Feminist transformations of the world religions* (pp. 65–86). Maryknoll: Orbis Books.

Gutschow, K. (2004). *Being a Buddhist nun: The struggle for enlightenment in the Himalayas.* Cambridge, MA: Harvard University Press.

Gutschow, K. (2010). The delusion of gender and renunciation in Buddhist Kashmir. In D. Mines & S. Lamb (Eds.), *Everyday life in South Asia* (pp. 250–262). Bloomington, IN: Indiana University Press.

Habib, I., & Jha, V. (2004). *Mauryan India. A people's history of India 4.* New Delhi: Tulika Books.

Hiltebeitel, A. (2010). *Dharma.* Honolulu, HI: The University of Hawai'i Press.

Michaels, A. (2004). *Hinduism: Past and present* (Trans. B. Harshav). Hyderabad: Orient Longman.

Mookerji, R. K. (1989). *Ancient Indian education: Brahmanical and Buddhist.* Delhi: Motilal Banarsi Dass. (Original work published 1960)

Olivelle, P. (2002). Ascetic withdrawal or social engagement. In D. S. Lopez (Ed.), *Religions of Asia in practice: An anthology* (pp. 122–135). Princeton: Princeton University Press.

Olivelle, P. (Ed.). (2019). *Grhastha: The householder in ancient Indian religious culture*. New York: Oxford University Press.

Omvedt, G. (2003). *Buddhism in India: Challenging Brahmanism and caste* (pp. 53–85). New Delhi: Sage.

Ortner, S. B. (1974). Is female to male as nature is to culture? In M. Z. Rosaldo & L. Lamphere (Eds.), *Women, culture, and society* (pp. 68–87). Stanford, CA: Stanford University Press.

Paul, D. Y. (1979). *Women in Buddhism: Images of the feminine in the Mahayana tradition*. Berkeley, CA: University of California Press.

Rangarajan, L. N. (1992). *The Arthshastra*. New Delhi: Penguin.

Thapar, R. (2002). *Early India from the origins to AD 1300*. London: Allen Lane, Penguin.

Tharu, S., & Lalita, K. (Eds.). (1991). *Women writing in India: 600 B.C. to the present. Vol. 1: 600 B.C. to the early twentieth century*. Delhi: Oxford University Press.

# 4
# THE DELHI SULTANATE AND MUGHAL DYNASTIES

When the Prophet Mohammad (573–647 CE) communicated his revelations to his followers, he did not seek to bring about a revolution in gender relations, whereas he did in social relations and the idea of the community. But insofar as social relations are unavoidably related to gender relations, ideas about both did shift and find new places. These include the reform of marriage and *meher*, the bride's personal savings; the nature of the household, with a maximum of four wives, all to be equal in every respect; the guarantee of marriage and rights of widows and divorced women; the inheritance of property equally by sons and daughters; and other legal rights of men and women. In this chapter, we will look at these practices during the centuries circa 1100 to 1750, which historians call the centuries "before Europe" (Asher & Talbot, 2006). The anthropological study of Muslim women in India today belongs to a later chapter.

The Prophet's life and teachings, together with the Holy Book and commentaries, formed a trio, of the Qur'an, the *shari'a*, or law, and the *hadith*, or sayings of the Prophet and records of his actions. These were continually debated and commented upon over the following centuries. We cannot assume that "Islam" was a normative ideology that went unquestioned. People, including Sultans, were more or less religious and acted according to criteria other than religion, both by choice and inclination and because of political and economic considerations. Then, we should remember that there is a change in practice over the approximately six centuries of Islamic rule in North India, also a variation over the spread of the territory, and a difference in the practice of differently placed communities and classes.

The role of a normative Islam was complicated in two other ways. The Delhi Sultans, and then outstandingly the Mughals, were the inheritors of Turkic, Afghan, Persian, and Mughal traditions, along with Arabic Islamic ones. Thus,

DOI: 10.4324/9781003393252-5

a possible obsession with the chastity of the female body in an Arabic Islamic discourse was tempered by the sensuality and open revelling in the embellished form of the female body in the other traditions, although any kind of strict characterisation of "a tradition" is itself questionable. The historian Harbans Mukhia points out that even the most pious of the Emperors of the period, Aurangzeb, did not think of giving a religious name such as Fatima or Khadija to his daughters. Instead, princesses had names such as Gulbadan, or "The Body of a Rose"; Gulchihra, "Rose-Faced"; Jahan Ara, or "Adornment of the World"; and Roshan Ara, "Adornment of Light" (Mukhia, 2004).

To different degrees over the whole period of the eleventh to eighteenth centuries, and in an overtly dramatic form during the reign of Akbar (1556–1605), the influence of different non-Islamic Indian communities, especially the Rajputs, permeated the followers of Islam. In this case, as different from the influence of Persian culture and politics, the relationship was reciprocal, alive, and fluid. Hence there is one more reason to call this the Sultanate and Mughal period, the eleventh to eighteenth centuries, "India before Europe," or the "Post-Gupta Empires," rather than any version of an Islamic or Muslim period.

The Delhi Sultanate, named after its capital, Delhi, consisted of the Mamluk dynasty (1206–1290), the Khalji dynasty (1290–1320), the Tughlaq dynasty (1320–1414), the Sayyid dynasty (1414–1451), and the Lodi dynasty (1451–1526). We will have space to look at only the first of these, with a mention of a Khilji ruler. The Mamluk dynasty was founded by the slave Qutb al-Din (1206–1210), a general of Mu'izz al-Din Ghuri (1173–1206), and *his* slave Shams al-Din Iltutmish (1210–1236). Mu'izz al-Din Ghuri, better known to us as Mohammad Ghuri, was a cultured Persian speaker from Afghanistan whose armies were led by a Turkish slave. This slave, manumitted, transitioned from general to governor of the conquered territories and set up the first Islamic dynasty in India, the Mamluk popularly known as the Slave dynasty. This new kingdom was made legitimate by setting up the first congregational mosque, the famous Qutb Minar, and the campus with mosque, shrine, tomb, and minaret, called Qubbat al-Islam. The term translates as "Sanctuary of Islam" and has become controversial when interpreted as "the Might of Islam," or a deliberate attempt to aggrandise Islam in the face of Hinduism, including by building mosques out of the destroyed pieces of temples. As the historian Sunil Kumar describes, the unusual fact of a dynasty of slaves may be explained by an understanding of the power of well-trained slaves, in turn the result of a deliberate policy of education, acculturation, conversion to Islam, and bonding in several ways of men captured when they were young boys.

> in the steppes the Turks were nondescript, indistinguishable from each other in power and wealth, but when they came within the Muslim world, the further [the Turk slaves] are taken from their hearth, their kin and their dwellings [*har chand az khanawa aqriba' wa wilayat-i khud durtar uftad*] the

more valued, precious and expensive they become [*qadr wa qimat wa baha'i-yi o ziyadat gardad*] and they become commanders and generals [*umara' wa sipahsalaranshawand*].

(Kumar, 2007, p. 83)

Kumar hinges much of his argument on what his sources describe to be the special ethnic quality of these Turks captured or recruited to be slaves: their ability to distance themselves from their natal homes, to forget and disown their places of origin and their kin. If this led to a new loyalty to the court and sultan, an additional bonding was constructed between the slaves themselves. The Sultan would order the exchange of women as wives among the new lineage of privileged slaves.

> The Sultan commanded that the daughters of Ilduz should marry Qutb al-Din Ai-Beg and Qubacha; two daughters of Qutb al-Din were married, one after the death of the other, to Qubacha. Mu'izz al-Din sought to tie his slaves not merely to himself through his affection, close association, and via the political and economic opportunities proferred to the select, he also wanted them to bond with each other through a unity of interests and social interdependence.
>
> (Kumar, 2007, p. 86)

Three points follow. One, this approach to bonding meant a direct role for women in the building of the Sultanate since the bonding happened through marriage ties. However, this was a circular ideology where parenting by biological parents had to be constantly downplayed in favour of the master's paternalism, followed by an instrumental use of marriage and extra-marital bonding. Two, we can make an educated guess that the women must have created their own bonds of solidarity among themselves, a point that will be documented with reference to the Mughals later. And three, there was likely little companionship between men and women and a case of separate worlds for the two, characterised by homosociality in each. The heightening of interest in trained male slaves and a reduction of the role of the family suggest a smaller role for women as companions when wives, and as educators and socialisers when mothers. It would be exciting to discover more details from sources untapped yet. Meanwhile, the evidence from extant texts paints a picture of reduced male–female companionship and one of friendship and homoeroticism among men (Vanita & Kidwai, 2000: Part Three).

> A slave whom one has brought up and promoted, must be looked after, for it needs a whole lifetime and good luck to find a worthy and experienced slave. Wise men have said that a worthy and experienced servant or slave is better than a son. On this subject the poet says:

"One obedient slave is better
Than three hundred sons;
For the latter desire their father's death.
The former his master's glory"
(al-Mulk in Sunil Kumar, 2007, p. 115)

As we shall see later, there were indeed frequent cases of regicide, and succession occurred much of the time by siblings assassinating the ruling Sultan and competing for the throne. This occurred not only with biological sons but equally with adopted slaves (regardless of what the poet says), including with the competitors to the very first Sultan Qutb al-Din. When new regimes *were* set up over North India by freed and honoured slaves, they sought stable relationships in their new homes. One way was to use local idioms, as for instance, on their coins. It is interesting to find among Sultanate coins, coins that give on one side an image of Lakshmi, the Goddess of wealth, and on the other side, in local Devanagari, the name of the new Sultan. This was parallel to, and apparently consistent with, an articulation of the new homeland as heathen and in need of sacralisation by the building of mosques and shrines.

The gradual consolidation of the Sultanate, the projection of domains in India as sanctuaries for Muslims, and the steady immigration from Iran and Afghanistan of male emigres of all varieties of skills to finally settle down and call India home led to a curiosity about the nature and size of the corresponding female migration, and the overall experience of the newly arrived woman in a foreign land. We have tantalising mentions of marriage and family life but really no glimpses of either the structure or experience of the family, either emigre or second generation. When one of the strongest Sultans, Shams al-Din Iltutmish (1210–1236) ascended the Delhi throne, he married the daughter of his predecessor Qutb al-Din. This was a political move, enabling Iltutmish, among several rivals, to claim a privileged relationship with the previous Sultan. An act of usurpation came to seem over time an act of logical succession. That brides were supposed to be given only to peers or to socially superior lineages, and that this was therefore an unusual move, was obscured in the later record. However, it must have been an intense, even perhaps a dramatic experience for the bride concerned – on whom came to hinge, if we like, the legitimacy of the Shamsi lineage and the solidity of the Delhi Sultanate.

Then there were female slaves or *kanizakha*, who were concubines. In a carefully constructed table, Kumar (2007, pp. 182–183) details the mothers of Iltutmish's children, some with question marks. Some were married wives, some were important women in the harem, and some were servants or slaves. The Turks, we are told further, were strictly delineated as a superior ethnic group through rites of passage, naming, and so on, but we do not know enough as to how their "purity" was also a contribution of various performances by their women folk, including marriages and children's socialisation.

In the category of "great women in history," we have the case of the queen Razia, a daughter of the Khilji ruler Iltutmish, who became the Sultan in 1236 after very brief reigns by two of his sons. Minhaj-i Siraj Juzjani, a jurist and historian at

Iltutmish's court, justifies her succession by evoking the judgement of her father, Iltutmish, that she was the most competent to rule among all his children. The brief rule by her brothers was, therefore, illegal, and her father's will was finally honoured when she ascended the throne. While one may understand the support given to her by nobles who could well prefer a puppet to a powerful ruler, why did the jurists and *ulama* support her as well? Juzjani avoids this tricky issue by mentioning the gender problem only in the context of her dethronement in 1240 after four years of rule. In this inconsistent and gendered account, Juzjani explains that Razia was fated to fail in spite of all her excellent qualities because she was a woman. Apparently, suddenly, at the height of her power, she gave up all the practices of modesty that were appropriate to her sex, and gave up the veil and appeared in male clothing and headdress. There was a revolt and she was deposed. Historians find that Juzjani protests too much. Recognising Razia's leadership acumen, and indebted to her for his own position, he still has to play the correct Islamic card and does so through the medium of gender in a rather transparent way.

The Delhi Sultanate in North India was succeeded by the Mughal dynasty. Research on the Mughal period, 1525 to circa 1750s, tells us about more "great women in history" and also gives us further insights into the Muslim family and kinship systems. The research on the Mughals can give us clues and indirect information about the Sultanate as well, while remembering that each period, indeed every few decades, has its own specificity. As Ruby Lal, a historian specifically of Mughal women, puts it, we may "posit a domain of 'domestic life' as a heuristic device" (Lal, 2005, p. 4). This is a fundamentally important domain because, through reproduction, it carries forth the dynasty, and, through love and care, creates the family and support structures. In this domain, women are powerful agents. At the same time, this domain does not really exist – that is, as fixed or already knowable. It needs critical enquiry to reveal it, and a questioning of the very meanings of "private" and "public." How boundaries were constructed, when, and with what results, are all open to investigation.

Of the Mughals, those who have left the greater imprint on history are the six so-called "Great Mughals": Zahir al-Din Babar (1526–1530), Nasir al-Din Humayun (1530–1540, 1555–1556), Jalal al-Din Muhammad Akbar (1556–1605), Nur al-Din Jahangir (1605–1627), Shah Jahan (1627–1658), and Aurangzeb Alamgir (1658–1707). Starting right from the beginning, from Babar's conquest of India, we have outstanding historical records. Babar wrote an autobiography called *Babur Nama* in Turkish. In this he speaks, with candidness, about his amorous and sexual preferences. Two excerpts will give us a picture. The first is about his first marriage; the second about his first love. They date between 1499 and 1500.

> Ayisha-sultan Begim whom my father and hers, ie., my uncles, Sultan Ahmad Mirza had bethrothed to me, came [this year] to Khujand and I took her in the month of Sha'ban. Though I was not ill-disposed towards her, yet, this being my first marriage, out of modesty and bashfulness, I used to see her once in 10, 15, 20 days. Later on when even my first inclinations

did not last, my bashfulness increased. Then my mother Khanim used to send me, once a month or every 40 days, with driving and driving, dunnings and worryings.

In those leisurely days, I discovered in myself a strange inclination, nay! as the verse says, "I maddened and afflicted myself" for a boy in the camp-bazar, his very name, Baburi, fitting in. Up till then, I had had no inclination for anyone, indeed of love and desire, either by hearsay or through experience, I had not heard, I had not talked. At that time I composed Persian couplets, one or two at a tie; this is one of them:

May none be as I, humbled and wretched and love-sick;
No beloved as thou art to me, cruel and careless.
From time to time Baburi used to come to my presence but out of
    modesty and bashfulness, I could never look straight at him.
(Vanita & Kidwai, 2000, p. 161)

In his autobiography, Babur gives, with dates, names, and details, the parties that he set up and attended, the drinking, eating, and merry-making at them, and how he enjoyed them and missed them. He fills his writings with descriptions of men: the habits, dress, looks, and minds of all kinds of men that he encounters. This interest in men and their company is remarkable, even if it *is* a homosocial society, but Babur's sheer forthrightness about it is what makes it doubly important. The corollary is a weak interest in women. Babur writes briefly and blandly about them, and often with a sense of reporting a duty fulfilled. In the quote above the duty is towards his first wife. In others, it is towards the senior women in the court. But overall, there is an inability on Babur's part to see the women he was close to as lively, complex human beings.

Babur's daughter, Gulbadan Banu Begum, gives us an opposite picture. She composed the *Ahval-i Humayun Badshah*, or the history of Emperor Humayun, her brother, upon the request of her nephew Akbar. Born in 1523 in Afghanistan and brought to India as a little girl when her father had made some noteworthy conquests, Gulbadan was exceptional in the "history" she wrote – *Ahval* meaning literally conditions, situation, or circumstances – and has left us a precious record of everyday life in the Mughal courts of Babur and Humayun. It tells of the same world of perpetual warfare and peripatetic existence as does Babur in his autobiography, and of how the whole court, women, children, servants, and all were constantly on the move. Where Babur's world, as we learn of it from his memoirs, is populated by seemingly almost only men, and almost everything interesting and wonderful is performed by them, Gulbadan's description of the same world presents a canvas with strong, lit-up female characters who are everywhere that men are and demonstrate often the same qualities of aggressiveness, ambition, and love for life. She does not do this purposefully. She had lived through it all and her genius as a writer lay in her ability to convey that the empire, her world, was indeed a world in the making, and the making of it was the work of women as well as men. Further, the wonderful quality of Gulbadan's history lies for us in its evocation of the details of a woman's world wrongly characterised as "private" in opposition to the "public." It shows how important considerations of prestations, rituals and relationships were central to empire-building, and how they were all profoundly interwoven with more overtly political and public action.

The Emperor Humayun led a peripatetic life for at least a decade of his reign, 1540–1550. For those ten years of exile, he moved from province to province, gaining and re-gaining friends and supporters. During this time of war and tension, family life continued, marriages took place, children were born, and interpersonal relationships were conducted. Gulbadan gives details, taking special care to emphasise the niceties of courtly life. She elaborates on the story of Humayun's marriage to Hamideh Banu Begum in a way that conveys to us the will and agency of the women and the ritual and protocol that was considered essential. Hamideh Banu refused to marry, or even see again, Humayun after an initial visit. However, she was persuaded to accept the suit by the joint effort of her mother and her suitor but not before a heated exchange regarding both the courtesies that had *not* been observed and the feelings of Hamideh Banu that she would rather marry a king whose collar her hand could touch, and not one whose skirt it could not reach, as she put it (Lal, 2005, p. 101). More interesting still is the fact that this story of courtship was reported by Gulbadan in her book, indicating how important seemingly private matters were to the overall nature and functioning of the empire.

The kind of data that describes royal transactions and *adab* (etiquette, appropriate behaviour) can shed further light on this overlap or mutual construction of the "domestic" and the "political." Lal's discussion of an incident in Bayazid Bayat's *Tazkireh-i Humayun va Akbar* in which Haran Begum objected to the people sent by Humayun to ask for her daughter's hand for his son is enlightening (2005, pp. 94–95). She was affronted at his choice of ambassadors and explained rather curtly what he should have done. Such incidents, and many more recorded in the histories available to us, indicate a great attention to rules of *adab*. Many rules of hierarchy and privilege operated in Mughal society, of which gendered divisions were a crucial one.

We come to the interesting question of the *haram*. As Harbans Mukhia puts it,

> The dominant popular image of the Mughal family is a vast number of women crowding a harem, all for giving pleasure to one man, the Emperor, whose sexual appetite was insatiable. The term harem itself evokes images of an immense fortified playground for carrying out one man's sexual fantasies, with hundreds of women of all shapes and sizes, colours and ethnic groups at his beck and call.
>
> *(Mukhia, 2004, p. 113)*

This kind of picture was largely an eighteenth- and nineteenth-century construction. Earlier travellers including those to the Mughal court certainly showed interest in the ruler's private life but did not fantasise about or vilify it in the way that it came to be in James Mill's *History of British India*, published in 1818,

> In truth, the Hindu, like the Eunuch, excels in the qualities of a slave. . . . But if less soft, the Mohammedan is more manly, more vigorous. [In both of them however there is] the same insincerity, mendacity, and perfidy; the same indifference to the feelings of others; the same prostitution and venality are conspicuous. . . . The Mohammedans are profuse, when possessed of wealth, and devoted to pleasure; the Hindus are almost always penurious and ascetic.
>
> *(Mill, 1858, pp. 365–366, quoted in Lal, 2005, p. 26)*

Such pictures of debasement of Mughal life became the stock in trade for colonial writers and created a discourse that there could be no quarrelling with as it gradually assumed the visage of a well-documented scientific truth. Mill's successors in history-writing, Mountstuart Elphinstone and Stanley Lane-Poole, carry on the tradition of few details and a great deal of pre-formulated generalisation. Lane-Poole's tale of sensualism and self-indulgence goes:

> [Shah Jahan's] favourite wife [Mumtaz Mahal], the lady of the Taj, had died in 1631, in giving birth to their fourteenth child, and her husband had centred his affection upon his eldest daughter, Jahan-Ara, with so much fervour as to cause no little scandal, while he also denied himself none of the more transitory joys of the zenana. He had been a grave stern man in his prime, an energetic soldier, and a prudent counsellor: at the age of sixty-four he was a sensual pleasure-loving pageant of royalty, given over to ease and the delights of the eye. . . . The burden of the state interfered with his enjoyment. . . . In 1657 he was afflicted with a malady which, in the words of Bernier . . . "it were unbecoming to describe." The self-indulgence of the old sensualist had brought its retribution.
>
> *(Lane-Poole, 1908, pp. 16–18, quoted in Lal, 2005, p. 28)*

The absence of a picture of the harem in earlier periods is followed by a flippant and imprecise description in the later. The historian Harbans Mukhia tries to give an estimate of the number of women in the harem. It was "modest" during the times of Babur and Humayun, their wives neither being nor shown by chroniclers as being, more than a dozen, with an additional couple of concubines. It is only when we come to Akbar that the number swells to hundreds and even thousands, at least in the fantasy of Father Monserrate (300 wives) and Abul Fazl (5,000). Before we address the implications of these figures, Mukhia encourages us to explore a few other concepts. The mother is one such. She was the guardian of the women's quarters and the acknowledged authority. As a *buzurg*, or respected senior, she was given the ultimate possible respect by Emperors in succession.

> Abul Fazl records the early days of Babur, when his grandmother Shah Begum had set up Khan Mirza against him. Babur went up to her, knelt before her and said disarmingly: 'If a mother has special affection for one child, why should that cause resentment in another? There is after all no limit to her authority.' He then added: 'I have been up long and have travelled a long distance,' and, leaving his head in her lap, went to sleep.
> 
> (Mukhia, 2004, p. 115)

Akbar's mother Hamideh Banu, whose marriage has been related earlier, was given the title Mariam Makani, or "similar to Mary," and there are many anecdotes about Akbar's devotion to her, or at least ritualised performances of devotion. He carried her palanquin on his shoulders at one time, welcomed her to his court with the utmost courtesies, acceded to her intervention on behalf of his rebellious son, and her grandson, Salim, and shaved off his hair and moustache at her death. The one other time he did the shaving was at the death of his wet nurse Jiji Anaga. Jahangir, similarly, showed the most refined etiquette towards *his* mother, *Hazrat* (a term typically used for the King) Mariam al-Zaman, the "Mary of her age."

The primacy given to the biological mother also had to correspond to the status of *begum*, a term exclusively used for princesses and queens of royal blood. An *Agha* or *Aghacha* was inferior, even if also royal, favoured by the King, or married to him. The haram consisted of several mothers, aunts, and other elders. It was the place where domestic rituals and life-cycle ceremonies, birthdays and betrothals, took place. One of the more interesting accounts has been left by Francois Bernier, a French doctor who spent most of his years in India (1655–1668) in the court of Aurangzeb. Arriving when the latter had just dethroned Shah Jehan and declared himself Emperor, Bernier first wrote about the deposed Shah Jehan and his two daughters Jahanara, called Begum Sahib, and Roshanara, the younger one. Both were intelligent, "vivacious," and politically active. In the succession struggle, Jahanara sided with Dara Shukoh who was finally defeated and killed, and Roshanara supported Aurangzeb. As the fortunes of either brother rose and fell, the sister on his side took action for his family, and again, the more interesting thing is not their dynamism, but that their actions and personalities are recorded by the likes of Bernier and Manucci not as if they were trivial women's pastimes but of importance to the empire. Apart from the scandal (as some would have it) of Shah Jehan's unbounded love for, and trust in, Jahanara, Bernier was a doctor who could occasionally visit the harem. He was also keen to write the most extensive possible account and gathered information from everyone he could. He tells us, therefore, that

> the *Seraglio* contains beautiful apartments, separated, and more or less spacious and splendid, according to the rank and income of the females . . .

> nearly ever chamber has a reservoir of running water at the door; on every side are gardens, delightful alleys, shady retreats, streams, fountains.
>
> *(Constable, 1968, p. 267, quoted in Lal, 2005, p. 44)*

In his description, Bernier, as well as other observers, describes a world where women were involved in mutual care, including of co-wives' and relations' children as well; their bonds extended to resistance against efforts to control them, such as by Aurangzeb's about wine drinking by women. The two important points to remember from the countless anecdotes about women in the harem are (i) that it was a secure world for women that provided in many parallel ways what the men's world provided them: companionship, pleasure, support, identity; and (ii) it was not an isolated "private" world with a kind of sub-culture but was deliberately conceived of as the locus for activities important for the well-being of the larger "public" world. The key lies in not imposing the "public–private" dichotomy we are familiar with on those times, and equally to construct a vocabulary and conceptual tools to imagine a world lacking our precise divisions, although complete with its own.

The key is also to see it all as a process and not something that appeared fully formed. A history can be traced from the time of Babur to Aurangzeb in which the Emperor emerged as "a divinely aided patriarch whose household was the central element in government;" members of the army were dependent on the emperor, the administration "a loosely structured group of men controlled by the Imperial household," and the emperor's travels were a significant part of administrative activities (Blake quoted in Lal, 2005, p. 12). Akbar, particularly, constructed himself through spatial and ritual strategies as an emblematic masculine, imperial monarch (O'Hanlon in Lal, 2005, p. 12). Akbar had the need for a strong political base, and one of his strategies was to marry extensively, including into clans with whom he needed alliances. One of Akbar's main pillars in empire-building was to gain the support and loyalty of various Rajput rulers, starting with Raja Man Singh of the Kachhwahas at Amber. Rajput princesses were married into the Mughal dynasty and bore sons who were effectively "Indian," and the men served, often in the highest of positions, under Akbar. This was not only an opportunistic strategy but also a powerful declaration of the Emperor's power and benediction. Whereas all marriages in the Mughals were made with illustrious partners, well matched to bring forth superlative offsprings to keep the flag of the lineage flying, it was the many marriages with Rajput princesses and non-Mughals that give us an insight into the idea.

> It is as if the emperor was accommodating the entire world through a marital grid. Daughters of kings and nobles of all cultures and every domain were seeking his protection, and Akbar was extending shelter far and wide. . . . These [other rulers'] large *harams* may well be seen as signs of the virility and power of kings or rulers. However, the presence of the large numbers

of women in Akbar's *haram* is perhaps better read as a sign of the supremacy of the monarch as the center of the empire.

*(Lal, 2005, pp. 171, 173)*

We may judge Akbar's strategy to have been successful. He was accepted by the Rajputs as a protector of the realm, and the master of a universe totally under his beneficence. But what about the experience of the women in his life? His harem was constructed to be unique. It was a place of respect, indeed a sacred and inviolate space, delineated by its physical separation and its rituals. It gave credence to the sacredness and inviolate nature of the Empire. There is no doubt, however, that the women themselves became progressively invisible. From riding alongside the Emperor in Humayun's time, or going on independent pilgrimages in Akbar's early years, or taking on the mantle of the governorship of Delhi while the Emperor was at battle, the women closest to him gradually ceased even to be even named. When Salim was born, his mother was not mentioned by name and all the eulogies were to the father, Akbar. We have complimentary but also contradictory readings of this process. Ruby Lal's argument is that "the feminine is produced and erased at the same time. . . . [Their] lives were not for themselves, but for creating other lives" (Lal, 2005, p. 85). On the larger canvas, however, the role of the harem was certainly not to act as the private or the margin of the Empire but to *add* to the power and sanctity of the Empire.

The case of Nur Jahan, wife of Jahangir, and de facto Empress in her own right, leaves us with another version of the same conundrum of power versus powerlessness. She was an older widow with a daughter when she was courted by an Emperor apparently passionately in love with her and was given ever more gifts, powers, and autonomy of action with passing years. Historians differ only slightly in interpreting her rise as due to her personality, together with the dissipation of the wine and opium lover, Jahangir. Nur Jahan began to perform many of the duties of the monarch, as well as to patronise and conduct many activities that were her own specialty such as designing buildings and textiles. Though she stands forth as an exceptionally talented woman and ruler, there is no discernible difference to women or change in the overall gender balance in the Empire due to her rule.

We have focused on the Sultanate and the Mughals, and neglected North India between these two dynastic formations and away from the centre, such as the regional kingdoms of Bengal, Oudh, Rajasthan, Maharashtra, and others. We have been obliged to neglect the states of South India. While a detailed narrative of their history is not possible here, some relevant points about developments that round up our picture of gender in South Asia are as follows. Rana Kumbha (r. 1433–1468), the ruler of Mewar in Rajasthan, whose clan had an ongoing conflict with the Delhi Sultans, built several forts. The fortress and palace at Chittor dating from mid-fifteenth century give an idea of the uses of domestic space. There were several courtyards, some only for the use of women. Raja Man Singh Tomar of Gwalior (r. 1486–1516) built a palace with an even more clearly designed women's section with screens for the women to observe through. The designs of the Mughals are similar, for example, the Jahangiri Mahal in the Agra Fort, including its carved brackets (Asher & Talbot, 2006, p. 132). The practice of women's seclusion has been described as "Islamic," which then influenced indigenous/Hindu practices, particularly Rajput ones. On the other side, it has also been argued that these practices were already indigenous to India and influenced incoming Muslims to start adopting them. Clearly, the original practitioners of *parda* and their imitators operated with a different set of values than their critics today.

Another practice that was common across Indian rulers of different regions and religions was of using marriage alliances as a political tool. In the powerful kingdom of Vijayanagar, the largest precolonial urban centre in the South, Krishnadeva Raya built a new, fortified residence *outside* the city supposedly for his queen Chinnadevi, who had been a courtesan before marriage. As in many Hindu ceremonies, public rituals included the man and his wife/wives. Thus, Krishnadeva Raya visited newly conquered territories with his two queens: Tirumaladevi, a princess, and Chinnadevi, a courtesan. He donated life-size copper images of himself and the two queens, showing himself to be permanently worshipping at the predominant temple (Asher & Talbot, 2006, pp. 68–70).

There are two developments in this period, however, that we have to take note of. The first is the aesthetics of the period and the second is mysticism, and we will see an extraordinary overlap between them. The aesthetics is gendered in two ways. One is that poetry, performance, and art are suffused with *rasa*, particularly of *sringar rasa*. *Rasa* is part of an aesthetic system that attributes both the emotion (the artistic expression) and its taste (audience reception) to certain set categories. Within a range of nine categories comes *sringar*, or sensual beauty, including beautification and attractiveness, and linked closely to it is the state or emotion called *viraha*. *Viraha* is not a *rasa* but is as powerful in artistic expression. It translates as the anguish or pain of separation, without which, indeed, the depth of attachment cannot be measured. *Sringar* and *viraha* are particularly gendered concepts, because they imply desire and longing between two partners, of the same or the opposite sex, and characterise love between non-partners as well. In both folk and what came to be defined as classical culture, there is a prolific production of texts that glorify the physical form, the body, typically female but also male, the irresistibility of its beauty, the nature of desire, and both the consummation and the separation of partners.

As Charlotte Vaudeville reports, the *Duhas of Dhola-Maru*, a love story of the two characters Dhola and Maru from Rajasthan, demonstrates a passion and a lyricism that is both extraordinary and common to many other such oral narratives in other parts of India. There is the story of Lorik and Chandni, Chandaini, or Chanda in North India and that of Heer-Ranjha and Laila-Majnu in Punjab, among others, that are all passionate tales of love that date from this period in several versions. Malik Muhammad Jayasi's *Padmavat*, composed in Awadhi in

1540, has Ala al-Din's supposed attack on Chittor because of his infatuation for the legendary queen Padmavati, his capture of the fort and the discovery that she has already killed herself, and also an elaborate description of a fantastical space of love (Metcalf, 2009). Jayasi's language is Awadhi, a precursor of Hindi, and both a language of the people as opposed to the elite Persian and one suffused with Persian vocabulary. Mir Sayyid Manjhan's *Madhumalati* is also in Awadhi. Dating from 1545, the idea of *rasa* is combined with Persian love poetry to become equally popular, creating a double motif of Sufi spirituality and a tale of two lovers in an idyllic Indo-Islamic world. Among the illustrated manuscripts produced in Akbar's reign is the *Tutinama*, originally written in the fourteenth century by Zia al-Din Nakhshabi. It consists of stories within a story about a parrot who tells a story each night to a woman to keep her away from her lover while her husband is away. It was likely of interest to Akbar because of his own extensive and growing haram and the earlier control on his throne and state by elder women such as his mother Hamideh Banu Begum (Asher & Talbot, 2006, pp. 136–138).

In the South, Ibrahim Adil Shah II (r. 1580–1627), ruler of the state of Bijapur, showed his love for the *rasas* and the arts in diverse ways. He wrote *Kitab-i Nauras*, "Book of the Nine Rasas," a collection of songs and commentaries that begins with an invocation to Saraswati, the Goddess of the arts. He founded a new city, Nauraspur, near his capital, which was a kind of cultural centre with designed spaces meant for performances and celebrations. His love of music was combined with mysticism, and his portraits depict him with beads and castanets. His peer was Muhammad Quli Qutb Shah (r. 1580–1611) of Golkonda, who wrote, as did Ibrahim Shah, in Dakhani. His poetry, too, is suffused with mysticism and devotion, addressing god in the feminine voice and celebrating beautiful women from different castes and religions.

Although the concept and approach of "the feminine voice" were applied in many places, one other good place for us to find it would be *bhakti* poetry. "Bhakti" means love and devotion. "Bhakta" is a term applied to a group of people, unrelated to each other, and Bhakti has become known as a "movement" exemplified by their common characteristics. Also called "saints" and "gurus" (teachers), they lived from the eighth century to the sixteenth century in all the states of India. They were typically low caste and low class. Their poetry and teaching proclaimed the love of a personal god, the desire to submit totally to their god, rather than to institutions and man-made laws, and to do so through challenging social structures and constraints. The god they conceived could have the names of Ram or Krishna but would either be personalised (*sagun*, or with traits) or be abstract (*nirgun*, or without traits). In either case, the poet-saint could express their love and desire for one-ness with their god by adopting a feminine voice. As Jack Hawley explains, the particular location of women in society as relatively weak and helpless, as well as the stereotypical presentation of a woman as more guileless but also self-aware of her instincts, combined to present a ready metaphor for the human's relationship to a supreme being. Male poets often wrote in the female voice and put on conceits supposedly reflecting a woman's style: devoted, maternal, romantic, lover-like, alluring, coquettish, jealous, bereaved, dependent, but also confident of reciprocity. There were some "original" expressions of this feminine role and many instances of a mechanical application of an established style and genre. And of course, the art fed back into reality: the feminine-voice poetry made women more socialised into playing just the role that was depicted as naturally theirs. The poetry of Sur Das (c. 1551–1640), one of the most famous and beloved of the North Indian bhakti saints, illustrates the ways in which *rasa* and *bhakti*, or emotion and devotion, come together. Here, Radha's physical beauty is dissected, climaxing in consummation with the Lord.

> Radha is lost to the onslaught of love.
> Her braid . . . .
> The honey of her voice . . . .
> Her hands . . . .
> And the full moon in her face . . . .
> Her despair, her desperation – the Joy of the Yadus [Krishna] sees it and appears at her side just in time.
>
> (Surdas, quoted as "NPS 1744" in Hawley & Juergensmeyer, 2004, p. 107)

Radha, as we shall see in Chapter 9, may also be worshipped as a goddess; here she epitomises the human soul longing and searching for the Supreme Soul, (in this poem) Krishna, referred to in the poem as "the Joy of the Yadus" and "Surdas' Lord." In poem after poem, Surdas elaborates on Radha's beauty and passion, on Krishna's beauty and *his* passion, and the subtle, sometimes elusive, point that there is reciprocity and even equality between them. The desire is mutual, and the Lord does come and cools down the flames of desire, only to disappear again and have to be searched for. Powerful as Radha is, she cannot permanently be Krishna's. She symbolises our helpless, longing selves. The theology is complex but for us to draw gendered conclusions, suffice it to say that personal devotion to one's chosen god, or *bhakti*, and the artistry used to present union and separation (largely through *sringar* and *viraha*) are constituted as metaphors for each other.

Surdas is only one of the many bhakti poets to worship god in a feminine voice. Chaitanya Mahaprabhu (1486–1534) was a Krishna *bhakta* (devotee), as respected and beloved in Bengal as Surdas was in North India. Chaitanya is famous for his dedication to his Lord, his intense love and passion and the impulse he gave to Vaisnavism, the worship of Visnu, of whom Krishna is an *avatar*. An interesting complication arises in the case of *bhakti* saints who are women. Andal (8th century) in the South and Mira (1498–1546) in West India had most likely a double project they negotiated. They had not only a ready-made female voice and did not need to adopt one, they had female bodies that were in many senses a burden in the societies they lived in. We see various strategies to deal with the body. Akka Mahadevi

(12th century) apparently walked about naked, covered only in her tresses. Mira used folk motifs in her poetry, and her voice is that of a village woman with its complications of housework and in-laws. At the same time, she is a *bhakta* and the only real value in her life is that of submission to her lord, the only "man" before whom every devotee is a female. Her body is thus erased and of no importance.

Since Mira was a live woman and a princess at that, her hagiography produces a model and spaces for women's freedom. She left her husband and home, was directly "disobedient" to men in her family, and was victorious over them when they attempted to trick her, catch her, and even poison her. Thus, she is a role model but also semi-divine, while always claiming for herself an identity of lover and worshipper of Krishna in a self-obscuring way that remains a model of *bhakti* poetry. In Mira's poems, she weds Krishna, whom she prefers to evoke as "the Lord of those who live in need" and "the mountain-lifting Lord" (one of his feats of lifting a mountain to shelter his people) – all because of the merits of her past life (Hawley & Juergensmeyer, 2004, p. 137). As Krishna's bride, Mira is a radical contrast to Radha, the cowherd lover of Krishna. Radha is a metaphor for the human soul, a soul best rendered as female, that is, weak (except in its voice and its longing). Mira is a poet who adopts this voice as well as other voices and can directly reflect, in her voice, the desire of a human for union with the Lord. That there is often a conflation between the two positions only shows how artistry and devotion could not be separated by the artist/devotee *or* the audience. That finally explains the female voice of men poets and performers. In the courts of the Ahmed Shahs of Gujarat, they claimed that their music made it superior to the courts of the gods. Males would perform as women, including as the goddess of music and art herself, Saraswati (Asher & Talbot, 2006, p. 96).

Akka Mahadevi has three hundred and fifty *vacanas* or verses that bear her signature, the name she chose for her Lord, Shiva, *Chennamallikarjuna*, literally, Mallika's beautiful Arjuna, or "Lord white as jasmine." Like Mira does with Krishna, Akka claims to be married to Shiva. At the same time, her love is illicit because she is married to a human, whom she rejects. The themes of love as forbidden, then fulfilled, then as longing in separation, are all beautifully rendered by her. The intimacies of carnal love mark spiritual progress.

> It was like a stream
> running into the dry bed
> of a lake,
> like rain
> pouring on plants.
> (Tharu & Lalita,
> 1991, p. 77)

The centrality of erotic love and desire gives rise to one of the debates in Indian historiography and art. Regarding both origins and the ultimate nature of the emotion, did "Indian" values influence a Middle Eastern or Islamic tradition, or did values coming from outside influence Indian practices? It would be a futile debate, however, because every influence was reciprocal according to the rich data on the subject, and the product was truly syncretistic. Most important, the question of origins and categories was of no value to the artists and audience, and is ultimately a misleading one when applied to the art, aesthetics, and devotional philosophy of the twelfth to the eighteenth centuries. It was, however, an important question for some reformers, and the question has become highly politicised today in the twenty-first century.

## Bibliography

Asher, K., & Talbot, C. (2006). *India before Europe*. Cambridge: Cambridge University Press.
Behl, A. (2009). The soul's quest in Malik Muhammad Jayasi's Hindavi romance. In B. D. Metcal (Ed.), *Islam in South Asia in practice*. Princeton, NJ: Princeton University Press.
Beveridge, A. S. (Trans.). (1997). *Babur-nama (Memoirs of Babur) of Zahiru'd-din Muhammad Babur Padshah Ghazi*. Delhi: Motilal Banarsidass. (Original work published 1921)
Chakravarty, U. (1989). The world of the Bhaktin in South Indian traditions: The body and beyond. *Manushi, 10*, 50–52.
Findly, E. B. (1993). *Nur Jahan: Empress of Mughal India*. New York: Oxford University Press.
Hawley, J. S., & Juergensmeyer, M. (2004). *Songs of the saints of India*. New Delhi: Oxford University Press.
Kaul, H. K. (1985). *Historic Delhi: An anthology*. New Delhi: Oxford University Press.
Kumar, S. (2007). *The emergence of the Delhi sultanate 1192–1286*. Delhi: Permanent Black.
Lal, R. (2005). *Domesticity and power in the early Mughal world*. Cambridge: Cambridge University Press.
Lane-Poole, S. (2015 [1908]). *Aurangzib and the decay of the Muhal Empire*. London: White Press.
Metcalf, B. D. (Ed.). (2009). *Islam in practice in South Asia*. Princeton, NJ: Princeton University Press.
Mir, F. (2010). *The social space of language: Vernacular culture in British colonial Punjab*. Berkeley, CA: University of California Press.
Misra, R. (1967). *Women in Mughal India 1526–1748 A.D.* New Delhi: Munshiram Manoharlal.
Mukhia, H. (2004). *The Mughals of India*. Oxford: Blackwell Publishing.
O'Hanlon, R. (1998). Kingdom, household and body: Gender and the instruction of imperial service under Akbar. *Journal of Economic and Social History of the Orient, 42*(1), 47–93.
Ramanujan, A. K. (1973). *Speaking of Siva*. Harmondsworth: Penguin.
Ramaswamy, V. (1992). Rebels – conformists? Women saints in medieval South India. *Anthropos, 87*(1/3), 133–146.
Ramaswamy, V. (1996). Madness, holiness, poetry: The vachanas of Virasaivite women. *Indian Literature, 39*(3), 147–155.
Tharu, S., & Lalita, K. (1991). *Women writing in India 600 BC to the present. Vol. 1: 600 B.C. to the early 20th century*. Delhi: Oxford University Press.
Vaudeville, C. (1999). *Myths, saints and legends in medieval India*. Delhi: Oxford University Press.

# 5
# THE COLONIAL PERIOD
## Changes in Work Roles

This chapter gives a broad overview of the economic and occupational changes as the colonial state expanded from the 1750s to the 1850s first as the territory of the East India Company, then recast as part of an empire under the Crown from the 1850s to its end in 1947. Colonialism is a specific economic formation, one of its characteristics being limited industrialisation of the colony. The limited industrialisation of India compared to the Industrial Revolution in Europe was a problem identified by Indian nationalists in the second half of the nineteenth century and admitted to by the colonialists. As studies of Europe have shown, the changes brought about by its industrialisation were not merely economic but social, ideological, political, and psychological as well. Many modern-day connotations of "male" and "female" that are accepted as natural, particularly of men's and women's work and relative status, were historically developed in the eighteenth–twentieth centuries in association with economic and technological changes. We will see in this chapter whether profound changes in gender roles occurred in India even without an industrial revolution. We will look briefly at the nature of economic change and how it impacted women. The economic history of this period has itself shifted in emphasis over the last three to four decades from concern with the national product, per capita income, etc., to the quality of life in terms of education, healthcare, and democracy. Studies of labour history, the informal economy, and environmental history have all contributed to giving attention to a more gendered study of economic activities. At the same time, because of the fluctuations within the discipline of economic history, and because of contemporary liberalisation of the economy, there is a new approach among some economic historians of not seeing colonialism as central to the region's economic fate. This new approach has its own gendered dimensions. For instance, economic stagnation, according to Tirthankar Roy, occurred at the turn of the

DOI: 10.4324/9781003393252-6

twentieth century for many reasons, among which was "risk." Risk from the monsoons and other uncertainties meant a "demand" for more children – obviously a decision that centrally affects women (Roy, 2004, p. 3242). In this chapter, we will not weigh the economic history debates as much as we will tease out all their implications regarding gender.

If colonialism is the domination and exploitation by one nation over another territory, and in the eighteenth century it was the domination by Britain over South Asia, we can refine this definition from our gendered perspective to say that colonialism was the domination by one group of males, British males, over another group of males, those in the pre-national states of India. True, the ruling monarch in England when the East India Company was chartered in 1600 was a woman, Queen Elizabeth I (1533–1603), and the ruling monarch when the Crown took over the Company's territories in 1858 was another woman, Queen Victoria (1819–1901), soon to be declared Empress of India. But it was exclusively men who opted to buy shares in the East India Company, or to serve it as clerks or as soldiers who fought skirmishes and battles with the male armies of assorted Indian states. Women were not even the prize; the land of India was. India was feminised. It was *entered, looted, raped*, and then *mastered* and *domesticated*. The early phases of European presence in India saw a more equitable gendered relationship between East and West in that Europeans often had Indian wives or mistresses and were partially assimilated in the new civilisation. In his historical fiction, *White Mughals* (2002), William Dalrymple claims that one out of three British men in India in the eighteenth century had an Indian wife or mistress. This changed radically to a racial inequality that put *all* men and women of South Asia below those of Europe. There continued to be heterosexual and homosexual relationships between European and Indian people, but they were fewer and lacked legitimacy, equality, or power.

Towards the end of the eighteenth century, the East India Company introduced three major administrative changes that percolated down to the most intimate levels of life. First, they installed a singular uniform law to replace the many customary laws that people observed. This resulted in the growth of new classes of middlemen who worked for the new courts, to whom women had less access than did men. It meant new conflicts regarding property, as *customary* patriarchal practices regarding marriage and succession, including adoption, became transformed into rigidly enforceable laws. It led to new relationships between and within families, and a sense of a new regime of power that controlled people's lives. Overall, it resulted in a huge discursive change in the definitions of "governmentality," which the historian Indrani Chatterjee explains as "the entire gamut of desires, habits, aspirations, beliefs, and attachments – the making of subjectivities" (Chatterjee, 2013, p. 58). As fiction set in a later period shows us, the very feelings of family members towards each other become modulated on the basis of new legal relationships. Rabindranath Tagore's short stories describe women and girls bereft of inheritances leading troubled lives because their attachment to brother or family became worthless in the face of a competition for the estate. In Chapter 8 we will see how legal history was not linear either. At every step, a British action did not have only repercussions for Indians but was met by reaction, manipulation, and resistance as well.

Second, the East India Company introduced revenue-related changes, notably the Permanent Settlement in Bengal in 1793. This empowered an older landowning class with newly defined private ownership of land and also created a new class of absentee landlords with no interest in the well-being of the countryside owned by them. Peasants and wage labourers became impoverished and indebted. The subordination of women was both further entrenched and newly enforced. Matrilineal laws of succession, to the degree that such as had existed, were replaced by patrilineal ones. Customs such as that of *karewa*, or the marriage of a widow to her late husband's brother, were reinforced by the colonial state in pursuit of political gains. A new gentry was created with its own separation of spheres in its gender relationships and over time; other classes were encouraged to aim for a similar high-caste, high-class status through control of women. Underlying the process was a perception of danger from both financial control by women of property and practice of social autonomy. The film *Sahib, Bibi aur Ghulam* (Alvi, 1962) and the novel it is based on, *Shahib Bibi Golam* by Bimal Mitra, picturises a decadent, feudal family in which the males are defined by their upper-caste, invulnerable patriarchal identity, and their wives by their lack of rights and freedoms. When one of the women is perceived as a threat because of her expression of discontent, she is murdered.

The third major change introduced by the colonialists was a policy to use English as a vehicle for higher education and official jobs. This meant not only a new course of study in new buildings but the re-definition of knowledge, the transformation of relationships, and a shift in the power of learning. English education had been introduced first by missionaries as a choice and was now pushed by *diktat* and pressure by the state. The changes in gender relationships this brought are discussed in detail in Chapter 7. Suffice it to say here that the new education supported and in many ways worked powerfully to create the new middle classes, which like middle classes elsewhere in the modernising world, had new ideas and values regarding gender. Alongside, it produced numerous less tangible changes in work patterns. Older professions of doctor (*vaid, hakim*), advocate (*vakil*), teacher (*guru, ustad*), and clerk (*munshi*), based on indigenous educational training, were replaced by newer versions of the same professions based on colonial education. A range of work, such as of ritualist and entertainer, that had been supported by older lifestyles were now explicitly scorned and reformed out of existence. The new educated classes developed a progressively stricter reform agenda over the latter nineteenth and earlier twentieth centuries, the impact of which will be studied in a later chapter.

The coming of new professions affected women as well, always with a time lag. Modern medicine was such a profession. In 1885, much after the profession was available to men, the Dufferin Fund was set up by the Viceroy Dufferin's wife to train doctors and nurses, and set up hospitals and dispensaries. Kadimbini Basu (b. 1861) was a beneficiary of the scheme and one of the two first female modern-style doctors in India. Brought up in a liberal household and then married to a Brahmo Samaj reformer, she succeeded in combining her career with apparently a happy family life. We cannot know fully what her personal experiences were. We know that she was severely taunted by others for her freedom, even winning a libel case against one such critic. Another beneficiary was Anandabai Joshi (b. 1865), whose case is more tragic. Married very young, she was encouraged, even pressured by her husband to study, and at 18 won a scholarship to study medicine at the Women's Medical College, Pennsylvania. She was traditional in her food habits, and the combination of her severe living conditions and intense labour, as well as perhaps other factors, led to her early death at the age of 22. She never had a chance to practice medicine. Muthulakshmi Reddy (b. 1885) was the daughter of a Brahman and a *devdasi* and did practise after completing her medical degrees, combining professional with family life. In her autobiography she writes, "Medical women, if they really love the profession and wish to practice should not think of marriage, because they cannot perform two functions at one and the same time" (Forbes, 1996, p. 105). She rose to be India's first woman legislator and worked on behalf of *devdasi* reform and other women's issues. (An aside: her birthday on 30 July was marked by the Google search engine, testifying both to a recognition of her life as an important one in the history of women and equally to the presence of Indian coders working at Google who felt that it gave them importance to recognise her.)

Other elite women, even while they participated in politics or social reform, did not choose to adopt a feminist posture. Sarojini Naidu (b. 1879), a pioneer in women's organisations and the Indian National Congress, wanted to emphasise the spiritual nature of women's work. She was not a feminist, she declared, because a feminist is one who admits "her inferiority and there has been no need for such a thing in India as the women have always been by the side of men both in councils and the fields of battle" (Forbes, 1996, p. 158). Rokeya Sakhawat Husain (b. 1880) was a contemporary who still stands out for her radical feminist stand. She succeeded in conceptualising a reversal of men and women's work in her famous *Sultana's Dream*, a science fiction novella featuring a utopian society called Ladyland, led by women, with men safe behind walls in the *zenana*. Rokeya Husain believed strongly in women's economic independence, and that education was the key to it.

While the three changes in law, administration, and education comprised India's modernisation, many Indian communities manipulated most economic and political processes on the ground to conform to their own values. Caste had historically been a manipulable structure. Fluid economic and legal situations had enabled caste groups to move up the social ladder. In the colonial period, one way to do so, as partly explained by the sociologist M. N. Srinivas, was through what he calls "Sanskritisation." First, the profession associated with the caste was adapted, for instance, from trading in hides or oil to trading in other, more neutral commodities, hides or oil being seen as lowly. Or the profession was totally changed, for instance, from trading to "service." Second, the lifestyle associated with the profession and the caste was revised to now include vegetarianism, more elaborate life-cycle ceremonies and rituals, and the seclusion of women. Sanskritisation was a process of change often followed by modernisation. The same community would first follow one, then the other, with often an overlap. Both the processes of change had women at the centre. The social-symbolic representation of their women by a caste group or sub-group marked them as moving up the social ladder or as staying behind, and the pace at which they did so.

While these were processes observable in most castes and communities, there was also an inertia based on a self-satisfaction that characterised some higher castes as well. The important changes introduced by the colonial state were resisted and an older identity was objectified and sharpened in reaction to a perceived threat of change from outside. Christopher Bayly (1983) explains how a business firm had its own ethos. This consisted of its reputation for honesty and integrity. This in turn depended upon impeccable book-keeping, which in its turn depended on expertise in book-keeping and accounts, accompanied by a reputation that was worth more in a court of law than a written document. This reputation and the ethos it was built upon had to be preserved through any changes. Here entered the roles played by women. They were the indispensable links in the chains of continuity. It was of crucial importance to make the right matches as weddings converted two unrelated families into closely allied ones and produced the precious sons (and, indirectly, daughters) that comprised the lineage that the whole merchant class depended on.

As the East India Company consolidated its rule, approximately 1760s to 1830s, there were new opportunities in trade and commerce, banking, and moneylending for Indian merchant classes, specifically in Bengal. An example of such a beneficiary of the new era was Dwarkanath Tagore (1794–1847), who became an honorary "Prince" from his profits and laid the foundations of the patrimonial house of Tagore. His wife, Digambari Devi (1802–1839), showed the courage to oppose his new intermingling and interdining with British men and women, and broke off marital relations with him and ostracised him from their house. His son Debendranath (1817–1905), given the epithet of "Maharishi" (Great Sage) because of his learning and asceticism, was similarly opposed by Jogmaya Devi, the wife of his younger brother, who divided the Tagore family into two, the so-called Hindu and Brahmo branches. Yet another sister-in-law, Tripura Sundari, fought to the end a legal battle with Debendranath for the right to retain her property willed to her by her husband's father after her husband's death. Men such as Dwarkanath and Debendranath are celebrated for their brilliance in commerce and letters, but they were also patriarchal figures who directly constructed lives that we regard in a modern feminist perspective as "limited" for women. The openings provided by East India Company trade for Indian men were accompanied by a gradual shrinking of the space for action by women.

Another example is Rammohan Roy (1774–1833), also like Dwarkanath, a Raja or "Prince" who made money partly in the service of, and partly through moneylending to, East India Company officers. He became a figurehead of social reform, particularly of wrongs against women that we will go into later in detail. His mother, Tarini Devi, about whom we know far less than we know of him, opposed him in his iconoclastic activities and sought to disinherit him. But the new property laws of the East India Company disinherited her instead. Like many widows and elder women, she found herself propertyless, if not debt-ridden. The Company had introduced "the Permanent Settlement" in 1793 as a result of which new taxation laws made property often change hands, creating radical social turmoil. In this change, as historian Indrani Chatterjee has shown, older practices of owning and transferring property by women were also replaced by new British ideas of taxation that favoured certain kinds of people, all men. That Tarini Devi spent her last years as a temple servant is both an indication of her agency to choose a mode of life that could provide survival and her helplessness before the forces of economic and political change.

Rammohan Roy founded the Brahmo Sabha that was later changed by Debendranath to the Brahmo Samaj in 1843. Seeking to reform Hindu practices of ritualism, dogma, and icon worship, this society also targeted many features of women's lives as needing change. Brahmo women were unusually free to move around, get an education, and marry at a later age and of their choice. There is no question that in the earlier phase of the East India Company's impact upon India, and specifically Bengal, the new Indians benefited from the relationship. They made money but were also socially active and took up leadership roles in education, religion, and society. The women of their families were affected in both a positive and a negative way. These elite women were also gradually leading new lives, even if only privately and never comparable to their husbands' roles as social leaders. They created new private worlds and were new kinds of mothers and wives. In a few cases, they were able to join the man's world and also study, practise law or medicine, write and publish, and be a reforming leader in society. The second effect on women was the actual loss of rights that they had earlier had, which did not continue to be recognised by the British under their new legal system, and therefore a loss of status, which extended beyond property rights to respect as a certain kind of actor in society. As the momentum escalated of "reform" of the many ills of women's position in society, they vanished in history as people and became transformed into problems, issues, and symbols. Historians of South Asia have been much more interested in these issues, collectively called "the woman question," than in women.

In the eighteenth and nineteenth centuries, because of the opening up of trade and banking into new directions with the East India's Company's markets, the merchant classes in many parts of India became more entrenched in their "traditional" ethos and identities. In Bombay and in Banaras, merchant communities resisted modernisation or even dependence on English and colonial education. Their relatively fixed occupations that were not as radically altered by colonial rule as many other occupations were the cause for what they would have called their "rootedness." But even for them, it is very likely that the position of men and women became more separate. Women were relegated more precisely to the inside, domestic spaces of the home, and men were the natural inhabitants of the outside, public, commercial, and political spaces. While women continued to have an indigenous education and power over certain spheres, they necessarily became weaker.

The "rootedness" of merchants is a contrast to the new middle classes that emerged first in the metropolises of Calcutta, Bombay, and Madras, and then elsewhere. At the heart of the new middle classes were the new professions of doctor, lawyer, journalist, bureaucrat, and teacher, all based in the new colonial and missionary education slowly introduced at the end of the eighteenth century, then with speed after the 1830s. This was a new bourgeoisie in India based, as in Europe, on urbanisation and new economic relationships. But, in a way different to Europe, the new Indian middle classes sought to define themselves by measuring their identity and image against the yardstick of the West. They launched reforms of what they saw as "backward" practices in their communities: practices of caste, worship of icons, seclusion of women, prohibition of widow remarriage, child marriage, polygamy, polytheism and an overall absence of a liberal, rational consciousness. Many of the problems that were seen as needing reform were seen as women's problems. The campaigns for reforms resulted in new gender relations, all within a patriarchal framework. In some cases, the new gender relations meant more freedom for women and more equality with men. In others, they meant new repressions where there had been more fluid rules, and disciplining where there had been agency. By and large, a new powerful ideology of domesticity, housewifery, and mothering emerged everywhere among the middle classes.

Because of their base in this new colonial education, the new middle classes tried to internalise an ideology of progress. For their women, it meant attempts at education but also separate spheres. Childcare and housecare became occupations that had to be carried out with diligence and self-consciousness. The next generation was being formed and had to be formed carefully in a progressive mode. This economic-educational-gendered change took root in a striking way in Bengal (Bose, 1995) and has continued up to the present. Indian educated middle classes reproduce their education and professions in their children. Margit Pernau, in her study of the emergence of the Muslim middle classes, shows the same process at work. She analyses the book *Mirat ul Urus* by Nazir Ahmad, the story "Majalis un Nisa" by Altaf Husain Hali, the *Tahzib un Niswan* by the Begum of Bhopal, and *Bihishti Zewar* by Ashraf Ali Thanawi. All these authors, which include one woman, set up the domestic sphere as the proper site of woman's work, wherein lay her professional success and her personal salvation. And it was not only for the children that the new woman in her new domestic private space was crucial. She was essential for her husband as well. Displacing the authority of his mother and other senior women of the family, the husband now became the axis around which the household revolved. Whether the woman preserved custom, such as in researching old herbal remedies, or innovated by educating herself about time and space discipline, it was all to support and promote the image of the man as a progressive, successful representative of a changing society. The great intellectual Khwaja Altaf Husain Hali became aware of the central role of women from his own experience. As he succeeded in the public world, their children and household was managed single-handedly by his wife.

Thus, for a variety of reasons, including Sanskritisation, Ashrafisation, modernisation, and emulation of Europe, there was a change in women's situation (less for some communities such as merchants) that was akin to what happened in Europe, even without its industrial revolution. In England, as a result of industrialisation, the "workplace" became separated from the "home place," and the former became the space of men, the latter the domain of women. This doctrine of "separate spheres" was a physical and ideological separation.

> The physical artifact "home" came to be associated with a particular sex, "women"; with a particular emotional tone, "warmth"; with a particular public stance, "morality"; and with a particular form of behavior, "passivity"; while at the very same time, "work" became associated with "men," "hardheartedness," "excitement," "aggression," and "immorality."
> *(Cowan, 1983, pp. 18–19)*

In India, modernity had its birth in colonialism. There was no industrial revolution, no Protestant ethic, and no consequent ideology of individualism and liberalism. Or, if all these did come into existence they were inflected in Indian ways. There were many similarities: the rule of the father was already a fact, and to this was added a new weight with colonial inheritance laws. The differences were many as well. The Bengali middle class, for example, was conflicted about "*chakri*," or service and its work ethic.

> What made *chakri* intolerable was – its connotation of impersonal cash nexus and authority, embodied above all in the new rigorous discipline of work regulated by clock-time. Disciplinary time was a particularly abrupt and imposed innovation in colonial India. Europe had gone through a much slower, and phased, transition spanning some five hundred years. . . . Colonial rule telescoped the entire process for India into one or two generations. . . . Chakri thus became a 'chronotype' of alienated time and space."
> *(Sarkar, 1992, pp. 1549–1550)*

The major changes in India's economy were structural ones. Instead of technological or administrative innovation, the emphasis on labour-intensive farm work remained. As the historian Sugata Bose explains,

> [t]he premium on family labor capacity meant relentless exploitation of women's reproductive capacities and largely unremunerated productive capacities as an expenditure-saving device, and of children's labor capacities as both an expenditure-saving and an income-earning mechanism. Among families of landless laborers at the bottom of the agrarian hierarchy, women, relatively unconstrained by cultural norms of segregation, also joined in the ranks of income-augmenters. Survival resting solely on family labor power has been achieved largely at the cost of exploitation within the family.
> 
> *(Bose, 1993, pp. 36–37)*

In some cases, agricultural production stagnated. In other cases, subsistence and mixed farming were replaced by commercial and single-crop farming in many parts of East, West, and South India. Cotton, tea, indigo, coffee, jute, and for a time, opium, became profitable crops to which acres of land were dedicated. India turned to becoming a supplier of raw materials and cash crops instead of being a combination of subsistence farming and small-scale manufacturing. Tasks on the cash-crop plantations, such as tea plucking and cotton picking, were performed exclusively by women. As scholars have found, while these were at least paid tasks, others such as rice transplanting or rice husking were not always paid, and went unreported in the censuses and surveys, leading to a picture of a very low statistic of women in the agricultural workforce.

Sugata Bose gives detailed attention to one kind of women's work in Bengal, rice husking. First, an important part of a poor family's earnings, and of a poor village's economy, was provided by women's labour in rice husking. Second, this income-generating capacity permitted women a certain autonomy and the ability to identify as providers of sustenance alongside and equal to men. Third, as mechanisation of rice husking in mills was introduced, mills expanding from 24 in 1911 to 369 in 1946, women's incomes plummeted. The new mill workers were mostly men. While rice husking may be a special feature of Bengal economy, the overall reduction of opportunities for women's income-generating labour caused a change everywhere in India in the value of women. In a peasant economy, much of the gender-bias comes from the perception of economic value and contribution of an individual. Women had been exploited for their reproductive labour, but perhaps valued for their productive, that is, economic labour. When that was devalued as well due to structural economic changes, they suffered both sexual and economic exploitation and devaluation. As the historian Paul Greenough (1982) has shown, during a famine, women were the last to receive food, and as the economist Amartya Sen (1984) argues, some part at least of gender inequality is due to the often invisible inequality in economic opportunity and therefore earning capacity between men and women. This inequality became intensified during colonialism.

Perhaps for the vast majority of the masses of Indians in agriculture or animal husbandry, there were significant ups and downs but not profound structural changes. Crops replaced each other, commercial farming became important, land changed hands from smaller croppers to larger landlords, new lands became irrigated, and old lands became barren. In Bihar, with new destitution, farmers migrated to cities for work and overseas to labour. In Punjab and Haryana, new farms rose and fell. In North, Central, and West India, there were cases of overtaxation leading to a permanently impoverished and debt-ridden peasantry.

But for all of India, modernisation in India did not mean industrialisation, but de-industrialisation. The best-studied example of this de-industrialisation is the textile industry of India, which was more or less destroyed between 1820 and 1860, mainly because of the tax and trade policies of the colonial state. Spinning and weaving, which had been done by women alongside men, became redundant as yarn and cloth came to be imported from Britain. The few cotton mills in Bombay employed women as between 20% and 25% of their labour force. The jute mills of Bengal had the same figures. An ironic complication arose when the International Labor Organization was established in the beginning of the twentieth century, and India was given representation in it in 1922. The ILO started recommending that India pass legislation to improve workers' conditions, such as regarding medical benefits, maternity leave, and restricted hours of work. This was seen as a problem by both employers and employees. The former preferred to get rid of now-expensive female workers for unregulated male workers. The women simply took on additional work, preferring to earn more rather than have shorter hours or fewer days of work.

The understanding of women's changing work during the colonial period is extremely important but remains challenging because of the relative lack of data, both raw and analysed. Census reports themselves have to be critically interpreted. When a historian says that in 1921 almost one-third of the women in India were working women, this figure excludes women in agriculture, home-based manufacture, and the sex industry. Information is obliquely obtainable. We know, for instance, that in rice cultivation women have always worked in the fields, either as waged labour or as family labour, in which case it includes all castes and sects. The number of working women was probably closer to two-thirds than one-third of all women. The other delicate question was about their exploitation on numerous fronts. Not only were they discharged in favour of male workers once ILO regulations were put on employers, they had no voice to represent them. There could be the occasional voice, such as of Lakshmi Menon, who represented India at the UN. Forbes reports how she explained the situation quite unequivocally:

> When laboring women turned to prostitution it was to supplement their inadequate wages, she said. Menon criticised the Madras Regional

Conference on Social Hygiene for its 1935 program of rescue work, propaganda, and VD clinics. They were ignoring issues of employment and wages for women. . . . Guaranteed employment, training programs, protective policies, and "a new sex code" which abolished the double standard seemed to be the answer.

*(Quoted in Forbes, 1996, p. 188)*

The economic changes produced great unevenness in development. The very nature of colonialism meant that there was no redressal from arbitrary processes: whole swathes of population could become more impoverished, indebted, or underemployed. The gendered results of the economic change of the eighteenth to nineteenth centuries are described for Bengal by Nirmala Banerjee by the use of the concepts of "modern sector" and "traditional sector" referring to factory work versus home-based production.

> workers of the region, both men and women, were made increasingly dependent on agriculture for their livelihood. Men were somewhat more fortunate: the bulk of the employment opportunities in the modern sector went to them. After 1931 the share of agriculture in the male workforce declined steadily. For women, the process meant a permanent shift towards the periphery of the economy. Their non-agricultural occupations in the traditional sector suffered a serious setback mainly because of the intervention of the modern sector into the village economy. Women had neither the skills nor the capital to resist these changes. Nor were they in a position to claim their share in the modern sector though, at least initially, employment opportunities had been created for them in these activities. The traditional sector had always imposed stringent constraints on their mobility between regions and occupations. . . . Therefore, the mere fact that jobs were available did not always bring forth an immediate response from the local female population. . . . The demand of the modern sector was in fact so small compared to the negative impact it had created in the traditional sector that any fresh increase in demand was quickly met by more and more very needy workers pouring into the city from further and further afield.
>
> *(N. Banerjee, 1989, p. 297)*

The scholar of popular culture in Bengal, Sumanta Banerjee, describes how a fairly unified, eclectic Bengali culture in the early nineteenth century split into two. "By the 1870s the cultural forms of expression of the Bengali *bhadralok* had developed a stylistic unity which resulted from the patronage of a social group that had become economically, culturally and politically unified." The unity was partly based on a distancing from the masses, who came to be characterised as ignorant, backward, and even dangerous and therefore to be avoided. These lower classes became more fragmented. "The social ties that used to bind them together in their old villages and, later, in early nineteenth century Calcutta snapped as the years passed and the first generations of the urban *nouveaux riches* disappeared" (Banerjee, 1989, p. 199). The new middle classes had different tastes and sensibilities, based on their English education and colonial mentality. They were unlike the older patrons who savoured performances and narratives produced by "low-class" performers. Functional products, such as textiles or domestic appliances, along with entertainment genres, became divided into "old" and "new," "low" and "high," and "theirs" and "ours." In turn, lower classes protested through the arts. They lampooned the products of the new education, often targeting women. A song in Calcutta ended with the lines:

> Men have lost their power,
> They're tied to their wives' apron-strings.
> (N. Banerjee, 1989, p. 111)

If we turn westwards to the state of Haryana, studies show it to be a poor, drought-ridden province where women and men worked equally hard on the fields, and women inside the house as well. While regarded as strong and wilful, they were yet oppressed by the same systemic practices as in other patriarchal structures. They veiled their faces (*ghunghat*), were sold for a bride price among many castes and given against dowry in certain others, and then could be married again after their husband's death by his male kinsmen. In all these cases, colonial law served to make the problem more emphasised. The veiling did not save them from work in the fields and when it did was explicitly condemned by the colonial authorities as an indication of the backwardness of agricultural productivity of the province. Whether through bride price or dowry, the wedding practices of Haryana served to represent a woman as a burden on the family, even while she was a worker all her life. The practice of levirate was something the women could not fight without state help and the state chose to treat it as a community practice they could not interfere in (Chowdhry, 1989, pp. 302–336).

In Oudh (present-day Uttar Pradesh), according to the Taluqdari Revenue Settlement of 1858, the *taluqdars*, or landowners, were considered the absolute landlords with full ownership of the land and rights over their tenants and labourers. These peasant tenants were now further impoverished as they came to be subjected to exploitation from both the government and the new landlords. For instance, they had to pay *nazrana*, a kind of premium on rent, an external amount that translated to a total burden on the peasant. As Kapil Kumar tells us, some people went to the extent of selling their daughters to meet their revenue needs (Kumar, 1989, p. 339). Premchand (1880–1936), a writer who drew graphic pictures of village life in India, has many short stories and novels in which his peasants suffer from tax demands, and the women characters suffer cumulatively from this as well as domestic burdens and a barrage of hardship brought on by the administrative structures of the colonial period. In *Godan* the wife of the chief protagonist Hori advises him strongly against giving up all his earnings to the landlord and then suffers with him and their family through rounds of impoverishment, indebtedness, and loss of crops and land.

Among others, Indrani Chatterjee, in her discussion of the extinction of women-based households by colonial law, shows how women came to be economically disempowered in subtle, nuanced ways (Chatterjee, 2013). Widows were often evicted from their land after the death of the husband. Both men and women could be fined for so-called illicit relations with people of another caste. At the same time, we must remember that taluqdars, and all landlords, could be women, and women landlords were as capable of exploitation of the peasants, male or female, as men were. Major General Sleeman, as he travelled through Oudh in the 1850s, could not help but note that some of his landed gentry were ladies, and that wealth, effects, and status passed down along channels in which men could be missing (Sleeman, 1858 I, p. 142). Sleeman is acerbic about the pageants and processions of Lucknow, an "overgrown city" into which its ruler poured all his wealth. From Sleeman's accounts, we can see the development of a new gender division. Some work is clearly feminine and feminising, such as composing and performing poetry, music, and dance. There were some problems that were both men's and women's, of which there were some that were *worse* for women than for men. Among these were child marriage: in 1921 there were over 50% more girls than boys under the age of 15 who were already married (Kumar, 1989, p. 343). There were some problems that were peculiar to women or girls, such as becoming widowed at an early age, and while men could also be widowed, the stigma on remarriage existed, when it did, only for women. There was female infanticide in some communities, according to Sleeman (1858, pp. 313–314). Infanticide and dowry are both problems associated with the image of women as non-economic assets. Inheritance laws made these two problems greater in the colonial period, at least for Punjab (Oldenburg, 2002).

Meena Gopal, along with others, points out that the work of women can best be understood as a complex of economic, caste, and gender ideology. Certain domestic work is considered at the bottom of the economic hierarchy and paid nothing, when performed by family women, or paid extremely minimally when performed by a female, hired labour. It is also considered lowly, especially garbage removal, sweeping, and washing up. It is always gendered. Women are made to bear the mantle of qualities of self-sacrifice, love and nurture, patience and dedication; the work becomes transformed into "a labour of love" (Gopal, 2013, p. 92). However, we need more research on women's work in India, both historical and anthropological (such as Daniel Miller, 1998).

Let us look first at low-caste work. Contrasted to the history of upper-caste women's work, where the process was one of domesticating the woman and keeping her from work outside the home, low-caste women shared historically in work outside the home. With their menfolk, untouchable women (today, *Dalits*) had the monopoly of the most servile work related to scavenging, and carcass disposal, and as with the men, it was very lowly paid. Among the most defiling occupations is considered midwifery. In modern India, the state tried to intervene, but by emphasising the notion of "cleanliness," kept intact the ritually polluting and low-caste status of certain jobs. Even upon institutionalisation of birth, the midwife or *dai* was rendered more marginal and left in the interstices, stigmatised twice over, as low caste and as unskilled.

The leather tanning industry is another one in which no protection is given to women while some of the most dangerous tasks are left for them to perform, at low rates of compensation because of the related status of the tasks as defiling and low caste. Similarly, manual scavenging of latrines, drains, and roadsides and railway tracks is also restricted to the lowest castes, and among them women are employed fully in these tasks. The state has assumed a high-caste mentality in not addressing itself to either a dedicated technological change that would remove the burden of such work from a hereditary worker or an ideological change where the work itself was not considered defiling and impure. The state and upper castes in positions of authority distance themselves from work that is considered filthy because it relates to waste materials such as shit, hides, blood, and placenta.

When caste and exclusion are not considered alongside gendered work, there could be a confusion of interests. In the case of bar dancers in Bombay, when the state prohibited the work, feminists opposed the prohibition as a violation of professional work choice for women. However, bar dancers themselves saw their work as a stigmatised one *because* it related to low caste and was not, in fact, voluntary. On a larger scale, the binary this partly rests on is between the "good" and the "bad" woman, the good being the wife, private and domesticated woman, and the bad being the public, working woman, at the extreme of which is the prostitute. This group can include widows, deserted women, working-class urban and landless rural women, and women engaged in domestic labour. The group is characterised by poverty and stigmatisation. The number of domestic workers particularly is large and comprises a huge informal economic class.

The history of women's work in the colonial period brings out a different, related binary as well. Upper- and middle-class, or "cultured," women (*bhadra, sharif*) simply did not *know* about the dimensions of lower-class life. They did not because they were socialised into an identity that saw itself constructed partly out of a contrast with the uneducated, lower caste, poor, and disenfranchised other. This basic class difference made it impossible for women to feel that they were one even when women's organisations and reform work burgeoned. An ethnography of servants and working-class women from the 1980s to the present explores the different kinds of prejudices that operate in elite women's minds, even when gender is supposed to be a unifying identity. Foremost among them are prejudices that are born of education, which serve to negate gender solidarity (Kumar, 2007).

Women are consumers as well as producers, especially upper-class women. This became pertinent when they were aroused to confront the idea of the "nation," as in a national economy and national production. When the Swadeshi movement developed in the late nineteenth century, inspired by the Drain theory of economic nationalists, the idea was to replace imported British goods by indigenous Indian ones and to stimulate manufacturing in India that had become weakened or destroyed as a result of British trade policies. Men were at the forefront and women assisted them by doing *dharna* in front of shops stocking British goods as well as throwing away their own foreign goods (when they could afford to do so and were sufficiently moved by swadeshi propaganda). Then, some educated women made more direct efforts. Swarnkumari Debi, editor of the *Bharati*, used her journal for calls for swadeshi. She started the Sakhi Samiti in 1886 to train widows to become self-reliant, which was the chief call of women reformers. She started an annual women's handicrafts fair to promote domestic manufacture and self-reliance. Pioneering women, such as her and her daughter Sarala Debi, had to fight social resistance to their new public presence. They were given a role model in fiction such as Shanti, the warrior in Bankimchandra's *Ananda Math* (1882) but of course they remained just a few leaders. Swadeshi was progressively aimed at women as consumers, and more gradually, women as producers.

The final word has to be reserved for that work of women that is the most determined and the most undervalued, in practical and not figurative terms. As the evocative title of the book by Patricia Jeffery *Labour Pains and Labour Power* (1989), indicates, women's procreative work *could be* seen as of the same stature as wage work, but is not. A woman is postulated as a certain kind of being who always has child-bearing capacities but who could do waged work or not, mostly depending on if the compulsory child-bearing will permit her. There is a firm class difference in this truth, which holds for all women. In high-caste and high-class households, the woman is secluded, and "protected" from work because it would go against the honour of the male – who stands for the "family" – were she to earn. The only rare time she may start working is when the family is in dire trouble. In low-caste and low-class households, the woman easily does double work: mothering and wage work. According to al-Wazedi, both Jashoda in Mahashweta Devi's "Standayani" and Bibi Haldar in Jhumpa Lahiri's "The Treatment of Bibi Haldar" demonstrate approaches to motherhood that are alternative to the norms of mainstream patriarchy. "Motherhood" is a male-defined institution that establishes essential patrilines for the community/nation, and "mothering" is the experience of women that can vary according to circumstance, choice, and ability. These two stories, of Jashoda and Bibi Haldar, are perhaps feminist counter-narratives of motherhood that show us through their imagining and implementing agency and autonomy, a view of motherhood that is a potential site of power (al-Wazedi, 2016). We will look further at the fate of woman as mother in later chapters.

## Bibliography

Al-Wazedi, U. (2016). Power(ing) mothers. In R. Badruddoja & M. Motapanyane (Eds.), *New maternalisms?* (pp. 201–215). Ontario, Canada: Demeter Press.

Banerjee, N. (Ed.). (1984). *Women and industrialisation in developing countries*. Delhi: Orient Longman.

Banerjee, N. (Ed.). (1989). Working women in colonial Bengal: Modernization and marginalization. In K. Sangari & S. Vaid (Eds.), *Recasting women* (pp. 269–301). New Delhi: Kali for Women.

Banerjee, S. (1989). *The parlour and the streets: Elie and popular culture in nineteenth century Calcutta*. Calcutta: Seagull Books.

Banerjee, S. (2010). Blurring boundaries, distant companions: Non-kin female caregivers for children in colonial India (nineteenth and twentieth centuries). *Pedagogica Historica, 46*(6), 775–788.

Bayly, C. A. (1983). *Rulers, townsmen and bazaars: North Indian society in the age of British expansion, 1770–1870*. Cambridge: Cambridge University Press.

Bose, P. K. (1995). Sons of the nation: Child-rearing in the new family. In P. Chatterjee (Ed.), *Texts of power: Emerging disciplines in colonial Bengal* (pp. 93–117). Minneapolis, MN: University of Minnesota Press.

Bose, S. (1993). *The new Cambridge history of India III: 2. Peasant labor and colonial capital: Rural Bengal since 1770*. Cambridge: Cambridge University Press.

Chakrabarty, D. (2000). *Provincializing Europe: Postcolonial thought and historical difference*. Princeton, NJ: Princeton University Press.

Chatterjee, I. (2013). Monastic governmentality, colonial misogyny, and postcolonial amnesia in South Asia. *History of the Present, 3*(1), 57–98.

Chowdhry, P. (1989). Customs in a peasant economy: Women in colonial Haryana. In K. Sangari & S. Vaid (Eds.), *Recasting women: Essays in colonial history* (pp. 302–336). Delhi: Kali for Women.

Cowan, R. S. (1983). *More work for mother: The ironies of household technology from the open hearth to the microwave*. New York: Basic Books.

Devi, M. (1987). Breast-giver. In G. Spivak (Ed. & Trans.), *In other worlds: Essays in cultural politics* (pp. 222–240). New York: Routledge.

Ditrich, T. (2005). Human and divine mothers in Hinduism. In M. Porter, P. Short, & A. O'Reilly (Eds.), *Motherhood: Power and oppression* (pp. 137–151). Toronto: Women's Press.

Farahbakhsh, A., & Bozorgi, S. (2013). The Cixousian woman in Jhumpa Lahiri's 'the treatment of Bibbi Haldar'. *Journal of Language, Literature and Culture, 60*, 118–131.

Fitz, B. E. (2005). Bibi's Babel: Treating Jhumpa Lahiri's 'the treatment of Bibi Haldar' as the malady of interpreters. *South Asian Review, 26*(4), 116–131.

Forbes, G. (1996). *Women in modern India*. Cambridge: Cambridge University Press.

Gopal, M. (2013). Ruptures and reproductions in caste/gender/labor. *Economic and Political Weekly, 48*(18), 91–97.

Greenough, P. (1982). *Prosperity and misery in modern Bengal: The famine of 1943–44*. New York: Oxford University Press.

Guha, R. (1983). *Elementary aspects of peasant insurgency in colonial India*. Delhi: Oxford University Press.

Jeffery, P., Jeffery, R., & Lyon, A. (1989). *Labor pains and labor power: Childbearing in India*. London: Zed Books.

Kapadia, K. (1995). *Siva & her sisters: Gender, caste, and class in rural South India*. Boulder, CO: Westview Press.

Kumar, K. (1989). Rural women in Oudh 1919–1947: Baba Ram Chandra and the women's question. In K. Sangari & S. Vaid (Eds.), *Recasting women* (pp. 337–369). New Delhi: Kali for Women.

Kumar, N. (1988). *The artisans of Banaras: Popular culture and identity, 1880–1980*. Princeton, NJ: Princeton University Press.

Kumar, N. (1991). Widows, education and social change in twentieth century Banaras. *Economic and Political Weekly*, *26*(17), 19–25.

Kumar, N. (2007). The scholar and her servants. In N. Kumar (Ed.), *The politics of gender, community and modernity: Essays on education in India*. Delhi: Oxford University Press.

Lahiri, J. (1999). The treatment of Bibi Haldar. In *Interpreter of Maladies* (pp. 158–172). New York: Houghton Mifflin.

Mencher, J. (1998). Review of Geraldine Forbes, *Women in Modern India*. *The Journal of Developing Areas*, *32*(4), 580–583.

Miller, D. (1998). *A theory of shopping*. Ithaca, NY: Cornell University Press.

Oldenburg, V. T. (2002). *Dowry murders: The imperial origins of a cultural crime*. New York: Oxford University Press.

Pernau, M. (2013). *Ashraf into middle classes: Muslims in nineteenth-century Delhi*. Delhi: Oxford University Press.

Premchand. (2002). *Gift of a cow (Godan)*. Delhi: Permanent Black.

Rich, A. (1976). *Of woman born: Motherhood as experience and institution*. New York: W. W. Norton.

Roy, T. (2002). Economic history and modern India: Redefining the link. *The Journal of Economic Perspectives*, *16*(3), 109–130.

Roy, T. (2004). Economic history: An endangered discipline. *Economic and Political Weekly*, *39*(29), 3238–3243.

*Sahib, Bibi aur Ghulam*. (1962). Directed by Abrar Alvi.

Sangari, K., & Vaid, S. (1989). *Recasting women: Essays in Indian colonial history*. New Delhi: Kali for Women.

Sangha, J. (2014). Contextualising South Asian motherhood. In A. O'Reilly (Ed.), *Mothers, mothering and motherhood across cultural differences: A reader* (pp. 413–427). Bradford, ON: Demeter Press.

Sangha, J., & Gonsalves, T. (Eds.). (2013). *South Asian mothering: Negotiating culture, family and selfhood*. Bradford, ON: Demeter Press.

Sarkar, S. (1992). 'Kaliyuga,' 'Chakri,' and 'Bhakti': Ramakrishna and his times. *Economic and Political Weekly*, *27–29*, 1549–1550.

Sen, A. (1984). Family and food: Sex bias in poverty. In *Resources, values and development* (pp. 346–368). Oxford: Oxford University Press.

Sleeman, W. H. (2006). *A journey through the kingdom of Oude in 1849–1850*. New Delhi: Asian Educational Services. (Original work published 1858)

Spivak, G. (1987). (Elite) approaches: 'Standayani' in Marxist feminism. In G. Spivak (Ed.), *Other worlds: Essays in cultural politics* (pp. 247–252). New York: Routledge.

# 6
# THE COLONIAL PERIOD
## Changes in Socialisation and Education

This chapter proceeds chronologically over roughly the 1750s to the 1940s. It discusses certain themes in girls' and women's education that are first laid out here.

The first theme that runs through almost every history of women's education is that of evolutionary progress. Education, we are reminded, is not only about subjects, such as mathematics, social studies, and so on, but also about the "subject" being formed, that is, the student being worked upon to produce a person with a certain mindset. At the risk of generalising, we should understand formal schooling, such as became the norm in the nineteenth and twentieth centuries in most places in the world, to be partly about creating a certain kind of subject-figure. The person in pre-modern societies also had a persona, or subjecthood, someone who thought of herself as an intelligent human being able to make observations and decisions. But the person in modern societies is different: she imagines and desires herself to be autonomous and believes in choice and agency as her *right* in a different way to the pre-modern person, who typically accepted herself as part of a community. Education, along with economic and political processes, aims to produce this new subjecthood. There is an ideological dimension to this. The new education is seen to have a monopoly over "enlightenment" and is always spoken of in the singular. Instead of talking about various kinds of education, most discussions of modern, formal schooling contrast the dawn of such schooling with a period before when there was "no" education. With regard to women, this kind of loose usage cuts at the very roots of a historiographical enquiry seeking to be feminist.

A second theme is to see the restrictive as well as the emancipatory conditions of new, formal education. Education is meant to both develop a person to be questioning and socialise the person to fit in satisfactorily into her society. Systems of schooling differ in the best way to combine these two aspects, and in the ways to adapt to achieve their preferred combination. While this is true of both men and women, a further complication arises in the case of women. Because they are not the rulers, actors, and thinkers, in short, the public figures, of history, women are often treated symbolically. That is, they are treated, not as living, feeling subjects who have a right to speak and decide for themselves, but as signs of something else. We have seen elsewhere that in the late eighteenth and nineteenth centuries, they were considered signs of the backwardness or progress of a community. This idea was launched by the British as part of their overall interpretation of Indian society as barbaric and in need of civilised rule. It was accepted by Indians themselves as a reflection of their fall from a golden age and the necessity of reform. Whatever the merits of the argument, this resulted in women almost always being looked upon symbolically. If she could be educated, this would symbolise progress for her community. If she remained unschooled, this would symbolise backwardness. There were many variations on this theme and many levels at which it operated, some of which contradicted others. The way that formal education worked for women, however, was to subvert this symbolic role of women and provide them with experiences that signalled change. To go out of the home and be in a different site of action, the school, meant to already experience subjecthood. It did not matter how conservative the course of study was, or how narrow and controlling the vision of the educators. Like many boys in the new system of education, girls became questioning and subversive no matter what the plan of the educators was. Many became questioning of the symbolic role they had been required to play in their communities. Many subverted it for themselves, and many more were instrumental in having succeeding generations subvert it.

Many processes of education and socialisation for women which continued over the centuries can only be speculated about and are simply not researched yet. The new education *was* progress, with improvement in freedom and opportunities for *some* women that were truly seized by them like "tigers uncaged." However, it never addressed all women but emphasised and often increased differences of class, caste, and religion between them. What is the least understood in the history of girls' education is that, typically, even while women shared patriarchal ideology, they were the ones who took the lead in progressive change, rather than the state, or male reformers. Women were educators when educated and were educators even when not themselves educated. We will now turn to the chronological story and look at the case of individual women, and some men, to illustrate these historical themes.

Let us begin with the case of Azizunnissa Begum (1780?–1857). She was the eldest daughter of Khwaja Fariduddin Ahmad, who had served as a high officer in both the Mughal and colonial states. She had studied the Qur'an in Arabic, elementary Persian from books, and knew Urdu as her mother tongue. We know nothing about her mother but can speculate that she was partly instrumental in Arabic and Urdu language learning. Azizunnissa learnt high standards of teaching and learning from *someone*. Her son, Sayyid Ahmad, recounts her perfectionism and disciplining methods when studying Persian from her. Azizunnissa was in *parda*, or seclusion, but conducted many "public" services privately. This included scholarship, teaching, charity work for women through alms, and supporting causes such as widow remarriage, which was looked down by high-class Muslims as it was by Hindus. Sayyid Ahmad Khan, her son, is justly famous as an educationist and social reformer. He can be said to have been formed by his mother by both her direct teaching and her serving as a role model. As the historian Gail Minault says,

> Despite – or perhaps because of – the influence of his mother on his early life, Sir Sayyid saw no need for women's education other than home learning. He opposed starting schools for girls, and in a version of the trickle-down theory, preferred instead to emphasize the education of Muslim boys at Aligarh. . . . [H]e stated . . . ." The present state of education among Muhammadan females is, in my opinion, enough for domestic happiness, considering the present social and economic conditions of the life of the Muhammadans of India.
>
> *(Minault, 1998, pp. 18–19)*

This "present state of education" for women that Sayyid Ahmad was familiar with from his educated, dynamic mother, was largely restricted to Muslim upper classes, or the *ashraf*, and diminishing even there due to their impoverishment. Daughters of this class, along with the sons, learnt the Qur'an at home from a *maulvi* when young. As she grew older, the sister was separately taught by an *ustani*, or female teacher, likely to be the daughter or widow of a *maulana*, or male religious teacher. Such teachers were not educated to very advanced levels and could teach with fitful competence. The girl students were also given more household tasks and were likely to find themselves too busy to study well. Beyond everything else, there was the firm consensual belief of Muslim patriarchs that, while reading the Qur'an and even some other texts was all right, learning to write was a bad idea. Texts such as Sa'di's *Gulistan* and *Bustan* consisted of exemplary stories whose female role models displayed the qualities of modesty, adaptability, and tact. Azizunnissa Begum was therefore an exception in the extent of her learning but representative of her class in the uses she put it to: ethical conduct, patronage of education, and the direct mentoring and support of her sons. We have to see that the perceived promise of education for Indian men – the exposure to science, rationality and modernity – went together with a perceived threat from education for women – the loss of culture, a possible move into public space, and a possible break-up of the family. Given these perceptions, it was often the case that colonial education produced a further tightening of barriers against women's education and a heightening of conservatism. New categories of virtue/vice, appropriateness/inappropriateness, tradition/modernity, ours/theirs, and East/West were built up, with the first adjective in each pair standing for the correct and the desired. Movement between the two "opposites," or a fuzzing of the boundaries, became progressively difficult to do, and then to conceptualise.

Azizunnissa's case also exemplifies the class divisions in Indian society, such as the division of Muslims into *ashraf* classes and the masses, and how this led to a particular understanding by ashraf men and women of what women needed. The identity of ashraf, like all upper-class identities, could be constructed only in contrast to lower-class people. We do not know directly what Azizunnissa herself would have said regarding a modern education for women. Nor do we know how she would have regarded a prospect of democratisation of education. There are many arguments, such as the desire for harmony at home but also of retaining class privilege for themselves (such as lower classes do not have) that persuade women to opt for conservation rather than change. We do know that some *sharif* women did take up the reforming mantle themselves, and then they spoke with a wider vision. An example is Rokeya Sukhawat Husain (1880–1932), a full hundred years later.

About two decades earlier than Azizunnissa Begum, at the very dawn of British presence in India, is born the interesting Tarini Devi (?–1822). We know little of her biography. Her name is not usually mentioned in the histories of her son, Rammohan Roy (c. 1772–1834), when they talk about his reforms for women. More surprisingly, even when we are told that his iconoclasm was opposed by her, and that mother and son had a property dispute that went to court – in other words when we can see that she played an active historical role – it is only Rammohan's role that is given importance, and not hers. However, Tarini Devi was a Brahman of Shakta heritage, well educated in the ethical, spiritual, and ritual mores of her community. She fought to preserve them, as men on the conservative side of the reforming-revivalist divide were to do. We could look on Tarini Devi as an opponent, one of the first actors in the drama of colonial education.

We have the wonderful and well-studied case of Rashsundari Debi (c. 1809–?), who wrote *Amar Jiban*, or "My Life," a fascinating description of her routines of housework and mothering. In the middle of feeding babies and blowing embers in the stove, she secretly taught herself to read and write at a time when no one of her class and sex did. Her evocative explanation of that is:

> I was angry with myself to read books. Girls did not read. How could I? What a peculiar situation I had put myself in. What was I to do? That was one of the bad aspects of the old system. The other aspects were not so bad. People used to despise women of learning. How unfortunate those women were, they said. They were no better than animals. But it is no use blaming others. Our fate is our own. In fact, older women used to show a great deal of displeasure if they saw a piece of paper in the hands of a woman. So that ruled out my chances of getting any education. But somehow I could not accept this. I was very keen to learn the alphabet.

*(Tharu and Lalita: 1991)*

Rashsundari Debi's is the first autobiography we know of, the expression of a subject identity (Sarkar, 1993). Meanwhile, around the same time, the 1820s and 1830s, missionaries had already started various educational projects in the East India Company's three Presidencies, after being kept out of its territories until 1813. From the records of their initial contact with Indian society, as well as from piecing together other data, we can make a rough picture of pre-modern and home-based education. For both men and women, education was of two kinds: vocational and ethical. Men's vocational education followed the trajectories outlined by their caste or ancestral profession. Women did not directly have similar vocations but did play supportive and supplementary roles. They did learn vocational skills although not as men did, to earn a living. Apart from their essential work in the family professions, their vocation was that of the wife, mother, and housewife. Training went into that and overlapped with what I am calling "ethical." In every single family, and very differently in different families, girls and boys were socialised into a knowledge of their identities within a larger society and the values to which their communities adhered. This was done not through a reading of texts or scriptures but orally, through narratives, local and family histories, festivals, performances, life-cycle rituals, and practical teaching in a manner I have described as apprenticeship (see Kumar, 2007: Chapter 5). When missionaries and other Europeans first got to know the Indian family, they were aware that here was a holistic world. This very holism also meant control and conservatism, a subject of criticism by many including Bengal's premier author Rabindranath Tagore. In his stories, the men are always educated, the women not. They have intelligence and personalities that are no less strong than the men's, but they have feminine preoccupations. When the occasional odd girl or woman shows an interest in learning to read or study, her worst enemies are the other women of the family, who perhaps see in her a threat to their own well-wrought identity. We should be careful to read neither educational change nor conservatism as a simple black-or-white thing that goes either for or against women.

The work of the missionaries constitutes a history in itself. It is partly the story of idealistic men and women who came out from Britain (or elsewhere in Europe) and risked their lives in an unfriendly climate to which they made poor adjustment, all to recover the soul of the misguided heathen. It is partly the story of a racist state that, under the guise of liberalism, supported such ventures that were overtly based on a racial hierarchy. It is also the story of some Indians who benefited from missionary education, some who got converted to Christianity, others who resisted and even abused it, and still others who found various positive alternatives to it. In the larger scheme of things, the role of missionary education has been to act as a model for modern, progressive, and *good* education in India. Under the surface, the impact of missionary education has included the creating of a split between well-educated and less-educated Indians. This split, modelled on the original racial divide, continues in a quasi-racial mode till today.

The historian Tim Allender has divided missionary activity into pre- and post-1813. The missionaries in the earlier period deliberately reached out to Indian intellectual and spiritual traditions and earned the respect and reciprocity of Indians. After 1813, there was a new approach of the British in India that was a combination of Benthamite utilitarianism, evangelicalism, and an unprecedented vilification of the Indian present and past, given voice by James Mill's *History of India*. Allender traces how some efforts, such as that of the Calcutta Ladies' School for Native Females, were unsuccessful, and others, such as of the Baptist missionary William Carey and the Scottish Presbyterian David Hare, were successful. The British Church Missionary Society (CMS) took over assorted educational activities in Bengal. But though ostensibly successful in numbers, for instance, with the orphans it could serve, and more successful in Madras than in Bengal, it failed to make an impact on mainstream society. Allender contrasts the CMS efforts to those of Rammohan Roy (Allender, 2016).

Rammohan Roy set up the Brahmo Samaj in 1829 to reform many practices in Hinduism and to resurrect what some saw as the original monotheism of the religion. He had already petitioned for, and published on, the need for a modern education for Indians, for schooling for girls and many other reforms, and for an ecumenism and syncretism between East and West. The Brahmo Samaj was never very large but provided a model for reform. Its members encouraged the women of their families to be educated, and these women in turn became pioneers in education and the modern professions.

There were other communities who also had a different self-image of themselves and wished to show themselves as the proponents of change rather than conservatism. They, too, saw that education bore the brunt of responsibility for the changes that had to be made in Indian society. *The Bombay Courier* of 19 August 1842 rejoiced at the news of a young lady having been admitted at a seminary by her father (we should say more accurately: her parents). I give the extract here to show the eloquent case made by the state and its supporters for understanding the new education as enlightenment.

> We consider the man, whose mind is sufficiently enlarged to admit of his taking the initiative of breaking down the prejudices of country and of caste, in so good a cause, not only deserving of our humble applause, but of the approbation which is sure to obtain of the whole civilized world. There was a time, a period of European History when a premium was offered to ignorance – when reading and writing were left to clerks and considered badges of vulgarity by the Sovereign and his Feudal Chiefs – when the proud Peers themselves could only make their marks, or impress their signatures with a stamp. But this was in a time of barbarians. . . . Happily, knowledge superseded ignorance and a brighter day has dawned on the intellectual horizon. *Ex Oriente lux*. In the East arose the sun of human enlightenment, it travelled Westward, and confers that power which consists

in knowledge. We of the West are bound, therefore, and feel the obligation to return to its Eastern source, as far as files it our power, the blessings of enlightenment. The dissemination of knowledge over the whole earth is a paramount object with the philanthropist of every clime.

The Parsees, of all the inhabitants of this portion of the globe ought particularly to appreciate and prize the cultivation of the mental faculties, for to their education is to be attributed in a great degree, if not altogether, their wealth, their liberality, and their acknowledged influence. They know this and they prove their knowledge by the pains they take, and the expenses they incur, in the education of their male children. Why they have so long neglected their female offspring, can only be accounted for by their blind subservience to the usage they found established in a country which afforded them protection.

*(Jessawalla, 2002, pp. 14–15)*

The father of the new student is then praised for his courage in going against the herd, for his sacrifice, for an indication of superior intellect, and for a step taken to save women from concubinage and domestic slavery, towards a future where husbands and wives can be on the same level.

In Western India, Jyotiba Phule (1827–1890) worked against caste discrimination and women's illiteracy with the Satya Shodhak Samaj. He started the first girls' school in 1848. He taught his nine-year-old wife Savitri – himself 13 when he was married – to read and write and Savitribai (1831–1897) became his partner in his educational endeavours. He was from a low caste, and it was his experience of discrimination at a Brahman wedding that made him use education as a tool to fight both caste oppression and the backwardness of women. Together, husband and wife started the first school for women (O'Hanlon, 1985). Savitribai was the first modern woman teacher in Maharashtra, and also a poet and biographer. In defence of her work with low castes, for which she was much maligned, she wrote:

> The lack of learning is nothing but gross bestiality. It was the possession of knowledge that gave the brahmins their superior status. Learning has a great value. . . . Yes, we both teach the girls, the women, and the mangs and mahars. The brahmans believe that this will create problems for them and therefore they chant the mantra "Abrahmanyam" (Unholy!) and go on reviling us and poisoning the minds of people.
> 
> *(Tharu & Lalita, 1991, pp. 213–214)*

That effort was needed to motivate women is documented repeatedly. Anapurna Turkhad (1823–1891), married to an English College Vice-Principal, wrote in the press about "The Mental Seclusion of India." She described how it was the English who discouraged Indians from progress. Even if an Englishman were to visit an educated Indian gentleman, his wife would never accompany him, looking down on the Indian wife and baby. The Indian wife would have zero motivation to learn English. She described how the English did not know Indians, except as servants and official dependents, and did not care to. Natives were at fault for their sensuality, their caste system, and their subjugation of women. But the English too were at fault. "'Peace has her victories,' and these have yet to be won" (de Souza & Pereira, 2002, pp. 49–51). We see here another undercurrent of difference between men and women in India. Whereas men had the motivation of direct contact with the British through work and sometimes socialisation, women had none such. In provincial India, the inertia against women's education was all the greater. Leela Sharma, an educator in her nineties who passed away recently, shared her memories of the first schools for girls in Banaras. Well into the 1940s, girls had to be personally wooed to come to school. They faced derision at every step, from putting on footwear to leaving the house at all.

If we want to peg the progress of women's education to the educational landmarks that are typically recognised, the first one we have is the Charter Act of 1813, and the second one is Macaulay's Minute in March 1835. This set the Orientalist-Anglicist controversy to rest, by derisively rejecting the view that traditional Indian studies in Sanskrit, Arabic, or Persian should be given support or encouragement. Instead, only English language and literature, and other subjects through the medium of English, should be officially funded. Macaulay's vote was not only decisive in the History of Indian education, it bears a clear stamp of the social, political, and epistemological masculinity of the time. Everyone agrees that his ignorance of the classical languages was a tremendous handicap in the desired clarity of the judgement he was called upon to make. His ignorance of all kinds of other information on India is less often discussed. He says, for instance, that

> All parties seem to be agreed on one point, that the dialects commonly spoken among the natives of this part of India contain neither literary nor scientific information, and are moreover so poor and rude that, until they are enriched from some other quarter, it will not be easy to translate any valuable work into them. . . . We have to educate a people who cannot at present be educated by means of their mother-tongue. We must teach them some foreign language.
>
> *(Zastoupil & Moir, 1999, p. 165)*

Without saying anything directly about women, Macaulay broached two points that were of central concern to women: vernaculars and the mother tongue. Dismissing them both as savage, undeveloped, and therefore for policy purposes as good as absent, he committed women-subjects of the Empire to an abyss where what they owned was dismissed as worthless, even non-existent, and what was proposed excluded them. He underlines this last point by saying:

> it is impossible for us, with our limited means, to attempt to educate the body of the people. We must at present do our best to form a class who may be interpreters between us and the millions whom we govern[-]a class

of persons Indian in blood and colour, but English in tastes, in opinions, in morals and in intellect.

(Zastoupil & Moir, 1999, p. 171)

The task he envisioned, of interpreting between the rulers and the masses, came to be performed by the new educated men, and the people to whom they translated were first their wives. If we look for any direct references to the education of women in Macaulay's Minute, there are none. But in 1854 we have an important Dispatch promulgated by the President of the Board of Control, Sir Charles Wood, that marked a shift in government policy from elite to mass education, including for girls. It reads:

The importance of female education in India cannot be over-rated; and we have observed with pleasure the evidence which is now afforded of an increased desire on the part of many of the natives to give a good education to their daughters. By this means a far greater proportional impulse is imparted to the educational and moral tone of the people than by the education of men.

(Forbes, 1996, p. 40)

As Forbes shows, after the Mutiny of 1857, everything changed. By the 1860s Indian men were willing to have British missionary women visit their wives at home. The Ladies Association for the Promotion of Female Education among the Heathen was established in 1866. Missionaries who went out found themselves challenged because of poor health, maladjustment to the climate, and disease. As opposed to earlier missionaries, they targeted only upper-class women, but the impact was negligible. Neither did they succeed in converting Indians to Christianity, nor did the Indians succeed in learning modern content in any subject to any appreciable extent. But the lead shifted very quickly from the hands of European missionaries to those of Indian men, organisations, and gradually, women themselves.

The Brahmo Samaj, under Keshub Chandra Sen (1838–1884), started a society for men who supported the cause of women, and for women who met for instruction and discussion, and then Normal Schools, or schools for the training of female teachers. From Brahmo educational efforts emerged the first two women graduates of the British Empire in 1883, Kadambini Basu and Chandramukhi Basu. The Theosophical Society in Madras, under Annie Besant (1847–1933), started a women's college in Madras, and a school for girls in Banaras, North India, in the 1890s. She called the latter Central Hindu School (later College) and saw it as a place where the lost glory of Indian womanhood could be revived. In multiple speeches and writings, Besant put forth her view of Indian history, Hinduism, and the future nation. She called her formula, "religion + secularism," by which she meant a synthesis of the ancient glory of Vedic India, combined with the science and technology of Europe. The Western curriculum that she used was taken from British schools, as was the Principal she hired for her school. The Hindu portion had to be devised by her through textbooks and school rituals, since the kind of Hinduism she was proposing did not really exist on the ground.

Whereas the Brahmos had clearly been innovators, even as they sought the truth in their own ancient past, Besant claimed to only *revive* an authentic past. So did Dayanand Saraswati (1824–1883), an ascetic from the Punjab who founded the Arya Samaj in 1875. He believed in the infallible authority of the Vedas and opposed most aspects of caste and ritualism, as well as modernisation and westernisation. The schools set up by the Arya Samaj, significantly called "Anglo-Vedic," were a curious mix of old and new. They certainly provided an education for many girls, along with boys, but criticism is levied on them for being profoundly close-minded on the subject of what girls and women needed. As Madhu Kishwar puts it:

> In some ways it can be said that the Arya Samaj movement was intended to 'reform' women rather than reform the social conditions which oppressed them. Women were to be educated into becoming more suitable wives and mothers for the new, educated men.
>
> *(Kishwar, 1986, p. 185)*

Then there were individual reformers who played leadership roles. Ramabai (1858–1922), given the names Saraswati and Pandita for her learning, was born to a Brahman couple in Maharashtra. She was thoroughly educated in Sanskrit and the shastras. Orphaned at 16, she carried on her parents' work of preaching for social reform and the education of girls. Widowed at 24, she continued her work in education by setting up the Arya Mahila Samaj in Poona and giving evidence before the Hunter Commission. Her conversion to Christianity in 1883 was a shock to high-caste Hindu society, but she continued undeterred, authoring *The High Caste Hindu Woman*, raising money through lectures in England, USA, and Canada for her Sharda Sadan, a school for widows in India. Pandita Ramabai argues that she would rather not be under the yoke of any priestly class, including Christian. She describes, in a letter to Sister Geraldine, how she was selected to be a Sanskrit Pandit, given the title of Saraswati, and then her spirit was kindled by the Brahmos to "plead the cause of women" (de Souza & Pereira, 2002, p. 33). Hers is a strong vision of independence in, and passion for, work. Not only was her curriculum designed to make women stand on their feet rather than become better wives or mothers, she could grasp the nature of the opposition to her ventures. Criticised by British officials for her opposition to colonial rule, and by Indians for her religious beliefs, she correctly diagnosed it as a gendered response – a pact between patriarchal rulers and ruled, and a Brahmanical response – her widowed students were high caste, while her critics would have been fine with a home for low-caste widows.

A home and a school for widows were also set up by Dhondu Keshav Karve (1858–1962), a teacher of mathematics at Fergusson College, who learnt from leaders like Pandita Ramabai, and others. He himself married a widow, Anandibai, when his first wife passed away. Together in 1896, they set up the institution called Karve's Home, and Anandibai joked in her old age:

> Sometimes in fun I tell him that although people call him Maharshi, some of the credit is due to me. For if I had not managed the family affairs and set him free to carry out his public activities, he could not have achieved so much.
>
> (Karve, 1963, p. 79)

A second school was set up for unmarried girls in Poona, and then a University for Women that still exists today, relocated to Bombay, the SMDT (Shreemati Nathibai Damodar Thackersey) University. Interestingly, committed to women's education as Karve was, he believed that widows needed training in vocational work to support themselves, but unmarried girls needed to learn womanly subjects to prepare for wifehood and motherhood. That this was not just a male prejudice is born out by the fact that his wife's sister, Parvatibai, who chose to not get married after being widowed, and who worked voluntarily, also believed that a woman should marry and not work.

Away from the metropolises of Bombay, Calcutta, and Madras, and the large cities of Poona and Delhi, there was also activity for women's education by the beginning of the twentieth century. In many cases, the models for these provincial actors were the reforming leaders of fame, such as Pandita Ramabai. In some cases, the inspiration came from Gandhi. Women who were widowed and then placed in the pilgrimage centre and the holy city of Banaras, as was Sarojini Devi, did not spend their lives passively. Sarojini Devi set up a school for widows, teaching them how to earn money through weaving rugs and shawls. Next, she set up a school for children and poured her own money as well as raised donations for it. Vidya Bai came to Banaras around 1920, adopted Swami Gyananand as her teacher, and learnt not only philosophy and the shastras from him but all the tasks of a public institution, such as fund raising, managing trusts, and publicity. She founded the Arya Mahila College, which is today a school/college that starts at pre-school and goes up to post-graduate.

Many more such activists could be mentioned, but some larger points deserve mention instead. Widows were active in education for several reasons. Their bereavement freed them from the duty of *pati sewa*, or service to one's husband, which they would have consensually ranked as first among their duties. Their dharma could now be adapted from service to husband to service to a larger family. Their bereavement also made them radical in an unforeseeable way. They were not concerned with the issue of remarriage for widows, as so many male reformers were. Instead, they focused on economic security. They vindicated their own experiences: alone and unsupported, untrained and unable to earn their living, they asserted the necessity to prevent other members of their sex from possibly undergoing the same experience as them. If so alone and unsupported, how did they begin to act in public roles? They used the language of self-denial and sacrifice to explain how they had been summoned to a cause. The mission of working for the brighter future of girls was on the reformist as well as the nationalist agenda. Each activist widow recounts how a guru, or a leader like Gandhi, directly inspired them – often expressed as, "He called me to come and join him," or, "She came and said, "Join tomorrow!"

There were two levels of discourse here. At one level, the rationale for schooling was that it could provide support for a future of need. To set up a school was to provide security for girls. At another level, in almost all the schools, there was no discussion about the curriculum. It was the same as in boys' school, with the additional subjects of classical music, dance, and Home Science. If in the early twentieth century, school curriculum was generally regarded as of little practical relevance to a career in life, at least in smaller cities and towns, this irrelevance mattered less to girls than it did to boys. But as we know, the whole secret lies in simply learning to read and write. Many of the girls who attended schools set up by non-radical reformers who were engaged in simple social service and sacrifice went on to lead lives of autonomy and freedom, and earn as well as open up the pathways to earn for their own daughters.

In the twentieth century, there was also impatience with the resolution, as proposed by male nationalists, of the "women's question." The older prejudice that allowing a girl to read and write would be to earn her the fate of a widow was replaced by the idea that "educating a girl means educating a family" (Borthwick, 1984, p. 61; Engels, 1989, p. 60; Chanana, 2001, p. 45). This new woman had to be a proper partner for her husband, as Shudha Mazumdar lived out (Mazumdar, 1989), while being totally respectable. Begum Rokeya Sakhawat Hossain (1880–1932) was supported by her older brother, who taught her English in the dead of night, and her husband, who wanted an active companion. She started writing three years later, at the age of 21, and over her life was a prolific essayist. Though she wrote on social and religious topics as well, her favourite theme was the need to end women's oppression through education. Her most famous work is her satirical piece on the reversal of *parda*, called *Sultana's Dream* (Hossain, 1988). She ran a school for girls where physical training was compulsory. She found it necessary to have the students come and go in *parda*, totally against the custom as she was, and to have girls cover their heads while inside. Undoubtedly a strategist who wanted even conservative parents to accept education for their daughters, she was still bitterly attacked for her radicalism.

Quite evidently, much of the opposition to girls' schooling lay in the perception of the danger of the sexuality of girls/women. The only way to control the danger was to prevent girls/women from being outside one's vision. When schooling *was* allowed, it had to be in separate spaces and conducted by female teachers.

The other important role played by women in a story of education is as mothers who were not themselves formally educated. Almost all members of the intelligentsia described themselves as going back after their modern work experiences to a re-discovery of their nation's past history, literature, and philosophy, and to either studying and researching it or working to ameliorate problems in the national body. The inspiration for this, and the identity it was based on, came from early childhood socialisation and the learning of the mother tongue, both of which were typically produced by the mother's labour. Women, even if we are critical of the overdetermined nature of their role as mothers, have been instrumental in the much-vaunted "cultural continuity" of India. Even with seven to ten generations of English education for the elite, the education given by women at home has resulted in a counter-balance. While hardly equal to the role of formal schooling, the role of home learning is of an intangible and not negligible weight. To theorise this in some way, I have elaborated on the idea of "a plural education," where one set of values, histories, sciences, and epistemologies is taught in the modern school, and another set is taught, albeit much less coherently and consistently, at home. So the modern educated Indian *does* know the epics – from oral narratives, performances, festivals, and the "women's culture" that characterises most homes.

What, finally, happened with girls' and women's education in the twentieth century? The number of women who were educated in schools rose gradually and the prejudice against such education disappeared. There were new graduates who went on to professional work in medicine, law, and teaching. Almost all of them still remained plural individuals in that they were: wedded to a philosophy that confirmed them as wives and mothers, tied in to their communities, formed by vernacular narratives and texts, and transmitters of mother tongues and family knowledge. This other education in the site of the family did not cease for women, and they remained active as both the students and teachers of it.

## Bibliography

Allender, T. (2016). *Learning femininity in colonial India 1820–1932* (Studies in imperialism series). Manchester: Manchester University Press.

Amin, S. N. (1995). The early Muslim Bhadramahila: The growth of learning and creativity, 1876–1939. In B. Ray (Ed.), *From the seams of history: Essays on Indian women*. New Delhi: Oxford University Press.

Amin, S. N. (1996). *The world of Muslim women in colonial Bengal, 1876–1939*. Leiden: E. J. Brill.

Borthwick, M. (1984). *The changing role of women in Bengal, 1849–1905*. Princeton, NJ: Princeton University Press.

Broomfield, J. H. (1969). *Elite conflict in a plural society*. Berkeley, CA: University of California Press.

Chanana, K. (2001). *Interrogating women's education: Bounded visions, Expanding horizons*. Delhi: Rawat Publications.

Chatterjee, P. (1990). The nationalist resolution of the women's question. In K. Sangari & S. Vaid (Eds.), *Recasting women: Essays in colonial history*. New Brunswick, NJ: Rutgers University Press.

Chattopadhyaya, K. (1986). *Inner recesses/outer spaces: Memoirs*. New Delhi: Navrang.

de Souza, E., & Pereira, L. (Eds.). (2002). *Women's voices: Selections from nineteenth and early twentieth century Indian writing in English*. Delhi: Oxford University Press.

Engels, D. (1989). The limits of gender ideology: Bengali women, the colonial state and the private sphere, 1890–1930. *Women's Studies International Forum, 12*, 4.

Engels, D. (1996). *Beyond Purdah? Women in colonial Bengal 1890–1939*. Delhi: Oxford University Press.

Forbes, G. (1996). *Women in modern India*. Cambridge: Cambridge University Press.

Ghosh, D. (2004). Gender and colonialism: Expansion or marginalization? *The Historical Journal, 47*(3), 737–755.

Hossain, R. S. (1988). *Sultana's dream and selections from the secluded ones*. New York: The Feminist Press.

Jessawalla, D. C. (2002). *The story of my life*. Bombay: Times Press. (Original work published 1911)

Jones, K. (1989). *Socio-religious movements in British India*. Cambridge: Cambridge University Press.

Karve, D. D. (1963). *The new Brahmans: Five Maharashtrian families*. Berkeley: University of California Press.

Kishwar, M. (1986). Daughters of Aryavarta. *Indian Economic and Social History Review, 23*(2), 151–185.

Kopf, D. (2005). *The Brahmo Samaj and the shaping of the modern Indian mind*. Princeton, NJ: Princeton University Press.

Kumar, N. (2007). *The politics of gender, community and modernity: Essays on education in India*. Delhi: Oxford University Press.

Mazumdar, S. (1989). *Memoirs of an Indian woman* (Ed. G. Forbes). New York: ME Sharpe.

Minault, G. (1998). *Secluded scholars: Women's education and Muslim social reform in colonial India*. Delhi: Oxford University Press.

Murshid, G. (1983). *The reluctant debutante: Response of Bengali women to modernisation, 1849–1905*. Rajshahi: Sahitya Samsad, Rajshahi University.

Naim, C. M. (1984). Prize-winning Adab: A study of five Urdu books written in response to the Allahabad Government Gazette notification. In B. D. Metcalf (Ed.), *Moral conduct and authority: The place of Adab in South Asian Islam* (pp. 290–314). Berkeley, CA: University of California Press.

Nurullah, S., & Naik, J. P. (1964). *A students' history of education in India, 1800–1965*. Bombay: Macmillan.

O'Hanlon, R. (1985). *Class, caste and ideology: Mahatma Jotirao Phule and low caste protest in nineteenth century western India*. Cambridge: Cambridge University Press.

Pernau, M. (2013). *Ashraf into middle classes: Muslims in nineteenth-century Delhi*. Delhi: Oxford University Press.

Prakash, G. (1996). Science between the lines. In S. Amin & D. Chahrabarty (Eds.), *Subaltern studies IX: Writings on south Asian history and society* (pp. 59–82). New Delhi: Oxford University Press.

Sarkar, M. (2015). Changing together, changing apart: Urban Muslim and Hindu women in pre-partition Bengal. *History and Memory, 27*(1), 5–42.

Sarkar, S. (1997). *Writing social history*. Delhi: Oxford University Press.

Sarkar, T. (1993). A book of her own, a life of her own: Autobiography of a nineteenth-century woman. *History Workshop Journal, 36*, 35–65.

Tharu, S., & Lalita, K. (Eds.). (1993). *Women writing in India Vol. II*. New York: Feminist Press (First published in 1991 by Delhi: Kali for Women).

Zastoupil, L., & Moir, M. (Eds.). (1999). *The great Indian debate: Documents relating to the orientalist-Anglicist controversy, 1781–1843*. Richmond: Curzon Press.

# 7
# THE COLONIAL PERIOD INTO THE PRESENT
## Marriage, Widowhood, Reform

The story used to be this: "The British came; they recognized the depravity of purdah, widow burning, child marriage and female infanticide; sensible Indians immediately recognized a superior culture when they saw one, and, thanks to British tutelage, they began the 'regeneration' their society needed" (Metcalf, 1994, p. 1). Since the 1980s, this is a story that has been challenged by historians. The different story now constructed goes like this:

> The British came and quite quickly developed an interest in ruling; they needed justification; they picked on certain traditions relating to women and family as 'depraved' to legitimize their rule; ever since, the label of 'depravity' has stuck to those practices. English-educated Indians *still* try to reform their society.

In this chapter, we will elaborate on this latter story but add some more dimensions to it. Apart from the colonial construction of gender relations, we will look at the experience of women in marriage, the variations of marriage practices, the meanings of seclusion, and the voices of women in change and reform. Some of this is difficult to do. Even when there are pictures of the feelings of women as bride, wife, and daughter-in-law, there is little data on historical change. Moreover, the pictures we *do* have, mostly from memoirs and fiction, are all created by women in the upper ranks of Hindu and Muslim societies and are therefore about a select kind of woman. One bemused account goes:

> A photograph taken during the ceremony shows what looks like a couple of untidy bundles of washing. The one topped by the tricornered *pagri* can be identified as my husband; the other bundle could be anyone – or,

DOI: 10.4324/9781003393252-8

indeed, anything – but is, of course, me. The upper half of my face is covered by the overhang of the *dupatta* or bridal veil, decorously pulled down well below the eyes, the lower half is covered by chains of flowers. . . . Through the tiniest slit I have contrived to make in the folds of the sari over my eyes, all I can see of my husband-to-be are his feet, folded under him as he squats on the hard wooden board. I gaze at them as though hypnotised, and suddenly I am struck by the thought that they are the feet of the god I have adopted as mine since childhood, the Bal Krishna who became the Gopal Krishna, and to whom I sang the devotional songs of Meera. Meera had found her god.

*(Scindia, 1987, p. 131)*

In this evocative account, we see several things: the marriage ceremony (as always, everywhere) is itself a blur. In South Asia, a marriage is typically arranged by one's family and the marrying partners do not know each other beforehand. However, both, and especially the woman, have/has been socialised to accept this as normal and do/does not usually worry about it. She thinks of the impending new life as both frightening and exciting. She refers in her mind to assorted rules of behaviour that she has learnt, often informally, from mythology, ritual practices, and narratives. Marriage feels like a harmonious part of a holistic world view. And, of course, she cannot help laughing in the midst of the complex goings-on.

However, historians are piecing together the story of women's own consciousness and agency through other sources than highly educated women's memoirs. Among these are court proceedings, which tell us about how women fought for their conjugal rights and dignity (Anagol, 2020; Grey, 2011); oral culture that can serve as the basis of a film such as Aparna Sen's *Sati* (Sawhney, 2015); reading archives "against the grain" (Atwal, 2016; Walsh, 2004); and anthropological studies of narratives and songs, such as discussed subsequently.

In North India, a girl/woman has two homes, informants will tell a researcher. One is her natal, or parents' home, sometimes called "mother's," often "father's." All brides are sad to leave their natal homes, but younger ones are sadder. Most girls are married very young, and the age of marriage for girls has steadily changed from any time before eight years in colonial times to 18 at present. Even if in infancy and childhood, marriage meant betrothal, cohabitation was expected to start after the bride's first menstruation, or "coming of age." How well a girl understood all this is difficult to say. No bride is "unambivalent," as Lindsey Harlan reports of Rajput women (1992, p. 92). They may be excited at the prospect of a loving husband and a new home with adult privileges, but they realise that their parents' home gave them a different, childhood, freedom. An extremely painful experience is depicted in the opening scenes of the film *Bandit Queen* (Kapur, 1996). The little girl, perhaps ten, is childhood incarnate, splashing around bare-chested in the river with her peers, to be suddenly called in to her home and given in marriage to a much older man. She is taken away by him, put in a room, and raped, and her mother-in-law smiles with satisfaction outside. In the 1890s, as the movement for reform in girls' early age of marriage grew, evidence was collected that showed how much of the behaviour of older husbands towards their child-wives constituted marital rape.

If we search for women's own voices, we find that typically women's experiences are expressed in folk sayings and songs. From the moment of marriage itself, ambivalence is expressed in the two points of view put forward, the man's and the woman's. The man's is articulated in the main wedding rituals that almost all include ritual deference from the bride to the groom's side, and a transfer of the bride from her natal to her affinal family. The woman's is expressed in songs called *gali* (literally, abuse) in North India. The bride's kinswomen and friends caricature and imagine failings of the groom and his family, especially lampooning his mother's sexual preoccupations and his own sexual impotence. These *gali* songs are either ignored by men who pretend that they do not know them or treated with dislike by men who insist that they should be stopped. Women's journals, such as *Kamala* in the early twentieth century, carried on unflagging campaigns to cleanse life-cycle ceremonies of *galis*. Criticism of them by men and reformers couches them as being "indecent" and "crude." They are not explicitly considered to be the "woman's voice" in Indian culture, though they are given that stature in academia.

However, women *themselves* think that they have a voice through these songs. After the wedding, a ritual parting called *vidai* (also *bidai*) is the occasion for melancholic songs in which the end of the bride's phase of life in her natal home is mourned.

### Refrain

> Dear girl, today you've left your father's house,
> Today you've become 'other' (*parayi*).
> (Raheja, 1994, p. 57)

North India has patrilocality, or virilocality, that is, residence with the male's family. This is true particularly among high castes. Almost without exception, the bride leaves her natal home to live with her husband's parents and siblings. Typically, there is an "extended" family, consisting of two to three generations of males with their wives and children: thus, father and mother of generation one; two or three sons with wives and families of generation two; the first married sons of generation three; or altogether, two to six or even eight couples, some unmarried girls who will leave at marriage for their conjugal homes, and up to a dozen or more children of assorted ages. As families increase in size, they split apart, and conjugal units form, to start the cycle again. Progressively, with changing values, occupations, and technology, conjugal units today may not start the cycle and choose to live instead as a nuclear family. Even then, to have adult children living at home until convenience or preference locates them elsewhere is common.

In South India, while Brahman women speak of "father's house," all other women speak only of "mother's house." The importance of marriage for a woman in North and South India is the same: she is a full person or human being only upon getting married. Marriage is a social act for her and also for her family, so the choice of bridegroom is of prime concern to her family. The South Indian system has been described as "matrilateral" (Kapadia, 1995) to denote a preference for a groom from the mother's side. Of these, the mother's brother, or *Tay Maman*, had the predominant place. Traditionally, he preferably married the girl, his sister's daughter, himself, or his son did. If not, he chose or assented to the choice of bridegroom. In North India, in contrast, marriage within seven generations of a blood relationship is forbidden, although no one typically has records of, or a prejudice against, over two or three generations.

In both the North and the South, the superiority, inferiority, or equality of affinal males (the men whose families are contracting marriages) hides the larger fact that this representation of kinship is only about men and that women are *always* inferior to men. Not only is a woman inferior to her father and brothers, after marriage she is inferior to her husband, father-in-law, and brothers-in-law. This is borne out by a host of daily practices and habits, such as of performing household tasks, serving, eating, dressing, and talking. These are all more prevalent and dogmatically insisted upon among higher than lower castes. In both cases, a dilemma occurs. The same patriarchs who swear by Brahmanical values, or the values of sanskritisation (for instance, women's seclusion), are the ones who also recognise the values of modernisation (for instance, women's going out in public for education or work). There is a clash between these, which is often resolved only by saying and doing contradictory things. A high-caste male with a government job that marks him as "modern" might boast that he has educated his daughters up to their Bachelor's degrees. if asked whether they will now seek jobs, he will shake his head. "No," he might claim, "To work outside goes against the nature of womanhood." Or simply, "A woman should not need to, unless there is a crisis." If he is then told that actually modern women and their families are fine with women working, he may express a version of the great social-political dilemma constituted by the concept of *dharma*. Dharma, or "code of conduct" – a code that is also one's "nature" – should actually be in the plural, for any person has more than one, and the different *dharmas* either overlap or could be in conflict. Here it is the code of an educated, professional woman in conflict with that of a "virtuous," domesticated daughter, wife, or daughter-in-law. In the man's case, there is a conflict between the progressive man and the old-fashioned patriarch.

Insights on the experience of early marriage are plentiful but difficult to judge, partly because they so overtly clash with our ideas about childhood. Childhood is an idea, or a discourse, that is born in modern times, and its absence as an objectified idea is common in India. Therefore, many writings that strive to be sympathetic towards women might judge them harshly, as when Geeta Sane (in Kosambi, 2012) tries to understand her mother: "How could the poor woman know that everybody is reduced to the same state when bidding farewell to childhood. She had become a mother in her adolescence – she was perhaps unacquainted with the border zone between childhood and youth" (Kosambi, 2007, p. 177). Writers, men and women, have described the experience of early marriage, parting from parents and natal home, and the mixed feelings of loss of the familiar and welcoming of the new.

Typically, a new bride may spend more time with and have more to do with her female in-laws than with her husband. Her mother-in-law particularly is an important part of her life. Writings about this relationship are common as well. They range from supporting a mother-in-law, as in the story "Lending a Helping Hand" by Rajam Krishnan, in which the young, educated, working woman does not judge the mother-in-law in stereotypical ways but instead tries to share her own interests and succeeds in becoming close to her (Tharu & Lalita, 1991, pp. 208–216); to the more common depiction of being abused and overworked by her. Kashibai Kanitkar (1861–1948) in her novel *The Palanquin Tassel*, as well as Geetanjali Shree in *Mai*, paints this stereotype. Both also try to give the older woman's perspective, which is otherwise under-represented, but it is finally the voice of the daughter-in-law that we know.

> If I get up early and finish the housework, she suspects I haven't been thorough and makes me do it all over again. If I get up late, she scolds me for not getting up early. . . . She says whatever comes to her mind.
> *(Kosambi, 2007, p. 114)*

In the novel, the young wife is asked why she did not complain to her husband who loved her and replies that "she would never cause a rift between mother and son. She is but an outsider and a mother can never be criticised to the son or daughter. She also sees her mother-in-law as a victim of circumstance and not personally a bad individual. Nor can she ask for a servant even though her husband can well afford it because that would seem like shirking her duties. Finally, there's a saying, "The first four days belong to the mother-in-law, and the next four days to the daughter-in-law." "My time will come" (Kosambi, 2007, p. 115). In *Mai*, the young mother tells her son and daughter, who are angry that she accepts her mother-in-law's abuses, how the older woman had been abused by her husband in her youth and is not therefore to be blamed for a transfer of abuse.

Two painful examples of a woman's experience in marriage are given by Dharmvir Bharati in his short stories. In "Savitri number 2," the protagonist is called Savitri and alludes to the mythological character also called Savitri. This mythological Savitri is famous because in her tale, her husband was doomed to die on a certain day, but such was her devotion to him, that she impressed

Yamaduta, or the Messenger of Death, and cleverly won her husband back to health and a long life. But the second, live Savitri is herself at death's door, and she unwinds in terror and insanity as her cancer enfeebles her and empties her of all the health and beauty that had made her so beloved of her husband and family. Her mother meanwhile plans how to keep this husband, soon to be widowed, as a son-in-law married to her second daughter. The story depicts the precariousness of a woman's status. If, in the original myth, Savitri has wit and intelligence and emerges victorious, we do not know exactly how: we are not told the hidden part of the story. In this story, we are. Obviously, health, youth, beauty, personality, *and* intelligence are all necessary for a woman's safe passage in married life. And if *she*, perchance, is dying, as opposed to Savitri's husband in the myth, there is no one to save her. Her husband's duty is not to be dedicated to her through life and death as the mythological Savitri is celebrated to be. Savitri is a role model for women to inspire them to cultivate wifely virtues (*and* intelligence, beauty, personality, etc.). There is no role model for husbandly virtues.

All the many aspects of family relationships are well structured and articulated and reflect the internal politics of family life. Anthropologists Raheja, Gold, Wadley, Vatuk, and others describe how village women routinely sing about their lives, putting into their songs complaints, curses, and even vows of revenge. The challenge of the woman's voice extends from the normative definitions of the smallest to the largest construct. Other scholars, interested in a feminist version, report that the impact of virilocality has been over-emphasised. While a woman *is* socialised to be ready to fit into her husband's homes, there are important formal and informal practices to ensure long visits for her to her natal family and an ongoing exchange of visits and gifts between her and her natal kin. Despite all the authoritarian structures and discourses that mould a woman into her normative roles of good wife and daughter-in-law, the counter-discourse in song, proverb, and speech is staunchly anti-authoritarian. Depending on the context and location of the conversation, a woman could say that even after decades, she could never call her husband's home *hers*, and used "home" only for her parents' home; or, conversely, that *of course* the married home was her home, her parents had sent her away, hadn't they? As Raheja describes at length in another context, there are many possible answers to the question, "Should Sita's ideal of a dutiful wife be followed?" One is clearly the following:

> When in 1990 I naively asked several groups of rural women from the dominant landholding Gujar caste whether they aspired to be like Sita, the paragon of wifely virtue and self-sacrifice, my question was greeted with gales of laughter, and a plethora of anecdotes about outwitted husbands and independent strong-willed wives. No one is like Sita nowadays, they said, and they assured me further that no one has any desire to be a "second Sita" (Raheja, 1994, p. 72). Abusive songs, or *galis*, have no limits, apparently – a woman could sing; "May the house of my mother-in-law be ruined.
> *(Raheja, 1994, p. 60)*

We could debate about the value or impact of songs and stories, as Raheja does in the Introduction to Raheja and Gold (1992). Certainly, songs or stories do not directly change anyone's life. The woman, as wife, has been, and continues to be, subordinate to her husband and his senior male and female kin, even though as a senior woman she will one day rule the roost. Songs and stories, however, give expression to the different values and sense of worth that can exist for the dominated within dominant cultures. They do so even at the macro level. A story in the epic *Mahabharata* that is often recounted as testament to the committed nature of wifehood is that of Nala and Damayanti. In the epic version, Nala foolishly gambles away his kingdom and leaves his wife in despair; she remains committed to him and wins him back. Anthropologist Susan Wadley tells us of another version of this story:

> In the popular oral epic *Dhola* . . . the hero, Raja Nal, has two wives. The first, Motini, has extraordinary powers as the daughter of a demon who taught her magic. When Raja Nal's parents are jailed by a rival king, Motini devises the plan that frees them (and she is the lead figure in that escape). Even after she leaves earth to abide in heaven, she returns to aid Raja Nal whenever he gets into trouble. The second, Damayanti, is the passive, dutiful wife who follows Raja Nal into exile. Both the male singers of the epic and women from Karimpur say that Motini is the more admirable woman and the "better" wife.
>
> *(Wadley, 1994, p. 40)*

The tension between the intelligence and power of a wife, and her subordination to her husband, based on the presumption that she is less intelligent and powerful than he is, remains unresolved and finds expression in numerous folktales, performative genres, local songs, and narratives. The dominant discourse of women's subordination as wife is seen in the ideal of *pativrata* (literally, vow of loyalty, *vrata*, to husband, *pati*). An adjective that refers to a faithful woman or wife, it describes the virtue of dedication to the husband to death. For the *pativrata*, the man can never do anything wrong. He is lord and master. A woman's *dharma* is to serve him. In that lies her *moksha*, or salvation. Her most defining *samskara* or life-cycle ritual is therefore marriage. The classical treatise, *Dharmashastra*, by the eponymous Manu, lays this out, and although it is not ever read or cited by ordinary women, is notorious in feminist circles for its overt misogyny. In many communities, women change their names upon marriage. In almost all Hindu families, they become part of a new family unit, *sapinda*, or one body with their husband, adopting the culture and practices of the new family.

> Once a woman is married, she participates fully in all the traditions of her conjugal family and is expected to abandon traditions she has brought from her natal family that might conflict with those of her conjugal family. This is true even down to her style of dressing. Beginning with her marriage

costume, she must accept dress styles and patterns typical of her husband's region. Most families, however, allow a wife some latitude. For ceremonial occasions such as weddings she must wear traditional local fashion, but at home she may wear dresses that please her, including clothes from home and even full saris, which are not traditionally worn by Rajputs.

(Harlan, 1992, p. 43)

The ideal of *pativrata* is a Brahmanical or at least high-caste ideal that seeks to present itself across society as normative. It implies many other codes of conduct and includes many other tensions within its seeming smooth exterior. The most important relates to the control of women's sexuality. Obviously, a woman as wife and mother is a sexual being. However, one of the dominant male discourses is of the ascetic, of the desirability of men's self-discipline, as in withholding one's semen, which is then transformed into inner power and stored-up vitality. This discourse projects the woman as a temptress and a dangerous, predatory being, even while a second powerful discourse talks of the importance of procreation and of a continuing lineage with sons to perform funeral rites. The two rival masculine discourses of ascetic and householder construct two rival women: the wife and mother, with constrained sexuality, used purely for reproduction, and the vamp, or prostitute of unrestrained sexuality, who is much admired but also feared and reviled by both ascetic and householder. Women do not themselves hold this dual view of women. They often echo male discourses, but many studies of texts, folk culture, women's stories, and songs, all muddy the waters and show that there is not one consensual point of view among women about themselves, "women" as a certain kind of being. They are fine with being sexual, asexual (maternal), independent and dependent, all at the same time.

The *pativrata* ideal has a version that expresses itself in the wife becoming *sati*, or true to her husband even after his death by committing herself to the flames on his cremation pyre. *Sati daha*, or *sati*, as it came to be called in short, was a practice that drew a lot of attention in the colonial period and in colonial history-writing. There are plenty of scholarly debates at present regarding the practice and its reform in the nineteenth century. But more startling is the fact of the occurrence of a woman committing, or being made to commit, *sati daha* as late as 1987, an immolation in a cremation pyre that was cheered by hundreds of thousands of bystanders and audience. Difficult as it is to separate the "fact" from its interpretation, here is an attempt to summarise what we know.

There is a conceptual or ideological frame that may be used to frame *sati*. The term comes from *sat*, or "truth," and *sati* refers to the person, male or female, who is truthful to their vow. As many scholars such as Weinberger-Thomas in *Ashes of Immortality* (1999) show, over centuries there have been varieties of practices by which people proved or demonstrated their "truthfulness." A widow immolating herself on the cremation pyre of her husband was one instance of this. Because other practices perhaps dwindled in importance, or at any rate were less represented and publicised, the term *sati* was used progressively only for the widows who immolated themselves.

We have no idea how commonly held or faithfully believed this conceptual structure was. It has been recovered from a variety of data, pictorial, oral, and archival, but there are no sure grounds for claiming that one of the creators of the archive, for instance, the state, was more prejudiced than another, say the community, which generally means the patriarchs of the community. In Rajasthan, as Harlan (2002) tells us, there was, and is, veneration of the *sati-mata* (the woman committing the self-immolation) as the purest, most "authentic" being. Sati becoming or burning is not a subject of reform but of celebration, something that goes into the very image of the Rajput. It equally went *against* the very idea of the self for other Indians. In the early nineteenth century, the Bengali moderniser Raja Rammohan Roy, petitioned the East India Company's government to abolish the practice. Supposedly, he had direct experience of it in his own family. In Bengal, the Company's officers and visitors recorded the practice, often in grisly or fantastic detail, and it took on the colour of a characteristically "Hindu" evil that needed eradication.

However, the transformation of the practice to a characteristic trait of Hinduism, and an issue of reform, was not about the pain or helplessness of women. As scholars, starting from Lata Mani (1998), point out, women were only the grounds on which were fought some ideological battles between colonising men and colonised men. The actual conditions of women did become a cause for worry for some Indian men, but the larger discourse treated women as a sign or symbol of progress and not as people with bodies and pain, minds and choices, agency or emotions.

Lord Bentinck, the Governor-General of India in the years 1828 to 1835, did declare *sati* illegal in 1829. The action was supported by some members of the public and opposed by others. Tellingly, those who were in favour were those who condemned the practice as degraded or criminal, one of many degenerate Hindu practices that had to be reformed. Those who were against the legislation were upset at the East India Company's interference in their customs. The Company, and later the British Crown, was appreciative of Hindu orthodoxy. They wanted to practice a laissez-faire policy towards Hindu customs and considered it unpolitic to rock the boat of their empire by risking protest and discontent. Bentinck himself, as several Governors-General and Viceroys could individually do, is seen as taking a more liberal view (although he was the one who signed with a flourish under Macaulay's Minute, "I concur wholly with everything in his Minute" – the "everything" included a blanket condemnation of Indian intellectual systems). The *sati* episode demonstrates the sides that different parties stood for, and how their interests were not the same as the ideologies they espoused.

"Reformers" such as Rammohan Roy expressed appreciation of the self-reforming nature of Hinduism. They quoted from Sanskrit scriptures in defence of their reformist stand and did not see reform as threatening to their (orthodox) identity in any way. In other words, they were not "reformers" in a generic sense who would proceed henceforth to challenge every single problem in society. The "conservatives" or orthodox section of society believed in the principle that no foreign person or government should interfere in the workings of Indian society. They may have concurred with the reformers over Hinduism's ability to produce internal change. Where they differed was in seeing foreign interference as a threat, where the reformers saw none.

Apart from the *sati* issue, there were important reform issues of widow remarriage and raising the age of marriage for women. These were battles fought several times with arguments marshalled by the reformers as well as the conservatives, all of which give us insights into the ideas about the control of women and the discourses of patriarchy. Let us look at a certain kind of widow first, "the Bengali widow of upper-caste Hindu families." We simply do not know to the same extent about the low-caste widow, the widow in various other parts of India, and the Muslim, Christian, or Sikh widow to the same extent. About the Bengali upper-caste widow, too, we know more about her representation "as a general figure of suffering . . . an abstraction of relatively recent times" (Chakrabarty, 2000, p. 117).

> There have been widows, of course, in Bengali upper-caste families for as long as such families have existed. It is also true that there have been, from time immemorial, pernicious little customs in place for regulating and dominating the lives of widows. It is not that every Bengali upper-caste widow has suffered in the same way or to the same extent throughout history, or that there have been no historical changes in widows' conditions. Many widows earned unquestionable familial authority by willingly subjecting themselves to the prescribed regimes and rituals of widowhood. Many have also resisted the social injunctions meant to control their lives. Besides, factors such as women's education, their entry into public life, the subsequent decline in the number of child brides, and the overall increase in life expectancies have helped reduce the widows' vulnerability. Kalyani Datta's [author of "Tales of Widowhood"] private act of (public) recording of some widows' own voices is itself a testimony to these changes.
>
> *(Chakrabarty, 2000, p. 117)*

The women, particularly the widows who could hypothetically have been *satis*, did not leave behind a historical record of what they felt or thought. We could extend our history-reading practices, however, to imagine that they "spoke" sometimes through their brothers, fathers, husbands, or sons. There is no reason why they could not or would not have been close to the men in their families. The closeness translated into an understanding by the men of the families of the misery and distress being experienced by the women. The women did not hide it or pretend it did not exist. She could be furious, as some records show, when a relative did not respond with proper sensitivity or interest (Chakrabarty, 2000, pp. 146–147). Family members were drawn into a realisation that they were culpable as well in whatever the fate of the widowed aunt, mother, sister, or sister-in-law was. The men would then be affected by the problem and, in the cases of motivated men, resolve to take action. Women were not active public figures and could not thus resolve. In this respect, the work that men and women performed can be considered complementary: women "teaching" men domestically, and men undertaking certain tasks publicly. Now, all this needs to be qualified for women who were, by virtue of class background or personality, able to turn the essentialised nature of "woman" and "widow" on its head. Vasanta Raje Scindia's grandmother was widowed, and typically in a joint Hindu family the power passes on to the oldest son. But she was "an altogether remarkable woman, strong and sparkling with vitality" (Scindia, 1987, p. 22). In spite of having three adult sons, she took over as head of the family. In my own study of widows in Banaras, I found that the strongest advocates for girls' education were widows who, free from the trammels of service to husband and family, were preoccupied with fundraising, administration, and public work (Kumar, 2007: Chapter 9).

On the matter of the practice of *sati* itself, there was of course an epistemology behind it. A feminist historian would argue, however, that somewhere in the continuum of pain leading to death, one should draw a line, and the pain incurred by burning to death is an action that can only be ranked with culpable suicide or homicide. There are *no* justifications for the practice in modern times, even if there might have been at odd times in the past (but which past?), "an authentic *sati*," or a woman who actually believed in the virtue of the practice.

Women were also controlled more directly in the newly educated households because of the fears that men must have harboured of losing their patriarchal identity because of the new English education and new occupations. Child marriage was similarly not simply a legal issue as it was posed but a deep threat that stood for the loss of autonomy and power for Indian men. Let us look at some representative examples over the colonial period to understand legal reform and social change in marriage. Widow remarriage was made legal in 1856; female infanticide was banned in 1870; the Age of Consent Act was passed in 1891; and the Child Marriage Restraint Act in 1929. At least two cases, "Dadaji Bhikaji versus Rukhmabai" from 1884 to 1888, and the death of the 11-year-old Phulmoni in 1889 in Calcutta, or "Empress versus Harry Mohan Maiti," give further data on the ways in which colonial policy relied on gendered practices, including the most intimate relationships within the home and the bedroom. The wonder is how intimacy, sexual relations, and conjugality were all treated in this period as proper territory for the state to build its legitimacy on.

The colonial government succeeded, historians argue, because of the peculiar success of their hegemonic domination over Indians. This hegemony was visible in their newly introduced educational system, the charms of the English language, the soft power of lifestyle and discursive practices – and not least, in the nature of their law. The law was framed as liberal, humanitarian, and universal. Its stark contradiction was that the state also sought to keep on its side conservative patriarchal forces, both because these were seen as the dominant forces and their support was needed for stability, and because the state itself consisted of (white) male patriarchs who saw the control of women's sexuality as natural as did Indian patriarchs. Altogether, the workings of the British legal system and the British concepts of justice, and the myriad capillary effects of the law, changed gender relationships and values in modern India.

A good way into the topic is to look at a well-studied case, that of Rukhmabai, a 22-year-old woman who fought a Bombay High Court case in 1884–1885 against living with her husband to whom she was married at the age of 11. Rukhmabai watched, from the age of 11 to 22, her betrothed/husband show himself as turning his back on education, a balanced life, employment, and good health. In other words, he was close to a derelict. He was a relative of her stepfather, and her stepfather supported her when she declared that she could not go and live with him. Her husband filed a case against her demanding his conjugal rights. The Bombay High Court Judge, Justice Pinhey, ruled in her favour.

There was a conflict, however, between two types of state control that developed into a confrontation as appeals were filed and other judges overturned the ruling on appeal. One legal approach of the state rested on so-called classical Hindu law, which, even when the Hindu state did not exist as in former times, was preserved by the British in a codified form. The other was British-style law and British-style-law courts as imported from Britain. There was a kind of space that might be under the jurisdiction of both these approaches, but insofar as they were contradictory, the space went undefined. Rukhmabai claimed to believe in universal justice of the British type, and, all through, spoke and wrote as if that was non-negotiable. The Press was similarly divided between those who were loyal to what they saw as either of the two spaces of British and Hindu law. Newspapers like the *Times of India* celebrated Justice Pinhey's judgement as a victory for women's rights. It published letters from "A Hindu Lady" and against child marriage, and editorialised in praise of Pinhey day after day. *The Pioneer* added its voice to this growing chorus for the superiority of British law over Hindu law. The racist undertones of these writings were matched by the elaborate responses on the other side, such as of *Native Opinion* and the *Maharatta*. On this side was the view that the British were trying to create social chaos by questioning the very validity of the Hindu marriage, and that Justice Pinhey had overreached himself in deciding in favour of a Hindu woman, married in childhood, to deny conjugal rights to her husband. Pinhey, in fact, had based his judgement on legal more than moral grounds. He had made the important observation that British law was defective in this regard and was outdated in its permitting a suit for conjugal rights, while Hindu law gave no such space to the matter. He had remarked on the *superiority* of Hindu law in this matter, but his remark was lost by the Anglo-Indian pro-colonial press, and then by the "native" anti-reform press.

The battle, couched in discourse and language, became one between the coloniser and the colonised in the stake for superiority. The colonisers, at least according to its Press, if not Pinhey, were determined to assert British superiority on the subject. The Indians were determined to deny it, and to further deny the right of the colonial state to interfere in matters of religion and custom. The actual issue was distorted as convenient to both sides and the battle took off independently of the fates of Rukhmabai and her husband, who reached a simple settlement between them, which left her free to pursue a medical degree and start a career as a doctor. No reform of women's conditions was achieved because none was permitted by Hindu leaders. The judgement of Pinhey against Rukhmabai's restitution having been reversed, the British also supported this conservative Hindu voice. A patriarchal pact clearly existed between English men and Indian men, which confirmed the unapologetic desire to keep men and women grossly unequal on the subject of marriage rights.

A different case was "Harry Mohan Maiti versus Empress," 1890, where a 29- or 30-year-old husband was charged with the death of his 11-year-old wife because she was forced to have sex with him. The defendant was let off lightly, but the case came to be used for the 1891 legislation called The Age of Consent Bill. This Bill made cohabitation with a wife under 12 years of age illegal, pushing the marriage age for girls a mere two years forward, from the previous ten to 12. Small as the gain for girls was, it was met by amazing resistance from a large section of Hindus, especially in Bengal. They used the argument that a central Hindu rite was the *garbhadan*, or gift of the womb, that is, the first ritual consummation of marriage, supposed to occur within 16 days of the wife's menarche. One of the many Bengali papers that opposed the Age of Consent Bill wrote,

> It is the injunction of the Hindu shastras that married girls must cohabit with their husbands on the first appearance of their menses . . . and all Hindus must implicitly obey the injunction. . . . And he is not a true Hindu who does not obey it. . . . If one girl in a lakh or even a crore menstruates before the age of twelve, it must be admitted that by raising the age of consent the ruler will be interfering with the religion of the Hindus.
>
> (Sarkar, 2000, p. 603)

In other parts of India, protest was marshalled with reference to this and similar themes. A solidarity of interests did not emerge because the most important issues for different communities in different regions were actually not the same. However, a few things were probably in common all over India.

Women's views were neither sought nor collected on the matter of the age of consent. But the occasional woman, such as Phulmoni's own mother, did give evidence in court, and their testimonies are recorded, thus squeezing in a woman's voice where none was technically sought. The earlier silence of the woman, created by the attitude of the community that only *it* could speak for all its members, even when reform was being pursued, was forcibly changed. Now the community was forced to acknowledge its inner conflict between exercising a tight control over all its members and wanting the welfare of its members. The idea of "consent" was radical as well. On the one hand, the whole law seemed to revolve around simply a more or less mechanical functioning of the body – the occurrence of the woman's menarche – over which she had no control. She could not possibly be unwilling to cohabit with her husband, or indeed could still be physically unprepared. On the other hand, the community seemed to wish to stress that girls and women *wanted* what the law wanted. As widows, women themselves wanted either death or an asexual life, and as girls they wanted to be married and serve their husbands unquestioningly. The introduction of the term "consent" in the law, the debate and the overall discourse, introduced another crack in the tight wall the community wished to build around its rights.

The debate was ironical and also productive in another way. It did not mean a leap forward for reform as many reformers fell silent because of the strong argument that the British were an enemy and could not be made responsible for reforms in the Hindu community. The cause of reform suffered also in other tangible and intangible ways. At the same time, nationalism became stronger because even those who pushed the Bill through acknowledged their reservations in thus seeking the support of the British. the dilemma concerned society, social change, politics, and nationalism – but it was all centred on the body of the woman. "The Hindu woman's body, thus, became a deeply politicised matter, for it alone could signify past freedom and future autonomy" (Sarkar, 2000, p. 603). As historians have argued more recently, the fight, in fact, is about *children*, as those under 12 must be understood to be.

The third major event in the legal history of marriage in colonial times, the Child Marriage Restraint Act of 1929, established in clear terms the definition of a "child":

> 'Child' means a person who, if a male, is under eighteen years of age, and if a female, is under fourteen years of age. . . . 'Minor' means a person of either sex who is under eighteen years of age.
>
> *(Pande, 2012, p. 205)*

This Act made child marriage a criminal offence but remained ineffective in practice, with the government actually advising provincial and district officers to remain quiet about its passing and impact, and refrain from convicting an offender. This was to avoid dissension from hitherto loyal subjects. However, the Act created a space for a possibly new legal structure. Together with the control of the community over an individual, a parallel control, based on responsibility, of the state towards an individual citizen, was now acknowledged. This new citizen could be female as well as male, hence creating a visible path through the prison house of unquestioned male control over females. Some historians question this positive view of women's gains. Newbigin analyses the legal changes of the time on the subject of property, inheritance, and the Hindu family. She finds that the interest in changing the legal hierarchy of the family was from men who wished to have freer control over their property and inheritance. Women were important partly as the excluded in the Hindu joint family, and partly as sign of a new patriarchy. "By focusing on an image of the weak and vulnerable female individual, legislators helped to promote a new kind of 'maleness'" (Newbigin, 2010, p. 143).

There were regional differences in the pace and nature of change on the subject of women's rights. The so-called nationalist resolution to the "Woman's question" in nineteenth- to twentieth-century Bengal, as discussed by Partha Chatterjee (1990), divided up the world into private and public, inner and outer spaces, and then resolved their conflict by identifying the inner and private as the site for women and the outer and public as that for men. Such an attempted division was neither new nor ever complete. It had already been observed by historians as a change occurring in the thirteenth to eighteenth centuries, attributed to different extents as due to the influence of Islamic practices, or the desire to defend themselves from the influence of Islam. In both cases, the precolonial and the colonial, a stronger discourse of the private world as the proper world of women, was the result of patriarchal tendencies. The sides of "Indian" versus "British" or "Hindu" versus "Muslim" were not as opposed to each other as were "men" versus "women." The men's identity lay precisely in treating their women as property to be protected, and then embellishing this need with a discourse of women representing history and tradition. However, this happened almost exclusively among upper classes and castes. Middle and lower castes did gradually follow suit, albeit spottily, and the best way to understand that is as Sanskritisation, a formulaic effort to emulate the practices of upper castes, including by keeping women in seclusion.

To return to regional differences about *purdah* (also *parda*) and seclusion, Meera Kosambi in *Crossing Thresholds: Feminist essays in Social History* (2007) points out how the situation in Maharashtra differed from that in Bengal. In Maharashtra, the inner or domestic was both private *and* public, and, prior to colonialism, had been public and political without any rivalry from other sites that were exclusively public and political. In Rajasthan, as the ethnography of Lindsey Harlan (1992) shows, the public-private separation was entrenched among Rajputs and spoken of positively by women as part of *Rajput* identity, implying a superiority to Bengal and other regions. In Haryana, as Prem Chowdhury's extensive oeuvre shows, the veil was a part of Jat identity, even while Jat women typically worked in the fields at manual tasks. The author argues that while women were highly prized for their capacity to labour, patriarchal ideologies managed to put men first. Sons were more valued because a son brought a daughter-in-law, whereas a daughter was lost in marriage. She describes the sexual exploitation of women in the form of a woman's availability to her husband's brothers and occasionally her father-in-law (Chowdhry, 1994, pp. 117–119). Demography and economy played a role: men from Haryana were recruited into the military or went away to search for work, and women's reproductivity was therefore at a high premium. They were respected as mothers. Marriages could cross caste barriers, caste differences whitewashed in sayings such as "Women have no caste" (Chowdhry, 1994, p. 127). But by the same token, a barren woman was then looked down upon. In any and every case, a woman was kept in her place by being veiled.

One of the strongest voices raised against *parda* was that of the Bengali Muslim woman, Rokeya Sakhawat Hossain (1880–1932). In essays and books, she critiques, often obliquely through satire, the institution of *parda* and points out its many negative effects on women, and men. Especially in her *Sultana's Dream*, she showed the utter stupidity of endangering lives and spirits to an ideology and justifying the harm done with reference to human (male) nature.

Apart from *parda* and seclusion, there are regional, class, and caste variations in marriage practices. We have already mentioned the North-South difference in eligibility and desirability of marriage partner, and the possibility of calling the Southern system "matrifocal." We have already mentioned levirate, or the practice, in Haryana and elsewhere, of the widow being passed on to the husband's brother. Then there is polygamy and polyandry. Rajput princes and the sons of Rajput landlords, Scindia tells us in her autobiography (1987, p. 18), was the class

> which formed the entrenched rearguard of feudal privileges, in particular of multiple marriages for men and of the seclusion in purdah for women. . . . Any Rajput prince who did not possess half a dozen legal wives and at least as many concubines would have been regarded by his peers as something of an eccentric, or, worse, too impoverished to afford a properly-stocked harem or even, the ultimate insult, lacking in manly vigour.
> 
> *(Scindia, 1987, p. 18)*

As for polyandry, a celebrated case is in the *Mahabharata*, where the five Pandava heroes are all married to Draupadi. Polyandrous practices have been studied in North as well as South India, particularly in the Himalayan states and in Kerala, but also exist elsewhere. Berreman (1962, 1975) is one of the anthropologists who have written directly about current polyandry.

A common marriage practice related to caste that deserves mention is hypergamy, or the preference of marriage upwards for the bride. This ensures, of course, the superior status of the man's family. It also led to the prevalence of female infanticide in pockets of North India in the mid-nineteenth century, justified by fathers under the pretext that it would be impossible to find grooms of the right status for their daughters (Sleeman, 2007). For many castes and caste clusters, migration entailed the risk of losing status. Brides, therefore, were treated as a link to be forged and maintained with the older homes. Rajasthani Rajputs are the norm, not the exception, in claiming themselves to be so cultured that they don't want to give their daughters to other places with less culture. In Rajasthan, it is best to marry with those located westwards (Harlan, 1992, p. 43). In Bengal, the east regards itself as superior to the west.

Many other studies of marriage, family, and gendered relationships could be mentioned, such as by Trawick and Kapadia in Tamil Nadu (Trawick, 1990; Kapadia, 1995), Oldenburg in Punjab and Delhi (Oldenburg, 2002), and Seymour in Odisha (Seymour, 1999). The Uttar Pradesh (previously Northwestern Provinces and Oudh) data includes historical studies (Kumar, 1993; Singha, 1998) and ethnographies (Raheja, 1988; Wadley, 1994). The last word deserves to go to an author famous for her fiction. in her memoirs, Ismat Chugtai (2012) describes evocatively the cross currents of interests in a family on the subject of marriage. The parents decide that her older brother Nanhe Bhai will marry their niece, his cousin Shaukat. Nanhe agrees on condition that it be a spartan wedding since neither his father nor father-in-law-to-be can afford to be extravagant. But his mother borrows money on the sly, orders finery, and invites many relatives, because she cannot bear to be spartan. Nanhe threatens to call off the wedding. The father threatens to have him arrested. He (the father) says he does not want to humiliate the bride's family by calling off the wedding. "I too have daughters," he says, "I cannot humiliate Zafar" (Chugtai, 2012, p. 45). Nanhe and his brother then quietly un-invite the guests invited by their mother, telling them that the wedding is postponed. This had to be done quietly because the father was against it twice over: he thought it was impolite, and he did not want to hurt his beloved wife who had secretly concocted the whole scheme.

> [Nanhe asks,] "Shall we cancel the invitations then?"
> "No, we can't do this to people after inviting them. They will be annoyed."
> "Sir, this is sheer injustice."
>
> I've got used to bearing with the injustices done to me by your mother," Abba said, smiling. "I have never made her unhappy if I can help it." Amma's irresponsible acts were a source of both delight and misery for him. But his love for her always triumphed over his anger.
>
> *(Chugtai, 2012, pp. 45–46)*

We could take one *last* snippet from the same author on the subject of *parda*. Ismat Chugtai describes how she had to wear a *burqa* for the first time when travelling by train for a family wedding. She says, "I cannot put in words the sense of humiliation I had to suffer. So intense was this feeling of debasement that several times I thought of jumping off the train and committing suicide" (Chugtai, 2012, p. 49). Her sense of shame was stronger because her own older brother Azim Bhai was against *parda* and had written articles that stirred a controversy. Ismat Chugtai also had role models in "gutsy women," who were creating "a commotion" by appearing in public (even if they wore a burqa doing so). Revealingly, "the Muslim community felt deeply humiliated by their action. *If these women did not come from highly influential, educated and aristocratic families, they would have been severely dealt with*" (Chugtai, 2012, p. 49; italics mine).

Azim, the author's brother, tried valiantly to have his wife break her *parda* and come before his close friends. The same situation and the same trembling wife are described in Rabindranath Tagore's *The Home and the World*, evocatively pictured in the film of the same name as she crosses the bridge between the secluded inside chambers and the public drawing room. In the Chugtai case, the wife is totally unable to bear the strain and complains to her in-laws. Both father and mother-in-law threaten the son with dire consequences if he proceeds in his reformist cause. When the wife's brothers have wind of it, they declare that "if their sister was forced to break purdah and made to dance in the marketplace they would decapitate both their sister and her husband. Azim Bhai remained subdued after this" (Chugtai, 2012, p. 51). In Tagore's story, the woman gets carried away by the man she meets once brought "out" by her husband, and then funds this activist, leading to the death of her husband. Violence always accompanies a woman's putative transgression.

## Bibliography

Anagol, P. (2020). Historicising child sexual abuse in early modern and modern India: Patriarchal norms, violence and agency of child-wives and young women in the institution of child marriage. *South Asian Studies*, 36(2), 177–189.

Arondekar, A. (2005). Without a trace: Sexuality and the colonial archive. *Journal of the History of Sexuality*, 14(1&2), 10–27.

Atwal, J. (2016). *Real and imagined widows: Gender relations in North India*. Delhi: Primus Books.

Bagchi, J. (1993). Socializing the girl child in colonial Bengal. *Economic and Political Weekly*, 28(41), 2214–2219.

Banerjee, S. M. (2010). Debates on domesticity and the position of women in late colonial India. *History Compass*, 8(6), 455–473.

Bannerji, H. (1998). Age of consent and hegemonic social reform. In C. Midgeley (Ed.), *Gender and imperialism* (pp. 21–44). Manchester: Manchester University Press.

Berreman, G. (1962). Pahari polyandry: A comparison. *American Anthropologist*, 64(1), 60–75.

Berreman, G. (1975). Himalayan polyandry and the domestic cycle. *American Ethnologist*, 2(1), 127–138.

Bharati, D. (2003). *Band Gali ka Akhiri Makan* (in Hindi). Delhi: Bharatiya Gyanpith.

Bose, P. K. (1995). Sons of the nation: Child rearing in the new family. In P. Chatterjee (Ed.), *Texts of power: Emerging disciplines in colonial Bengal* (pp. 118–144). Minneapolis, MN: University of Minnesota Press.

Burman, E., & Stacey, J. (2010). The child and childhood in feminist theory. *Feminist Theory, 11*(3), 227–240.

Burton, A. (1998). From child bride to "Hindoo Lady": Rukhmabai and the debate on sexual respectability in imperial Britain. *The American Historical Review, 103*(4), 1119–1146.

Carroll, L. (1989). Law, custom, and statutory social reform: The Hindu Widows' Remarriage Act of 1856. In J. Krishnamurthy (Ed.), *Women in colonial India: Essays on survival, work, and the state* (pp. 1–26). New Delhi: Oxford University Press.

Chakrabarty, D. (1999). Nation and imagination. *Studies in History, 15*(2), 177–207.

Chakrabarty, D. (2000). *Provincializing Europe: Postcolonial thought and historical difference* (pp. 117–148). Princeton, NJ: Princeton University Press.

Chakravarty, U. (1998). *Rewriting history: The life and times of Pandita Ramabai*. New Delhi: Kali for Women.

Chandra, S. (1998). *Enslaved daughters: Colonialism, law and women's rights*. New Delhi: Oxford University Press.

Chatterjee, G. (2000). *Child criminals and the colonial Raj: Reformation in British jails*. Delhi: Akshaya Publishers.

Chatterjee, I. (2004). *Unfamiliar relations: Family and history in South Asia*. New Brunswick, NJ: Rutgers University Press.

Chatterjee, P. (1990). The nationalist resolution of the women's question. In K. Sangari & S. Vaid (Eds.), *Recasting women: Essays in colonial history*. New Brunswick, NJ: Rutgers University Press.

Chowdhry, P. (1994). *The veiled women: Shifting gender equations in rural Haryana*. Delhi: Oxford University Press.

Chugtai, I. (2012). *A life in words: Memoirs*. New Delhi: Penguin Books India.

Engels, D. (1989). The limits of gender ideology: Bengali women, the colonial state and the private sphere, 1890–1930. *Women's Studies International Forum, 12*(4).

Grey, D. J. R. (2011). Gender, religion, and infanticide in colonial India, 1870–1906. *Victorian Review, 37*(2), 107–120.

Harlan, L. (1992). *Religion and Rajput women: The ethics of protection in contemporary narratives*. Berkeley, CA: University of California Press.

Hawley, J. S. (Ed.). (1994). *Sati, the blessing and the curse: The burning of wives in India*. Xiii, 214 pp. New York and Oxford: Oxford University Press.

Hossain, R. S. (1988). *Sultana's dream, and selections from the secluded ones* (Trans. and Ed. R. Jahan). New York: Feminist Press at CUNY.

Kapadia, K. (1995). *Siva & her sisters: Gender, caste, and class in rural south India*. Boulder, CO: Westview Press.

Kapur, S. (dir.) (1996). *Bandit Queen*. Produced by Bobby Bedi.

Kosambi, M. (2007). *Crossing thresholds: Feminist essays in social history*. Delhi: Permanent Black.

Kosambi, M. (Ed.). (2012). *Women writing gender: Marathi fiction before independence*. Ramikhet: Permanent Black.

Kumar, N. (2007). *The politics of gender, community and modernities: Essays on education in India*. Delhi: Oxford University Press.

Kumar, R. (1993). *A history of doing: An illustrated account of women's rights and feminism in India 1800–1990*. Delhi: Kali for Women.

Mani, L. (1998). *Contentious traditions: The debate on Sati in colonial India*. Berkeley, CA: University of California Press.

Metcalf, B. D. (1992). *Perfecting women: Maulana Ashraf Ali Thanawi's Bihashti Zewar*. Delhi: Oxford University Press.
Metcalf, B. D. (1994). Reading and writing about Muslim women in British India. In Z. Hasan (Ed.), *Forging identities: Gender, communities and the state in India*. Boulder, CO: Westview Press.
Nair, J. (1996). *Women and law in colonial India: A social history*. New Delhi: Kali for Women.
Nair, J. (2008). 'Imperial reason,' National honor and new patriarchal compacts in early twentieth-century India. *History Workshop Journal, 66*, 208–226.
Newbigin, E. (2010). A post-colonial patriarchy? Representing family in the Indian nation state. *Modern Asian Studies, 44*(1), 121–144.
Oldenburg, V. T. (2002). *Dowry murders: The imperial origins of a cultural crime*. New York: Oxford University Press.
Pande, I. (2012). "Coming of age" law, sex, and childhood in late colonial India. *Gender & History, 24*(1), 205–230.
Raheja, G. (1988). *The poison in the gift: Ritual, prestation, and the dominant caste in a north India village*. Chicago, IL: University of Chicago Press.
Raheja, G. (1994). Women's speech genres: Kinship and contradiction. In N. Kumar (Ed.), *Women as subjects: South Asian histories* (pp. 49–80). Charlottesville, VA: University of Virginia Press.
Raheja, G. G., & Gold, A. G. (1992). *Listen to the heron's words: Reimagining gender and kinship in North India*. Berkeley, CA: University of California Press.
Ray, S. (1985). *The home and the world (Ghare Baire)*. Produced by National Film Development Corporation of India.
Sarkar, T. (2000). A prehistory of rights: The age of consent debate in colonial Bengal ("Points of departure: India and South Asian diaspora"). *Feminist Studies, 26*(3), 601–622.
Sawhney, R. (2015). Revising the colonial past, undoing 'nationalist' histories: Women filmmakers in Kannada, Marathi, and Bengali cinemas. In C. Gladhill & J. Knight (Eds.), *Doing women's film history*. Champaign, IL: University of Illinois Press.
Scindia, V. R., with Malgonkar, M. (1987). *The last Maharani of Gwalior*. Albany, NY: State University of New York Press.
Seymour, S. (1999). *Women, family, and childcare in India: A world in transition*. Cambridge: Cambridge University Press.
Singha, R. (1998). *A despotism of law: Crime and justice in early colonial India*. New Delhi: Oxford University Press.
Sinha, M. (1997). *Colonial masculinity: The "manly Englishman" and the "effeminate Bengali" in the nineteenth century*. New Delhi: Kali for Women.
Sinha, M. (1999). The lineage of the 'Indian' modern: Rhetoric, agency and the Sarda Act in late colonial India. In A. Burton (Ed.), *Gender, sexuality and colonial modernities* (pp. 207–220). London: Routledge.
Sinha, M. (2000). Refashioning mother India: Feminism and nationalism in late-colonial India. *Feminist Studies, 26*(3), 623–644.
Sleeman, W. H. (2007 [1844]). *Rambles and recollections of an Indian official* (Part 25, Vol. 1). Oxford: J. Hatchard. Digitised in 2007 by Google Books.
Spivak, G. (1988). Can the subaltern speak?. In C. Nelson & L. Grossberg (Eds.), *Marxism and the interpretation of culture* (pp. 271–313). Urbana, IL: University of Illinois Press.
Tagore, R. (2005). *The home and the world*. Delhi: Penguin.
Tharu, S., and Lalita, K. (1991). *Women writing in India Vol. II*. New York: The Feminist Press.

Trawick, M. (1990). *Notes on love in a Tamil family.* Berkeley, CA: University of California Press.
Uberoi, P. (Ed.). (1996). *Social reform, sexuality and the state.* New Delhi: Sage Publications.
Wadley, S. (1980). Hindu women's family and household rites in a North Indian Village. In N. Falk & R. Gross (Eds.), *Unspoken worlds: Women's religious lives in non-Western cultures* (p. 94). San Francisco, CA: Harper & Row Publishers.
Wadley, S. (1994). *Struggling with destiny in Karimpur, 1925–1984.* Berkeley, CA: University of California Press.
Walsh, J. E. (2004). *Domesticity in colonial India: What women learned when men gave them advice.* Lanham, MD: Rowman and Little Field.
Weinberger-Thomas, C. (1999). *Ashes of immortality: Widow-burning in India* (Trans. J. Mehlman & D. G. White). Chicago, IL: University of Chicago Press.

# 8
# NATIONALISM AND PARTITION

In order to understand women's participation in the nationalist movement, and the gendered nature of the movement, we need to take another quick look at the century and a half of colonialism. Indian nationalism was a direct product of that colonial experience. The rapacity that attended the first activities of the East India Company in the last quarter of the eighteenth century produced turmoil within the countryside in Bengal, the part of India where the Company had first landed. Their house was put somewhat in order with the regulation of revenue collection and accompanying land settlement. But these very actions, together with the Company's commercial activities and judicial reform, started a minor social revolution. New laws exerted new pressures, land changed hands, cities grew, and new professions took over from older ones. There were indeed many strands of social and cultural continuity, given the entrenched nature of Indian intellectual and social systems. But these subterranean strands consisted not only of continuity. There were internal processes within Indian society that also produced critique, protest, and reform. Meanwhile, the overall effect of British rule was to shake up the parts of India where their contact was greatest. The combined result of these two dynamic internal and external processes led to many changes, starting with Bengal, then Maharashtra and Madras, the three first British Presidencies.

The older ruling classes and dominant groups re-formed themselves as a new bourgeoisie that was mostly urban, commercial, and professional; progressively educated in English; and self-conscious about its identity. It saw itself partly in the mirror held up by British rulers and missionaries and targeted for reform certain of its practices that came to be deemed "backward" and feudal, such as ritualism, caste, idolatry, child marriage, seclusion, lack of girls' education, and prohibition against widow remarriage. In this effort for reform, they took various positions,

DOI: 10.4324/9781003393252-9

termed as reformist and revivalist, who saw themselves as opposed to each other. The reformist and revivalist efforts had many points in common, however.

First, these movements for change in the first half of the nineteenth century were all led by men. It would be several decades more till women took over the charge of the reforms that concerned themselves, and then outstrip the men in their demands. The leadership exercised by men in women's issues in this earlier period succeeded in making women into signs or symbols of the community. As signs, women's relative oppression or liberation signalled the presence or absence of progressiveness of the community, and not anything about women themselves. Women were not seen as living, feeling people as much as they became symbols of civilisation and progress. This trend was clearly created by the contact of Indians with the British, where Indians felt defensive about their image and sought to re-shape it. The repercussions for women were tremendous as they perceived they had to battle two related problems: their own empirical situation and the mirage of themselves as symbols. Literature in all the Indian languages expresses this familiar dilemma of women, how to be true to themselves while *also* trying to ensure the happiness of their family or community members who have a constructed image of womanhood.

Second, both revivalists and reformers looked at Sanskrit scriptures for validation. In the case of *sati*, for example, discussed in more detail in Chapter 7, William Bentinck, the Governor of Bengal and later the Governor-General of India, drew on the authority of the Chief Pundit of the Supreme Court to declare *sati* as having no sanction in the *shastras*. Raja Rammohan Roy had made the same case on the basis of scriptural evidence a few years earlier in 1815. In response, a hundred and twenty-eight pundits published a rebuttal re-interpreting the same evidence, and Rammohan then replied to their response with more scriptural exegesis. This dependence on the scriptures was a British invention, part of their larger work of codifying Hindu and Muslim law. Hindu practices had not thus far derived their legitimacy from any particular text or texts. Textual debates there had been in plenty in precolonial periods, but they were restricted to scholastic sites. The new permeation by textual models into everyday life had serious repercussions for women, as many of the fluid rights they had when oral and local authority was recognised were lost in the new regime.

An interesting difference occurred between the responses of middle-class Indian men and Indian women to colonial domination, challenges, and opportunities. Middle-class men, as they developed a new class identity, wished to both emulate their British masters in giving women liberal freedoms as British women seemed to be given and to preserve the distinctiveness of their Indian heritage. Middle-class women seemed to be fine with this project, of becoming more educated and equal in a liberal mode, retaining their different and complementary role to men. For both men and women reformers, the thrust for reform of women's condition was not to make women equal to men, or to question the authority of men and the nature of Indian patriarchy. It was to make, as in Victorian

England, women better helpmeets of the men, able to bear worthy sons, support them in their careers, provide a peaceful domestic life, and shine in their roles as wives and mothers. Women had therefore to be made educated and enlightened but also kept totally unequal and subservient to men.

Women's magazines, such as the *Bamabodhini Patrika* in Calcutta, reflect this contradiction as well. The new educated woman was also, up to a point, anxious to appear in a continuum with tradition. So, while taking up and promoting the new education with alacrity, there was a continuous refrain of dispatching duty to family and society and carrying the burden of tradition. The writing in this magazine, as well as in almost all other women's magazines, shows women's preference to develop themselves along the lines preferred by their husbands, to earn their appreciation, and to rise to the stature of worthy companions for these newly modernising men.

However, a difference occurred at a certain point in time between the responses of Indian men and women to colonialism. Many Indian women *also* developed a questioning of why the domestic sphere was the only locus of their identity, why they could not work or be active in public or be on a par with men. Gradually, there came to be a paradigmatic difference between reform as undertaken by men and by women. This was brought into sharp relief by women's participation in the nationalist movement.

The idea of building a nation state of one's own, or nationalism, was supposed to be a foreign, imported idea in India. Scholars have long debated the exact relationship of Indian nationalism to colonial education and colonial rule, and the consensus by now is that Indians turned to nationalism in spite of colonial education and not because of it. Just as men took part in the freedom struggle against Britain, so did women. The Indian National Congress, set up in 1885 to participate in political life on British terms, was to grow steadily through a "Moderate" phase, when it debated and memorialised, to an "Extremist" phase, when it went out to the street. It had some women delegates in its very first four years, such as Swarnakumari Debi (b. 1856) and Kadambini Ganguly (b. 1861), who attended the Congress meetings in 1889. Just as did the men delegates, the women at these early Congress meetings were polite and non-controversial. It is fair to say that they were quietly learning the earliest lessons of public participation in politics.

As men in the nationalist movement expanded their reach to include lower classes into the protest, so did women try to similarly extend their reach. 1905, which saw the Partition of Bengal, and a mass protest against it, marks the date for women's active participation in the freedom movement in Bengal. Some innovative steps had already been taken by a few women. Gymnasiums to build up the physique of youths and revolutionaries had been set up by Sarala Debi Choudhurani (b. 1872) around 1902. Swarnakumari Debi became editor of the journal *Bharati* and started several associations. In 1905, women in Bengal participated in boycotts and protests, both as followers and as leaders.

> Women like men are organizing meetings in towns as well as villages to express sorrow at the partition of Bengal, and are taking the *swadeshi* vows.

> At several meetings women are coming forward to inspire men, while at home they are initiating their sons, brothers and husbands to the worship of the motherland.
> (Bamabodhini Patrika *vol 43, Nov. 1905, quoted in Ray, 1995, p. 186*)

In August 1905, a decision was taken to boycott British goods. Women were reported to be active in attending pro-boycott meetings held in far-flung district towns and to organise meetings of their own. They destroyed British-made goods of their families, including accessories of their own, such as imported bangles. Upper-class women donated money and jewellery, and village women, reportedly, put aside grains as their contribution. The Bengal movement was welcomed by nationalists in Punjab who also called for a boycott of all foreign goods, echoing an earlier cry by Punjabi leaders for *swadeshi*. This was the term for homemade goods, and the call led to the larger cry for starting indigenous capitalist enterprises. In Lahore, a Ladies' section was organised at the Industrial and Agricultural Exhibition, and several women were reported in the files of the Home Department to be strong seditionists.

As the nationalist movement progressed, we may observe a gendered difference between men and women. Men could be categorised as those who fought for India's freedom, and women as those who struggled for national freedom *and*, gradually, also for women's freedom. Nationalist men were accused by the British of being elite and non-representative of their countrymen, of harbouring ideas that were simply learnt from outside and mindlessly mimicked, hence not "authentically" Indian and therefore not deserving to speak on behalf of the masses. Women could similarly be accused of disturbing a natural peace by bringing in foreign ideas that did not belong in India, hence of being "inauthentic" and trying to create trouble where none existed.

Women's organisations were set up all over India from the end of the nineteenth century to provide discussion platforms for women or, through self-help, to work for other women by giving medical and educational care. Such were the Aghorekamini Nari Samiti in Bengal and the Bharat Mahila Parishad in Banaras. The Ladies Congress in Madras sought to bring together women from all of South India in 1908 and was succeeded by the Women's Indian Association in 1917. Many thought of this as a new phase for women, seeing it as both feminist and unified. Its founders included Annie Besant, an Irishwoman active in education and nationalism, and an inspiring figure by 1916, when she started a Home Rule League. After her imprisonment and release, she was elected the first woman President of the Indian National Congress in 1917. In her Presidential Address, she spoke of women:

> The strength of the Home Rule movement was rendered tenfold greater by the adhesion to it of a large number of women who brought to its help the uncalculating heroism, the endurance, the self-sacrifice, of the feminine nature. Our League's best recruits and recruiters are among the women of

> India. . . . Home Rule has become so intertwined with Religion, by the prayers offered up in the great Southern temples – sacred places of pilgrimage – and spreading from them to village temples, and also by its being preached up and down the country by Sadhus and Sanyasins.
>
> *(quoted from Sumit Sarkar, 1983 in R Kumar, 1993, p. 55)*

As we shall see, Besant's tendency to bring together Hinduism, women's activism, and nationalism was part of a trend that continued through to Independence and beyond and brought tragedy to the nation. It was of doubtful use to women as well. The emphasis, in this view, was on women's special self-sacrificing and nurturing natures. Besant, as well as other women leaders such as Sarojini Naidu, saw this nature as noble, brave, and powerful, deriving from a Hindu past from the dim Vedas to the heroines of Rajput palaces, who could fearlessly commit themselves to the flames when their menfolk were killed on the battlefield.

When Indian women demanded equal franchise for women in 1917 – using the argument that their participation would be good for their children as well as for the political world – parliamentary response was to make individual provincial committees responsible for the decision. Madras was the first province to make women qualified for the franchise and to elect a woman legislator, Dr Muthulakshmi Reddy to the Legislative Council. In Bengal, a restricted female suffrage was approved in 1925, based on property and education. Men's wavering support for the franchise demand marks one of the many issues on which women and men stopped seeing eye to eye. Women accepted their predefined roles, but the grumbling behind the scenes rose in crescendo and finally came out to the front.

Meanwhile the "Extremist" phase moved on to the "Gandhian" phase, with the return from South Africa of Mohandas Karamchand Gandhi in 1915. At one of the earliest meetings in his address to a women's social reform organisation, he cited the epic heroines Sita, Draupadi, and Damayanti. This was not unusual since to look at India's past Vedic and epic ages and find many instances of greatness in them, including of women's outstanding purity and courage, was becoming a norm. In 1919, Gandhi took the bolder step of calling upon women to join the resistance movement he was calling. This peaceful resistance movement that he named *satyagraha* was partly learnt by him from his mother, and he had no hesitation in both ascribing its proximity to feminine strength and to expect women to be adept practitioners of it. Though he had to call off the campaign because of the massacre of hundreds of innocent people perpetrated in Amritsar by a British general, the nationalist movement was now legitimately joined by thousands of women.

> Shrimati Ambujammal, one of Gandhi's loyal followers from Madras, outlined how Gandhi touched the hearts of both Hindu and Muslim women. First, he explained to women there was a place for them in the movement, then he expressed his faith in their courage. It was possible to help the movement without leaving home or neglecting the family. "Do what you

can," Gandhi advised women, convincing them that every act counted. At the same time, he reassurred families their women would not sacrifice family honor or prestige. Sucheta Kriplani credited Gandhi for his special attention to male attitudes: "Gandhi's personality was such that it inspired confidence not only in women but in guardians of women, their husbands, fathers and brothers." Since his moral stature was high, "when women came out and worked in the political field, their family knew that they were quite secure, they were protected.

*(Ambujammal and Kriplani, quoted in Forbes, 1996, pp. 125–126)*

In 1921, in an extension of the *swadeshi* and *satyagraha* campaigns, many women were arrested by British soldiers in Calcutta and given public support from Indian communities across the board. Both the British and Indian nationalists understood the value of women agitators. Gandhi persuaded more women to join, and more women did, in the north, south, east, and west of India. There are numerous touching incidents recorded, such as the *devdasis* who held a meeting for him, where they donated their jewellery and thousands of rupees. Gandhi could easily collapse social reform issues and political ones, and argue for moral regeneration as the solution for political ills. This did not always accord with women's desire for legal change, such as for the franchise. Gandhi continued to speak to women with reference to Sita and other epic heroines. Women continued to fight for their rights, alongside, following him with all sincerity, calling themselves Gandhians and Gandhi, their Bapu, or Father.

Women were now actively recruited into nationalist fighters. They would picket shops selling foreign goods or liquor, spin yarn and teach spinning, sell *khadi* and propagate it through parades and songs, and the leaders got periodically arrested for doing all of this. Many of the leaders were related to male nationalist leaders, such as Basanti Devi, the wife of Chittaranjan Das; Urmila Debi, his sister; and Parvati Devi, Lajpat Rai's daughter. However, they did not simply follow in the men's footsteps or function in their shadow. Though cautious in their own ways, women now began to link women's rights with nationalism to make the argument that just as the nationalist movement could not be advised to be patient and moderate but rather to engage in a struggle *here* and *now*, so could the women's movement not wait for a ripe enough time. By the 1930s, a distinction between social and political issues was no longer tenable.

Even as nationalist movements in India were finding their anti-colonialist voice and shaping their unified approach, the effort by women to work for women as a group that could speak and choose for itself was not typically in favour with nationalist men. A delightful excerpt from a 1931 short story by a woman activist, Hema, and her male friend Bibhuti, goes:

> [Bibhuti asked] 'Would a confrontation between men and women lead to any benefit to the society at large?'

> 'At least there will be no harm done', Hema retorted. 'Women need some relief from the injustice they have been subjected to all these years'.
> .... Bibhuti continued, 'Injustice! This hostile attitude of yours to men, this suspicion that men have increasingly conspired to put women down, is nothing but imported ideas from Europe ....'
> [Hema] could have said that if every idea from Europe was to be discarded, then why did the Indian Congress subscribe to the theory of democracy? After all, the concept of democracy was not native to India. . . . [Bibhuti] then turned the direction of the debate and continued, 'When the nation is passing through a severe crisis, when all our energies are deeply enmeshed in our revolt against administrative and economic mismanagement, is it the right time to start a civil war between men and women? . . . all you are doing is to create disharmony between men and women. A great mistake'.
> *(Ray, 1995, pp. 175–176)*

Hema then announces that women have separate interests from men, and "For us the liberation of the country makes little sense if we, women, are to be kept shackled inside our homes. This we must declare unequivocally" (Ray, 1995, p. 176).

Gandhi's leadership produced the Civil Disobedience campaigns of the 1930s, which were particularly important sites for women's participation. To "disobey" non-violently was read as particularly well suited for women, since they had the qualities of patience, sacrifice, and nurture. In addition, given the British self-image of liberalism, it was strategically useful to have women at the head of picketing and protesting lines. In March 1930, at the symbolic gesture of making salt at Dandi in defiance of colonial laws, the front line of seven people included two women, Kamaladevi Chattopadhyay and Avantikabai Gokhale. The former writes:

> this was their [women's] first appearance in any modern militant political campaign and I could hardly suppress my excitement at the enormity of the occasion and my own good fortune to be amongst the first. . . . It seemed such a stupendous moment in my life, in the life of the women of my country.
> *(Chattopadhyaya, quoted in Forbes, 1996, p. 132)*

In the years following, women demonstrators and picketers were repeatedly arrested and jailed, and kept protesting. The RSS in Bombay and the MRS in Calcutta worked to achieve both, *swaraj*, or self-rule, and women's rights.

> MRS leaders argued that these goals were inseparable: until women's lives improved the nation could never be free; and until the nation were free women's condition would not improve. The first step to *swaraj* was the

education of women to their double oppression as colonial subjects and inferior sex.

*(Forbes, 1996, p. 136)*

An interesting historiographical debate has developed on the different meanings for men and women of the nationalist struggle. On the one hand is Chatterjee's claim about what he calls "the nationalist resolution" to "the women's question."

> He begins with the puzzle of why the 'Women Question' ceases to become an issue for nationalist discourse by the end of the nineteenth century and argues that it is in fact 'resolved' by a necessary kind of silence; a nationalist refusal to make the issue of women an item of negotiation with the colonial state. The 'home' then, becomes the discursive site of nationalist victory when the 'world' has been ceded to the colonial state. The male nationalist turns inward, reifying the home, and women's place within it, as a spiritualised 'inner space' that contests colonial hegemony. . . . it is possible to see a kind of logic at work: if the family or home is the site of nationalist silence, and women's subjectivities are located in the home, women's agency is itself subject to a kind of silencing.
>
> *(Visweswaran, 1996, pp. 85–86)*

On the other hand, there are calls for more pro-women and feminist readings of the same "nationalist resolution." One reading interprets more closely *how* and *why* the nationalists (nationalist men) come to share colonialist understandings of women as nothing but dependents of their husbands, confined to their domestic spheres and of no interest politically as active agents. The colonial rendering of women as passive and publicly ineffective is clear from the archival record. Sometimes, they are seen as weaker adversaries even when engaged in the same protests as men, and the force used against them is often less violent. When charged with the same offences as men, the jail sentences are patronisingly lighter and shorter. Even when described as making fiery or seditious speeches, they are simultaneously suspected of being mere mouthpieces for their husbands. In a rare instance of giving a woman power, a District Collector describes one such passionate woman agitator on 27 May 1930:

> My district was perfectly calm till Durga bai came here on the 21st. She delivered very violent and inflammatory speeches at Gudiyattam, Vellore, Arni, and Arcot on the 21st, 22nd, and 25th instants and openly incited the masses to disobey all order and authority. All the present troubles are the direct result of her speeches in the District.
>
> *(Visweswaran, 1996, p. 116)*

This excerpt is a rare exception; colonial officials more typically characterise women protesters as unimportant, and not worthy of being considered real political actors as their menfolk are. Even in the cases when the power of her speech is recognised, the woman nationalist is always categorised as the domesticated woman, a wife or daughter.

A man was judged by the property he owned, and women were seen as similarly divided. Since their economic power was different, the punishments that were appropriate for them were different. Lower class, poorer and less-educated women were considered so unimportant that they were not only treated as bottom-rung prisoners, they had abuse heaped on them in the official records and, therefore, we can be sure, in their actual treatment. This centrality of the hierarchy of caste, class, and status is important to bear in mind when talking about women and nationalism. Much of the time, when we use colonial records or nationalist writing, what we are talking about are women of property and status, while consistently ignoring poor women.

Apart from Gandhi's leadership, there were at least two alternative models of opposition to the British. One was Subhash Chandra Bose's, or Netaji, as he was called. He stood for an armed fight against the British and formed an Indian National Army for the purpose. This had a women's regiment as well, named after the Rani of Jhansi, famous for her stand against the British in the 1857 War of Independence. Another anti-Gandhian format was that of the terrorists, who stayed undercover, manufactured bombs and collected firearms, and attempted to directly assassinate the enemy, that is, British officers.

Historians have also traced the gendered component of the present-day rise of Hindu nationalism to nationalist developments. The gymnasiums set up by Sarala Debi were self-consciously Hindu sites that strive to build up a militant persona that could equal the Muslims' putative proclivity to masculine violence. She built herself up in the model of Bankimchandra Chatterji's heroines Shanti and Debi Choudharani. Bankim Chandra's novel *Anandmath* was a rallying cry to many who could now mould themselves in the ideal of a Hindu nationalist group dedicated, under a matriarch, to fight for their mother, India.

The idea of "Mother India" took flight. Artwork, posters, advertisements for Indian-manufactured goods, songs, speeches now presented India as a goddess-like female in a sari holding a flag unfurled, often with a tiger next to her like Durga, young, winsome, and very feminine. This sexualised figure was Mother India in need of worship and defence by her sons. She personified the land, tradition, history, and a distinctive identity. This particular image succeeded in giving men who fought for the country a more privileged position as the sons of the nation – suggestive of the powerful mother-son relationship in Hinduism. It also gave a further religious resonance to nationalism, insofar as the goddess-like figure was in the format of Hindu goddesses such as Durga, Parvati, Lakshmi, and

Saraswati. The first two verses of the song *Bande Matram* composed in 1872 by Bankim Chandra Chatterji for his novel *Anand Math*, and put to music and first performed by Rabindranath Tagore in 1896, are as follows (the mention of Durga and Lakshmi occurs in a later verse):

## Bande matram

*Bande matram*
*Sujjalam, suffalam*
*Malayaj shitalam*
*Shasya shyamalam matram*
*Bande matram*
*Shubhra jyotsna pulakit yamini*
*Phullakusamita drumadilshobhani*
*Suhasini, sumadur basini*
*Sukhadam maradam, matram*
*Bande matram*

## Mother, I praise you!

Rich with your hurrying streams,
Bright with blossoms and fruits,
Cool with delightful winds,
With dark fields, Mother of might,
Mother free.
Glory of moonlight dreams,
Your branches and mighty streams,
Your blossoming enveloping trees,
Mother of rest,
Blissful and sweet,
Mother, I kiss your feet,
Mother, I praise you!

The song was evocative and continues to be sung today in India as a national song. However, its two problems were its religious imagery, such as of kissing the feet of a goddess, and its feminisation of the nation, making the feminine inalterably an object, and not a subject, of decisive action – being praised, loved, wooed, sung to, and worshipped.

However, while we mark this rumbling of discord between Hindus and Muslims on the subject of the nation, we must note that many nationalists of both religions, including women, consistently saw beyond this divide and fought for unity. Kamaladevi Chattopadhyay (b. 1903) was one such. She lectured and wrote for attention to actual problems such as of work, exploitation, and class equality. She explained the new Hinduisation of nationalism thus:

> The [Muslim] League has no record of any constructive work for the amelioration of the Muslim masses. . . . Had the Congress from the earliest days countered this by courageously pursuing an economic programme for the masses . . . it would have effectively undermined the League's efforts at disruption and the two-nation theory would have failed to find the soil in which to implant its poisonous stem. . . . The Hindu section, on the other hand, partly through ignorance but more so because of the frustration caused partly by the absence of any positive programme of mass contact and social reconstruction work and partly by the tension produced by the long delay in the attainment of power due to Britain's reluctance to part with power, plunged deeper and more recklessly into a similar abyss of fanatical passions, unable and too ill-equipped to face the logic of a rapidly changing situation. It has however sought refuge in a demagogic past. . . . Unfortunately as the aggressiveness of the Muslim League has advanced, proportionately has the lure of this Hindu mirage deepened, ensnaring in its meshes raw immature minds who, thwarted by an overpowering present, fill the imagination with past achievements, which at least for the fleeting moment give them a sense of security.
>
> *(Guha, 2011, p. 254)*

The Muslim League was founded in 1906, as a delegation led by Muslim landlords to Lord Curzon, to extend the demand for separate electorates for Muslims. It was perhaps based on a fuzzy notion of Hindus and Muslims representing two nations, as Sayyid Ahmad Khan had outlined at the end of the nineteenth century. However, as historians, particularly Ayesha Jalal, have shown, and as Chattopadhyay's speech above illustrates, the Muslim League did not speak for an abstract group called "Muslims" while recognising the huge divides within the group based on class, education, property, and status. Only as late as the mid-1930s did Mohammad Ali Jinnah successfully revive the League and give it an all-India face. Events in the next decade, especially the promises opened up by electoral reforms by the British, and Congress and various Muslim parties' response to them, led to a situation where the League came to be seen as the one all-India Muslim party that was profitable for local Muslim parties to support. In 1940, the All-India Muslim League made a formal demand to recognise separate Muslim states on the ground that the Muslims were a nation. In the following years, the demand took clearer shape and gathered further support until, to the surprise of many, a Hindustan-Pakistan Plan was announced in June 1947.

The time of Partition was characterised by far more than the establishing of new national governments, the finalising of new flags and constitutions, and the drawing of new national boundaries. It consisted in fact of the wrenching apart of communities, villages, families, whole regional groups, and the painful reconstruction of new – seemingly artificial – identities and communities. Women are crucial to such splitting apart and reconstruction, as the terms "families" and "communities" themselves tell us. Every step of history has women at its heart. What is, however, of special interest in all gendered enquiries about the Partition is the fate of women within the violence that took place. Many were killed or widowed; many were abandoned or separated from their families. Many were kidnapped or abducted. Many of these were raped, then married when not killed. Some were rescued or returned, more were rendered homeless, and still more chose to stay or were forced into the decision to stay with their new families, whether of abductors or rescuers. Rather than statistics, we have narratives re-created through memoir, fiction, film, and interviews.

We do know that some 10 million people changed residences, Hindus and Sikhs migrating to India, and Muslims to Pakistan. This reciprocal migration was far from a peaceful one. It was utterly unbelievable to policy-makers and politicians, and a horrendous experience for those living it. At least a million people lost their lives and those who survived were traumatised and embittered. The brutality of the mutual movement and accompanying violence staggered any attempt at logic. The best description of it was as a "madness," when "normal" people are rendered insane and should be represented as inmates of a lunatic asylum as in Saadat Hasan Manto's story "Toba Tek Singh." One of the many painful stories on the Partition, this one has lunatics play out all the scenarios that actually happened during 1947: individuals asking where "home" is and receiving no answers; others refusing to move to a new place deemed "home"; some declaring that to live on a tree was preferable; some revolting by tearing off their clothes, not sleeping, or running around; and others laughing or crying uncontrollably or speaking gibberish. Chaos prevails, before which authorities throw up their hands. Manto's characters are all men, but one could say, "men" in the sense of human beings. He does mention towards the end that there were female lunatics too, and they were even noisier and more difficult to control.

Both Punjabi Muslims and Sikhs were seen as the first aggressors. There was a fever pitch built up by taunts of cowardice on the one hand and a vow to display "manliness" on the other – by both sides. As violence broke out, authorities saw clearly that women were being targeted by both sides. Unfortunately, this was not accidental. *Rape* was one of the facets of the violence. Men were attacked, forcibly converted, and killed; women were attacked, raped, and killed. The violence reached a climax in March or August 1947, in different accounts. In March, Punjab was ablaze, down to villages and hamlets. August saw the "Direct Action Day" of the massacre in Calcutta. Apart from the interview-based histories of Bhasin, Butalia, Das, Menon, and Pandey, there are films of varying quality. *Khamosh Pani* includes the story of the mass suicide of scores of women who threw themselves into a well, of a woman who survives, only to be rejected by both sides. *Pinjar* is a more romantic story of an abducted woman who chooses to stay with her new family while both sides are, finally (not initially), ready to welcome her. Through art, literature, and of course, memory, we can reach a little closer to the possible pain of the woman, doomed if she does and doomed if she does not, to the consciousness that has to play between danger at every turn and the cracks open for survival, and the violence that emanates from *one's own* community that would suddenly rather defend an abstract "honour" than their own kinswoman. As a young woman, left on the wrong side at Partition, then disowned by her brother, told him in a letter, "How can you talk of purity and honor? How can you denounce me for what was no fault of mine?" (Menon & Bhasin, 1993, p. WS 6).

As historians have documented, the subjectivity of women was not the focus of the post-Partition actions taken to "recover" those who had been abducted. Some women had resigned themselves to their new situations; born children become accepted by their new families, and were unwilling to be "returned." A new round of violence was involved at this expatriation that was legally mandated by both India and Pakistan. The women, on their part, continued to resist as far as possible. They challenged the legitimacy of a state that had once played false with its citizens. They taunted the social workers and police who forced them to return. As a social worker reported, "There was so much distrust and loathing for us in their hearts . . . they would say – if you were unable to save us then, what right have you to compel us now?" Another confronted her rescuers thus:

> You say abduction is immoral and so you are trying to save us. Well, now it is too late. One marries only once – willingly or by force. We are now married – what are you going to do with us? Ask us to get married again? Is that not immoral? What happened to our relatives when we were abducted? Where were they? . . . You may do your worst if you insist, but remember, you can kill us, but we will not go.
>
> *(Menon & Bhasin, 1993, p. WS 6)*

In all, some 30,000 women were restored to their original homes, over 20,000 Muslims and fewer than 10,000 non-Muslims. Jawaharlal Nehru, the first Prime Minister of India, pleaded with the country to extend love and care, instead of rejection, to abducted and returned women. Mahatma Gandhi made a similar appeal. The ministry of relief and rehabilitation strove to educate the public through pamphlets and broadcasts that women did not have to be rejected after a rape or illegal marriage. To little success – the record of India was particularly negative on this score, even as India and Pakistan made the whole project of recovery a competition of national honour. The Hindu articulation of the problem weighted more against the woman, finally, to the extent that many who were forcibly returned, preferred to live alone or in an *ashrama* than with a family likely to be abusive, and with children who were looked down upon by Hindu society. The state of India, meanwhile, while trying to act in a secular vein for its citizens, continued to echo the patriarchal concerns of its dominant Hindu community, and failed to be either humane or compassionate towards women. Partition was a tragedy for women in multiple ways. What we are left with is a clear picture – that violence is instigated by men, participated in by both men and women, but it is not for or against individuals equally. In the name of the community and the nation, and though they are hardly innocent of violence, women suffer more. We are also left with a blurry picture – our historiography does not enable us to yet create a finely etched enough picture of what women actually experienced.

## Bibliography

Bankimchandra, C. (1992). *Anandmath* (Trans. And adapted B. K. Ray). Bombay and Delhi: Vision.
Butalia, U. (1994). Community, state and gender: Some reflections on the partition of India ("On India: Writing history, culture, post-coloniality"). *Oxford Literary Review*, 16(1/2), 31–67.
Chatterjee, P. (1989). The nationalist resolution of the woman question. In K. Sangari & S. Vaid (Eds.), *Recasting women: Essays in colonial history* (pp. 233–353). Delhi: Kali for Women.
Forbes, G. (1996). *Women in modern India*. Cambridge: Cambridge University Press.
Ghosh, D. (2004). Gender and colonialism: Expansion or marginalization? *The Historical Journal*, 47(3), 737–755.
Guha, R. (Ed.). (2011). *Makers of modern India*. Cambridge, MA: The Belknap Press of Harvard University Press.
Hasan, M. (2001). *Legacy of a divided nation: India's Muslims since independence*. New Delhi: Oxford University Press.
Hasan, M., & Roy, A. (Eds.). (2005). *Living together separately: Cultural India in history and politics*. New Delhi: Oxford University Press.
Jalal, A. (2008). *Partisans of Allah*. Cambridge, MA: Harvard University Press.
Jones, K. (1989). *Socio-religious reform movements in British India*. Cambridge: Cambridge University Press.
Kumar, R. (1993). *The history of doing: An illustrated account of movements for Women's rights and feminism in India 1800–1990*. Delhi: Kali for Women.
Lipner, J. J. (2005). *Anandmath, or the sacred brotherhood by Bankim Chandra Chatterjee*. Delhi: Oxford University Press.
Manto, S. H. (2011). *Toba Tek Singh: In his Mottled Dawn*. Delhi: Penguin.
McKean, L. (1996). Bharat Mata: Mother India and her Militant Matriots. In J. Stratton Hawley and D. Marie Wulff (Eds.), *Devi: Goddesses of India*. Berkeley, CA: University of California Press.
Menon, R., & Bhasin, K. (1993). Recovery, rupture, resistance. Indian state and abduction of women during partition. *Economic and Political Weekly*, 28(17), 2–11.
Pandey, G. (2001). *Remembering partition*. Cambridge: Cambridge University Press.
Ray, B. (Ed.). (1995). *From the seams of history: Essays on Indian women*. New Delhi: Oxford University Press.
Ray, B. (Ed.). (2002). *Early feminists of colonial India: Sarala Devi Chaudhurani, Rokeya Sakhawat Hossain*. New Delhi: Oxford University Press.
Robertson, B. C. (1995). *Raja Rammohan Roy: Father of modern India*. Oxford: Oxford University Press.

Sangari, K., & Vaid, S. (1989). *Recasting women: Essays in Indian colonial history*. New Delhi: Kali for Women.

Sarkar, S. (1983). *Modern India*. Delhi: Macmillan & Co.

Sarkar, T. (1987). Nationalist iconography: Image of women in 19th century Bengali literature. *Economic and Political Weekly*, *22*(47), 2011–2015.

Sarkar, T., & Butalia, U. (Eds.). (1995). *Women and right-wing movements: Indian experiences*. London: Zed Books.

Tagore, R. (1919). *Ghare-Baire. The home and the world* (Trans. S. Tagore). Madras: Macmillan.

Tarlo, E. (1996). *Clothing matters: Dress and identity in India*. Chicago, IL: University of Chicago Press.

Visweswaran, K. (1996). Small speeches, subaltern gender: Nationalist ideology and its historiography. In S. Amin & D. Chakrabarty (Eds.), *Subaltern studies IX: Writings on South Asian history and society* (pp. 83–125). New Delhi: Oxford University Press.

# 9
# GENDER, WOMEN, AND HINDUISM

A class studying women and gender in South Asia would find the meanings of symbols and narratives in South Asian religions fascinating. They could also fruitfully debate the emancipatory values of these constructs for women in the present. Academics have also been preoccupied with precisely these questions. That there is female divinity in South Asia is not debatable. But are there many different, even contradictory, forms of the goddess, each with their own history, forms of worship, and meanings, or is there one overarching Goddess who merely manifests herself variously? If so, is she to be more broadly understood as a feminine *principle*, the immanent principle of the Universe? Or as an equal of the many Hindu gods, and one that a Hindu might forefront according to the practice of henotheism? What do we know about the historical continuities, from the Indus Valley period to the present, and about constructions of the Goddess, including colonial and nationalist constructions? What can we conclude about the elite-mass or classical-popular connections in goddess/Goddess worship? Finally, what does any of this mean in the lives of actual Indian women, and Indian men? What are the historical, political, psychological, and cultural interpretations of the relationship of the goddess to mortals?

This chapter gives an overview of how Hinduism produces and interacts with gendered formations and practices. It looks particularly at the meaning of the Goddess in its historical context and in the anthropological present. This chapter looks as well at discursive spaces within which feminist movements and scholars have sought to present religion as a resource rather than an alienating force. Other important issues find their place elsewhere, such as female infanticide, dowry and *sati* in the chapters on family and marriage, although they are often discussed as if they were a part of "religion."

An important historical source is the text called *Devi Mahatmya* (dated to c. 6th century CE). These are verses in Sanskrit that are a later addition to the *Markandeya Purana* of the fourth century CE, but which come to be read separately, and are also known as *Durgasaptasati, Durgapatha* or *Candipatha* (The 700 verses on Durga, the lesson on Durga/Candi). Translatable as "The Glorification of the Goddess," the *Devi Mahatmya* is a work that celebrates the Goddess as the supreme and autonomous principle in the universe through a series of stories.

The frame story is that of a dispossessed king and an unhappy merchant who are guided by a sage to think through their dilemmas by reflecting on stories of the Goddess. The *Devi Mahatmya* then presents three stories that display the Goddess' power in crisis, to save other deities who need help with their own dilemmas, thus suggesting that she has the power to save those earthly devotees who choose to turn to her. In the first story, she is the force underlying the universe who makes it possible for Vishnu to defeat two demons, Madhu and Kaitabha. In the second story, the creation of the Goddess is narrated. The demon Mahisa is threatening the gods, or *devas*, and they persuade Siva and Vishnu to create a new being through the *tejas*, or radiance, of the gods. This new being is the Goddess, shining and radiant, and equipped with all the weapons of the gods, riding a lion. She fights Mahisa and his armies and defeats him in whatever form he takes. The most famous, iconographically, is the form of the buffalo. Riding on her lion, she swings her spear and mounts, and kills and beheads the buffalo-demon. Among her many names is the popular *Mahisasurvardini*, or The Slayer of the Demon Mahisa. The gods and the world are saved and acknowledge the Goddess for accomplishing the task that needed to be done.

In the third story, Durga, the Goddess, is entreated to save the world from the twin demons, Sumbha and Nisumbha. A range of goddesses, all manifestations of Devi, appear: Parvati, Ambika, Kali, Chamunda, as do the "seven mothers," or *Saptamatrakas*. At the end of the story, the Goddess is addressed, beyond all her many names and forms, as being the one and most powerful creator, preserver and destroyer of the world, and the deliverer of her devotees.

The *Devi Mahatmya* is a text that makes coherent many strands of goddess worship that are already present in Hindu and pre-Hindu scriptures and practice. It is constructed as a work that may be recited and used for the purpose of resolving the kinds of existential questions that are posed by the king and the merchant in the frame story. Similarly, every single goddess has her own story, many of which are equally multi-layered and complex, and all of which are historically developed. It is true that the gods of Hinduism are better understood by scholars than the goddesses, but we must emphasise that goddesses are not merely their "consorts" or somewhat inferior partners but rather bear different, complex relationships with male gods that in each case may be understood by looking at the theology and the practices associated with them. In general, as Vaudeville tells us,

> If the male god is conceived as powerful, the consort goddess tends to be conceived as the embodiment of the god's power or energy, his *sakti*. If the male deity is conceived as the supreme lord and master of the universe . . . his consort may be identified with the great cosmic *sakti*, the force or energy that sets the universe in motion . . . this energy is personified as the great Goddess, Devi. . . . Ultimately the great Goddess controls even the supreme male deity whose emanation she is supposed to be.
>
> *(Vaudeville, 1982, p. 1)*

There are scores of separate goddesses and we can only discuss a few of them here.

Radha, the mistress of the god Krishna, is worshipped independently with love and devotion by her followers, as in the poetry of the Bengali poet Rupa Goswami (c. 1493 – c. 1564) and the North Indian saint Sur Das (c. 1478 – c. 1561). From being a personification of a human devotee's yearning for the Lord, Krishna, she becomes equal to Krishna. Descriptions of Krishna's hypnotic charms and unique cleverness in attaining his ends are matched by Radha's legendary attractiveness and distinctive sense of mischief. This equality is then accepted by the faithful, and texts such as the *Brahmavaivarta Purana* and *Sur Sagar* proceed to elaborate further on its implications. From the fifteenth to sixteenth century, theology proposes that Radha and Krishna are *prakriti* and *purusa*, the ancient correlates of reality that are fundamentally one, and inseparable. Radha then becomes the divine principle incarnate, the principle that is imminent in the universe. The creation theology that features her goes:

> The Goddess, Primordial Nature, incited passion in the heart of the Supreme Being.
> Krishna, infatuated with her beauty, embraced her in amorous sport for the lifetime of a Brahma,
> At last discharging his seed into her womb.
> From her exhausted limbs flowed perspiration which became the cosmic waters upon which the universe would float.
> From her labored breathing arose the vital breaths that would sustain all living beings.
> After a hundred eons, the goddess finally gave birth to a golden egg, which she kicked into the cosmic waters.
> From that egg arose, in due course, the entire universe.
>
> *(Brown, 1982, p. 57)*

Scholars have worked on the textual history of Radha's transformation from a minor figure to Supreme Mother. Equally interesting is the development of the styles of worship associated with her. Because she is love incarnate, and part of Krishna as well as a simple cowherd maiden, that is, part of us, she is an object of reverence as the channel or proof of access to the Lord. The intimacy that is possible with the Mother is accompanied by reverence or servitude, as to a teacher.

> You [Radha] are the Mother of the world, Hari [Krishna] is the Father.
> The guru of the Father is the Mother, to be worshipped and honored as supreme.
>
> (Brown, 1990, p. 70)

Then, we come to Parvati, the daughter of Parvat, the mountain or the Himalayas, also known as Uma or Sati. Originally an ambiguous semi-divine being, she goes through several historical transformations as well, while continuing to be represented at several levels simultaneously. At one level, she is the devoted consort who initially fasts and prays for the husband of her choice, Siva. As his devoted wife, she is the audience for several doctrines expounded by Siva, in which her role is almost equal to a mortal woman's. At another level, she is *already* the Great Goddess who has consented to marry a less-than-great God. She *pretends* to serve her husband but in reality controls him. For both Radha and Parvati, it is true that they shift (sometimes within the same text) from supplicant of the god to his controller, from human-like to supremely, remotely divine. Parvati is worshipped as a wife, as a mother, and as an intermediary to Siva, as well as the Supreme Mother and creatrix.

Sita, the consort or Rama and heroine of the *Ramayana*, is often considered to be the model Hindu wife. She says in the epic, asking her husband to accompany him in exile:

> A wife wins the fate of her husband, and not her own, O bull of a man. Knowing this, I shall live in the forest from now on. Here and hereafter there is only a single goal for a woman: her lord, and not her father, her child, herself, her mother nor her friends. . . . O take me with you, noble husband! Do as I ask, for my heart is devoted only to you. If you leave without me, I shall die!
>
> *(Dimmitt, 1982, p. 210)*

However, she has two important other levels in her characterisation. One is as the daughter of the earth, literally *sita* or furrow, and, as such, mistress of vegetation. The other is as *sakti* or the true power and energy of Rama, without whom he would not take action. Like Radha, she is worshipped as an invisible part of the male god she is associated with. Like Radha, she mostly keeps hidden her role as the provocateur of plot development in the story of the universe.

Lakshmi, or Sri, is the consort of Vishnu, and is pictured as sitting on a lotus or on the breast of Vishnu. She is addressed as Mother by devotees and is the archetype of the loving, forgiving mother who is always there for her children. She is incarnated as Sita, herself a mother, but is full of potential implicit in her very name, Sri:

| | |
|---|---|
| *sriyate:* | she who is resorted to |
| *srayate:* | she who resorts [to the Lord] |
| *srnoti:* | she who listens [to humans] |
| *sravayati:* | she who makes [the Lord] listen |
| *srnati:* | she who removes [past karma and hindrances from devotees] |
| *srinati:* | she who makes human perfect [for moksha] |

The words *Shri* and *Shrimati* are used as honorifics before male and female names to denote respect, literally translatable as "Prosperous" or "Auspicious," and loosely as Mister and Mistress.

We could trace the course of these goddesses, and others, in much greater detail. The point, however, is that there *is* this complex and weighty mythology. While *Maha*devi, literally, the "Great" Goddess, may be synonymous with *Sakti*, literally, power, *each* of the particular manifestations of the Goddess, such as Laksmi, Parvati, Durga, and Kali, may be identified with her, and have the prefix "Maha" or "Great" attached to them.

There are other goddesses discussed in the Puranas, and other Sanskrit sources, who are more abstract (if we consider the goddesses mentioned earlier as "concrete" because of the human-ness of their narratives), such as Aditi, the primal creator. Aditi has no similar narrative of birth and adventures, nor is she anthropomorphised. There are village goddesses as well, who may be identified with Mahadevi in full or part, as exhibiting specific aspects of her power. The earth, *bhu* or *dharti*, is also perceived as a goddess, as are various rivers, chiefly the Ganga. The Ganga is both a goddess and the quintessence of all sacredness, promising release or *moksha*. All rivers are present in her and she in all water bodies.

There is no question that Hindu goddesses provide a quite different space to their devotees, men and women, than do the gods of masculinist religions. At the village level, they stand for their association with nature and motherhood, that is, with preservation and nurture, and provide a valuable antidote to the masculine militancy of many religious movements, including the creation of female-dominated canons of religious beliefs and practices (Gandhi, 1992). For Dalits and low castes, as Ilaiah argues, a local village deity, such as Pochamma, is all about cure and procreation, and one who can be comfortably addressed by anyone in their own language (Ilaiah, 1996, p. 92).

Although we have told the story of the Goddess earlier, to know her story is not to know a goddess. Many devotees themselves may not know her stories and know her primarily through the rituals they perform. Indeed, the two things are complimentary. Some know her rituals rather than her stories, and some – relatively fewer – know only the narratives and do not perform the rituals. An excellent example of a goddess ritual and story that is local belongs to the pilgrimage town of Tirupati, in Andhra Pradesh. Here, the goddess Gangamma is said to expand, heat up, and become *ugra*, or "excessive," at a certain time every year. For a week, she is placated through various domestic and public rituals, while her "excessiveness" is also sought to be controlled by men dressing up as her, in *strivesham* (literally, a woman's outfit or disguise). This *ugram*, or excess, may be understood as *sakti*, or power, and desire, and *must* be contained to not spill over into anger or destructiveness. Fieldwork conducted by Joyce Flueckiger suggests that while both men and women are agreed on the power of Gangamma and how to appease her, men are afraid of the *sakti* as women are not. Flueckiger suggests that men dressing up as woman is to approximate some of the femininity that the world possesses, but that "men may feel overwhelmed by a female quality that they do not possess, but which women share with ease" (Flueckiger, 2013, p. 4). Her study of the goddess Gangamma is tellingly called *When the World Becomes Female*. Wearing a woman's disguise gives men the possibility of accessing *sakti* at least temporarily. This local narrative is tied together with the larger Sanskritic narrative of the Goddess when Gangamma herself divides herself into four parts, three to become the consort of the three gods (Brahma, Visnu, and Siva), and the fourth to become the hundreds of *gramadevatas* (village gods), who do not need consorts. At both levels, the local and the classical, the message is that *sakti* is female power, a power that is universal and immanent, that can transform men into different kinds of men.

In general, written texts of Hinduism are associated with male, Brahman priests, and oral texts with local, lower-caste ritualists and women (Sax, 1991, p. 23). In the Himalayan state of Uttarakhand, William Sax recorded several different versions of the songs of creation and origin, and underlying their differences was one similarity: the versions sung by women embodied a feminine perspective, whereas those sung by men ignored women's perspectives to reiterate narratives with male gods at the centre. The feminine versions state quite clearly that creation occurs from menstrual blood, that the Goddess is alone but then desires a male, that her fertility produces several males with none of whom may she mate, being the mother, and finally comes the convoluted narrative of resolution, in the course of which much else about creation, the cosmos, and the pantheon of deities is explained. Sax tells us that the male versions of the songs, sung by Brahman priests, are accompanied by sheer ignorance of the female versions.

This goddess of Uttarakhand is Nandadevi. She is the outmarried daughter of several local villages. She is carried in procession from her married home back to her natal village, her story being recited continuously, and her worship performed by everyone en route. Whichever village hosts her procession as it moves around becomes her natal village, in return for which she blesses them with the crops, sons, and good health they desire. Sax makes a detailed exposition of her pilgrimage as it travels through the mountains, showing that while the travels replicate the trope of the rule of the Goddess and her Brahman priests, to whom all the villagers are subservient, the ways in which the travel is controlled and closed, and the social relations of the mountains, are also projected and re-affirmed. These are inevitably gendered ones in which men have superior power. The *dhyani*, or outmarried woman, does return to her husband's home. She shares her *sakti* with her devotees, but it is finally controlled by the rituals performed for the purpose. The songs that tell her stories are privately, for women, still about her ultimate power, but the public, Brahmanic ones, chime fully with normative Hindu songs of creation and of power as being in the hands of male gods. In short, Nandadevi's worship in the mountains is one of the clearest cases of feminist streams of consciousness and performance in India being ultimately controlled by patriarchal ones, their power then restricted to women's spaces.

An interesting point to be made from the Nandadevi case is about Maya. The Goddess is routinely called that on the ground, as she is in the stories about her. The creation stories tell us that an undifferentiated – hence, lone – being feels obliged to divide, proliferate, and multiply. Why? For companionship, for the very sake of creativity. This creation has to be done unilaterally, acting on the self as the partner, since there is only one being so far. Many myths about this act of single creation narrate it as performed by the male deity, that is, they present the primordial being as male. There are also stories in which the creation is carried out by the female deity by herself, but they are fewer. However, the term and the concept of *maya*, or differentiation, is female, reflecting the fecundity and fertility of the female. Sax explains it thus:

> The creative activity of Maya depends on her power of multiformity, but it is motivated by desire. Earlier she emanated the world, and was "very happy" when she saw the results. But the presence of others soon gave rise to desire. "How can I live without a man?" she asked.
> "Without a man, for whom shall I live?
> Without a man, there is no wealth.
> Without a tree, there can be no shade.
> How shall I give birth to that shade-giving tree?
> Or must I remain a sad little girl?
> All of Maya's troubles, her subsequent actions and ultimately her self-decapitation, could have been avoided were it not for the power of desire, which, as elsewhere in Hinduism, quite literally makes the world go round.
>
> (Sax, 1991, p. 29)

Over two millennia earlier, the Indus Valley Civilisation shows evidence of the worship of a mother goddess. There is no evidence, however, that later goddesses, while also being seen as "mother" goddesses, are direct descendants of this earlier one. Some five hundred years later, the Vedic civilisation also gives importance to the female power, although less so than does the "extra-Vedic," all the forms of religion that continue on the subcontinent alongside Vedism and are gradually assimilated into late Vedic, Sanskritic, or Classical Hinduism. Vedic goddesses include Aditi, the mother; Prithvi, the earth; Ushas, the dawn; and Ratri, or night. We have to be careful both when making connections between antecedents that bear little resemblance to a later figure and equally about denying any historical connections altogether. The danger lies in over-emphasising "female-ness" as an essential quality of a deity. If two deities are otherwise distinct but are both female, one could slip into the easy generalisation that they are both manifestations of a "Great Goddess," whereas the many male gods are never typically subsumed under a "Great God." What we could then suggest is that we find in Indian history a "matriarchal worldview."

> The worship of the mother goddess does not constitute a matriarchy, but it does constitute a matriarchal *culture*, in the sense that it preserves the value of women as life-givers and sources of activating energy, and it represents the acknowledgement of women's power by women and men in the culture.
>
> *(Liddle and Joshi 55, q in Sunder Rajan, 1993, p. WS-35)*

Many goddesses, particularly unconventional ones such as Kali, are associated with a history of worship by village and tribal groups. Brahmanic religion, both Vedism and the later Hinduism, historically incorporated many local gods, goddesses, and forms of worship. We have to distinguish between some deities that do have a local origin but are then classicised clear out of their local roots and become part of the Brahmanic pantheon, and others that continue to be worshipped strictly at the local village and tribal levels. The latter are often called *mata*, *amma*, or *ma* (mother), or simply *grama devata* (village gods). While village gods could be either male or female, typically they are female, associated with fertility and the agricultural cycle. They are represented often as aniconic, as a pot, rock formation, a pile of rocks, a tree, or other natural feature, and sometimes as an image. Most are guardian deities of the places they are in, many control diseases, almost all have a jealous and aggressive nature, as is needed for their functions. They were often offered animal sacrifices in the past. They are regarded as "hot," full of martial energy, needing to be "cooled." When not raised up to be part of the more formal Hindu pantheon, they are often associated with lower castes and classes. When acknowledged as identifiable with the Great Goddess, they are given large temples and Brahman priests.

The goddess Kali is one that may well have had a local or tribal origin and is now properly a Hindu goddess. The scholar David Kinsley traces how historical processes such as her celebration by two poets and saints of modern times elevated her, while insisting that it was a two-way process.

> Kali does not make her way in the tradition solely on the basis of conflation with other goddesses; she makes her way in her own right. . . . Kali keeps her integrity despite various changes in appearance and function. She is not simply "used" by the Great Tradition: she brings something to that tradition, revealing herself to that tradition, and it is not an exaggeration to say that in this process the tradition itself is enriched.
>
> (Kinsley, 2000, p. 86)

Kali's earlier, more local, history is difficult to know for sure, but she makes her debut in the "Great Tradition" in the story of Durga in the *Devi Mahtamya* given previously. From this role of the helper of Durga, she becomes independent, a rich and complex character, worshipped in her own right as the Mother of the Universe and the embodiment of the highest divinity.

Worship of the Goddess is referred to as *Sakta-ism (Saktism)* and her devotees as *Saktas*, one of her names being *Sakti*, or power. *Saktism* is one of the three main sectarian divisions of Hinduism, together with *Vaisnavism*, or worship of Visnu, and *Saivism*, or worship of Siva, but sometimes difficult to separate from Saiva and Vaisnava worship insofar that Visnu, his avatars, and Siva, as well as other Hindu gods, all have female wives or consorts, who are worshipped as various manifestations of the Goddess. And of course they are not merely wives or consorts but also expressions of the female *sakti*, or power, of the male god they form a partnership with. Brahma, the Creator's consort is Saraswati; Visnu's is Lakshmi; and Siva's is Parvati. Thus, Saraswati, Lakshmi, and Parvati also constitute the *Tridevi*, or triad of Creator-Preserver-Destroyer in themselves, according to *Saktism*. But Saktism differentiates itself theologically by identifying the female principle that activates the world as the Absolute. This female power encompasses the male principle, which is passive, in a dynamic, energising union, which is the ultimate reality.

Tantrism may be related to indigenous agricultural societies with matriarchal practices, as opposed to Brahmanic religion, which was fundamentally patriarchal. But as to what Tantrism *is*, scholars such as David Gordon White show that it has a precise ritual approach and philosophy that has been fundamental in the formation of modern Hinduism, albeit forgotten by reinterpreters and apologists of Hinduism, who prefer a more puritanical approach that replaces ritualism with *bhakti* devotionalism. Tantra is about a group of divine powers called *yoginis*, who must be propitiated in ritual ways. The sexual aspects of these rituals are directly responsible for various desirable worldly powers. Another scholar, Vidya Dehejia's work on the Yogini cult and temples, connects the Yogini traditions with those of the *apsaras* (nymphs), *grahanis* (seizers), *yaksinis* (female dryads), *dakinis* (flyers), *matras* (mothers), and other representations of female divinity. Tantra is not identical with goddess worship, by any means, but the worship is imbued with Tantric elements, whether consciously recognised as such or not. The schools of Sakta Tantrism may be divided into the Kalikula, or the family of Kali, the black goddess, or Srikula, the family of the benign or auspicious goddess. These are regionally distinct as well, Kalikula strong in Bengal and the Northeast, and Srikula in Kashmir and the South.

As ethnographies inform us, until very recently, and to some extent even today, the proper ritual for a Goddess, especially of the village goddess, is a blood sacrifice, that is, an animal sacrifice. In a way, this sums up the bridging of the possible dichotomy in the female deity between fertile, creative, preservative qualities and angry, violent, and destructive action. The two poets of Bengal, Ramprasad (1718–1775) and Ramakrishna (1836–1886), exemplify this bridging in their devotion. Ramprasad describes Kali in the way iconographically familiar: black, ferocious, decorated with severed limbs and heads, a bloody tongue protruding from a terrible face, a body that is haggard and ugly, armed by lethal weapons, trampling on corpses and the body of Siva. she personifies the ambiguity of creation. Ramprasad writes:

> O Mother! Thou art present in every form;
> Thou art in the entire universe and its tiniest and most trifling things . . . .
> The whole world – earth, water, fire and air –
> All are thy forms, O Mother, the whole world of birth and death . . . .
> O Mother! Who can understand Thy magic [*maya*]?
> Thou art a mad Goddess; Thou hast made all mad with attachment.
> (Kinsley, 2000, p. 116)

These devotees' approach to her is that of helpless and forlorn children who will not give up on her in spite of her recalcitrance. Ramakrishna calls the human being a machine who has, if they only used it, the weapon of love. He writes:

> O Mother, what a machine is this that Thou has made!
> What pranks Thou playest with this toy
> Three and half cubits high!
> Hiding Thyself within, Thou holdest the guiding strong;
> But the machine, not knowing it,
> Still believes it moves by itself.
> (Kinsley, 2000, p. 123)

If we had to explain her fierce and unnatural look, we could ascribe it to the desire to represent both the dark side of creation and the power of transgression, of not being fooled by the many masks or illusions that "reality" puts on, but to see the reality of the power of death, and the freedom imposed by this knowledge. Tantra is a ritual practice in which the practitioner or *sadhaka* strives to unify the seeming opposites, such as male–female, Siva–Sakti, sacred–profane, body–mind, and beautiful–ugly. With the help of a guru, the practitioner seeks to use his body in precise ways to re-unite the partitioned world of illusion and reality, male and female, to a necessary wholeness. This *sadhana*, or ritual effort, can take dramatic forms that have been caricatured and vilified in different ways in the modern period by both Indians and colonials and other non-Indians.

Tantric discourse is a male discourse, and its canon is read and known largely by men. There is evidence that its peculiar form of asceticism may, in fact, as I argue later, run counter to the interests of women as wives and mothers and that its peculiar form of eroticism fans the male fantasy by combining ritual, ascetic, and sexual preoccupations in a single symbol system, albeit one that mostly consists of talk and almost never entails actual ritual practice.

There is an interesting spatial dimension to Sakta ideas and practice. According to a popular myth, Sati, the wife of Shiva, committed suicide upon her husband being dishonoured by her father. Different parts of her dismembered body fell in different regions of India, each of which became a *tirth*, or pilgrimage place, known as a *saktipitha*, or seat of power. This subtle unification of the space of "India" came to be evoked in the nationalist period as an ancient and original unity, a kind of ur-nation as it were. The Goddess became a pan-Indian deity, the country itself became "Bharat Mata" or Mother India, another form of the Goddess. The formal launching of the idea was done perhaps by the Bengali novelist, Bankim Chandra Chattopadhyaya (Chatterjee), in his 1882 novel *Anand Math* or *The Abbey of Bliss*. Its plot depicts a group of monks who have sworn to fight for their mother, that is, country. The novel has been critiqued for its celebration of a past ancient Indian glory that was rendered dim by an interlude of foreign rule, thus leading to a mindless xenophobia and false characterisation of the enemy as foreign and Muslim. From our perspective, it may be further critiqued because it places the highest value on asceticism, including celibacy. In the glorification of "Mother India," it devalues actual women. Indeed, it has no place for women at all, only men and the *idea* of a mother.

Hindu women do have spiritual heroines as role models, though "Mother India" is not one of them. Sita and Parvati are particularly venerated in North India, Draupadi is dear to the hearts of others further north, in the mountains, and in South India, and literary figures such as Savitri and Damayanti are worshipped everywhere. Apart from these, there are, as Lynn Denton tells us, woman saints, ascetics, and mystics, people who struggled in their own lives with spirituality and society. These Hindu "saints" are not the same as saints in other traditions. Hindu saints, as Lisa Hallstrom tells us in her book on Anandmayi Ma, are neither "saints" nor "women." They are divine, with different amounts of godhood in them. To say that the "divine" acts as a role model for ordinary women in everyday life is a difficult concept, and one on which more research needs to be done.

A possible way to look at the position of women is through the lens of performance. Ordinarily, the Indian woman performs the role of dutiful daughter, wife, and mother. She takes pleasure in performing the role well and savours the rewards of it, in terms of security and approval. When there are occasions of trial, of which there could be many, there may be a questioning of the role. Here, the goddesses and the saints come in. They all have complicated histories of social trials and challenges, to which they rise in a variety of interesting and powerful ways. The ordinary woman has their example to follow. Given the gendered configurations of society, many of these ways could be seen as "feminist," though certainly not all, nor is feminism necessarily a subtle enough concept to respond to all the varieties of challenges in social and human life. Whatever the response of the individual woman, she is still "performing" the response, deciding and acting on it as one choice out of many (not necessarily "pretending," as when performing means "play-acting").

Another way to understand the relationship of the Goddess to human women is to recognise the similarities in the experiences of both. The kuldevis of Rajputs, such as Ban Mata and Jamvai Mata, are homologous with the great Goddess and are often referred to as Durga, Kali, Shakti, Devi, etc., as by their local names (Harlan, 1992, p. 61). They are both maternal and militant. The kuldevi brings together the functions of protecting the lineage, the man's work, and protecting the family, the woman's work. The kuldevi might, at some times, symbolise the disharmony of the duties she performs. Women devotees experience the same disharmony or dissonance (Harlan, 1992, pp. 78–90).

> The traditional goals of a Rajput man are two: conquest and death on the battlefield.... A Rajput woman, as we have seen, aspires to preserve her husband's life, but at the same time, she understands that her *pativrata* duty requires her not only to preserve her husband but also to serve him and be obedient to him. She must sacrifice her personal desire to fulfill the desires of her husband. Thus, if her husband wishes to die a glorious death on the battlefield, she again experiences dissonance.... The warrior-*patrivrata* character of *kuldevis* reflects this dilemma.
>
> *(Harlan, 1992, pp. 106–107)*

Many stories from Hindu epics, Puranas, and other mythology are taken purposefully for application by modern-day feminists as well. Alf Hiltebeitel, in his essay "Draupadi's Question," ties together some of the ways in which the figure of Draupadi is used. Draupadi, as already mentioned in Chapter 3, is the woman born of fire, married to the five Pandav brothers, who suffers many times because of the tribulations brought upon their family by the miscalculations and recklessness in gambling (although never is one result ascribed to any one cause) of the oldest brother, Yudhishtra. One of the most complex scenes is that of the dice match between Yudhishtra and their Kaurava cousins. He loses, one after the other, all their wealth and possessions, then his four brothers, then himself, and finally his wife. The victor, Duryodhana, orders that Draupadi be dragged into the courtroom and disrobed. Her question is, did he lose her before or after he lost himself? Implying, was she his to lose? The question has a direct bearing on a possible woman's question. One meaning is related to Samkhya philosophy, according to which self-hood is challenging and debatable. The over-simplistic dichotomy of *purusa*, the male principle, and *prakriti*, the female principle, should rather be seen as a mind-matter unity, *prakriti* (matter), alive only through *purusa* (consciousness), and vice versa. In the *Devi Mahatmya*, as Cynthia Humes points out, the Goddess is extolled as *prakriti*, but as matter that is immanent in the universe, and is not passive, but active. "The text's creators posit that matter and spirit are both aspects of a single divine being, who is best understood as female precisely because she is plural, immanent, and active" (Humes, 2000, p. 131).

The more direct meaning has to do with Draupadi's actual disrobing. Yudhishtra was silent; someone or something else protected her. Was it Draupadi's dharma as a good wife – the more conservative explanation? Was it universal dharma, a kind of cosmic justice? Or was it Krishna, to whom she prayed – the most conservative, and most recent, explanation?

Among others, the author Mahasweta Devi gives a reading of the Draupadi story in her story about a Naxalite tribal woman, Dopdi Mejhen. When she is finally apprehended, tortured, and gang-raped, she refuses to wash or put on clothes. She challenges the government officials with,

> What's the use of clothes? You can strip me, but how can you clothe me again? Are you a man? . . . there isn't a man here that I should be ashamed. I will not let you put my cloth on me. What more can you do?
> *(Hiltebeitel, 2000, pp. 119–120)*

As Gayatri Spivak explains, "It is when [Dopdi] crosses the sexual differential into the field of what could *only happen to a woman* that she emerges as the most powerful 'subject'" (quoted in Hiltebeitel, 2000, p. 120).

Other scholars such as Agarwal (1995) and Menon and Bhasin (1993) have discussed how sexual violence has always been part of an authoritarian world view, one that cannot admit the legitimacy of women's sexual freedom. This ranges from an everyday attitude of valorising the dignity of "our" women and the potential shame of dishonour, to an attack on the women of "others" as a symbolic act of power. These scholars, in decrying the reification of god into nation and the use of women as a political weapon, note that goddesses are selectively chosen as role models. Sita is far more popular than Draupadi, even while both literary figures undergo a similar trial of rejection by their husbands. Sita chooses to withdraw, an independent gesture without doubt. Draupadi chooses to shout, question, and fight. As a sexually awakened woman, she poses a greater threat to the patriarchal nation than the independent but non-challenging, withdrawing woman. The patriarchal nation and its discourse closes its ranks against the Draupadi figure. Cynthia Humes, too, finds in the Vindyachal area, famous for its Devi temples, that there is a curious disconnect between the power of the Goddess and that of ordinary women. However, significantly, she finds that texts such as the *Devi Mahatmya* may be used in both feminist and patriarchal ways but that the discursive space of the text is potentially an anti-dualistic one, where the entrenched male–female or *purusa–prakriti* dichotomy is broken down. The Goddess remains a female, never a male –

> only by affirming and insisting on the integrity of her female nature does the Devi of our Glorification maintain her own integrity and truly ultimate position in the universal hierarchy. She is not diminished by being (only) female; and she is the Truly Ultimate, resident in all things, and thus imparting her nature to all of reality.
>
> *(Humes, 2000, p. 141)*

Another interesting contemporary light that is shed on the Goddess is by Karline McLain, who looks at the comic book (Amar Chitra Katha) issue that is about Devi. It is not "authentic" as its author and illustrator claim but derived from many sources and makes important changes from the Devi Mahatmya that it claims to derive from. These changes include framing the story in a way that belies the Sakta claim that the Goddess is "the supreme deity and the transcendent reality responsible for the creation of the universe and its preservation in the face of evil," but rather makes her an equal to others (McLain, 2008, p. 315). Moreover, the fact of her being a *woman* is underscored, rather than the fact of ultimate reality being feminine taken for granted. Kali is also sanitised, and not shown as drinking blood, as described in the scriptures. Altogether, as McLain shows,

> As an independent woman with martial qualities, Durga did not fit the established formula for either male or female heroes; but Mahisha, although a villain, was more suited to the male heroic template. The ambiguity concerning Durga's role as heroine also has important ramifications: it may suggest discomfort with the immanent power of the Goddess and her martial role as the "supreme ruler" of earthly creatures.
>
> *(McLain, 2008, p. 316)*

This would be in line with the modern, revisionist belief that Hinduism should be divested of its superstitions, including fear-arousing practices such as the worship of snakes and the violence of gods (Hawley, 1995, p. 118). This accords with the observation that those versions of power in Hinduism that

> are not unambiguously benign, such as those of the inauspicious Shani (Saturn), Krishna's cosmic form (*viraat roop*) revealed to Arjun on the battlefield in the Mahabharata, or Kali in her more terrifying aspect, have gradually disappeared from calendar prints, or have given way to interpretations with a quite different affective charge: the Krishna you see nowadays is much more the sweet, seductive, androgynous child, and similarly the sensuous treatment of Kali's tongue can sometimes verge on soft-focus eroticism.
>
> *(Jain, 2000, p. 162, quoted in McLain, 2008, p. 320)*

But ironically, recent political developments in India have chosen to use Hindu deities and symbols to construct their ideologies of violence and revenge, and this has included the use of goddesses. The "empowerment" of women in and by the Hindu Right is correctly problematised by critics, including from the left and secular feminist movements. Clearly, agency or empowerment is not something whose positive value can be left unquestioned. Female goddesses such as Lakshmi, Parvati, and Savitri, as well as epic figures such as Sita, Draupadi, Savitri, and Damayanti, to say nothing of apsaras and *viranganas* (heroic women), have complex roles in their various texts, oral and written. In Hindu nationalist ideology, however, they are subsumed to the power of men or cooperate with them in revisionist ways. There is no predicting how a goddess may be used: to dominate over women, to keep them passive, to arouse them to questionable action, or to liberate them and empower them to work in humanistic, democratic ways.

An interesting inversion occurs with the recruitment of women to the BJP (Bharatiya Janata Party), RSS (Rashtriya Swayamsevak Sangha), and VHP (Viswa Hindu Parishad) complex. While feeling empowered because they can move out of their homes, participate in rallies, get involved in national causes, and demonstrate seeming equality with men, they are simultaneously part of a political movement that is based on a mindset that is conservative through and through. It can include pleading the causes of polygamy, dowry, domesticity, and even widow immolation. It routinely does flaunt preference for male superiority and control of women's social freedom and sexuality, obscured under the fog of "*Hindutva jagaran* (the awakening of Hindu-ness." Among its contradictions is that without allowing women the freedom to do anything with it, they put emphasis on a trained and developed female body. As Tanika Sarkar says, "The specific deity that embodies their aspirations is the eight-armed Durga, a militant icon who subsumes Saraswati, Lakshmi and Kali. Sevikas see themselves as full-fledged soldiers in an impending apocalyptic war" (Sarkar, 1994, p. 204). There is, we can see, further potential for the Goddess to be used for political ends as the RSS movement expands and mines Hindu imagery for its own purposes. By the same token, the sheer contradiction between women's desire for freedom and the Hindu nationalist idea of a woman cast in a fixed image will make the political aspirations of the RSS, VHP, and BJP collapse under its weight. Apart from the worry that a feminist might feel about which turn things might take, there is a theoretical pleasure that gender is so transparently crucial to public life in India today, albeit for the wrong reasons.

## Bibliography

Agarwal, P. (1995). Surat, Savarkar and Draupadi: Legitimizing rape as a political weapon. In T. Sarkar & U. Butalia (Eds.), *Women and right-wing movements: Indian experiences* (pp. 29–57). London: Zed Books.

Brown, C. M. (1990). *The triumph of the goddess: The canonical models and theological visions of the Devi-Bhagvata Purana*. Albany, NY: State University of New York Press.

Coburn, T. (1984). *Devi-Mahatmya: The crystallization of the goddess tradition*. Delhi: Motilal Banarsidass.
Coburn, T. (1991). *Encountering the goddess: A translation of the Devi-Mahatmya and a study of its interpretation*. Albany, NY: State University of New York.
Dehejia, V. (1986). *Yogini cults and temples: A Tantrik tradition*. New Delhi: National Museum of India.
Dimmitt, C. (1982). Sita: Mother goddess and *Sakti*. In J. S. Hawley and D. M. Wulff (Eds.), *The divine consort: Radha and the goddesses of India* (pp. 210–223). Boston, MA: Beacon Press.
Eck, D. (1982). Ganga: The goddess in Hindu sacred geography. In J. S. Hawley and D. M. Wulff (Eds.), *The divine consort: Radha and the goddesses of India* (pp. 166–183). Boston, MA: Beacon Press.
Falk, N. A. (2006). *Living Hinduisms: An explorer's guide*. Belmont, CA: Thomas Wadsworth.
Flueckiger, J. (2013). *When the world becomes female: Guises of a South Indian goddess*. Bloomington: Indiana University Press.
Gandhi, R. (1992). *Sita's kitchen: A testimony of faith and inquiry*. New Delhi: Penguin Books.
Grimes, J. (1993). Feminism and the Indian goddess: Different models. In N. Smart & S. Thakur (Eds.), *Ethical and political dilemmas of modern India* (pp. 126–143). London: Macmillan.
Hallstrom, L. (1999). *Mother of bliss: Anandamayi Ma (1896–1982)*. New York: Oxford University Press.
Hansen, K. (1988, April 30). The *Virangana* in North Indian history, myth and popular culture. *EPW*, pp. 25–33.
Harlan, L. (1992). *Religion and Rajput women: The ethic of protection in contemporary narratives*. Berkeley, CA: University of California Press.
Hawley, J. S. (1982). A vernacular portrait: Radha in the *Sur Sagar*. In J. S. Hawley and D. M. Wulff (Eds.), *The divine consort: Radha and the goddesses of India* (pp. 42–56). Boston, MA: Beacon Press.
Hawley, J. S. (1995). The saints subdued: Domestic virtue and national integration in Amar Chitra Katha. In L. Babb & S. Wadley (Eds.), *Media and the transformation of religion in South Asia* (pp. 107–134). Philadelphia, PA: University of Pennsylvania Press.
Hawley, J. S., & D. M. Wulff (Eds.). (1982). *The divine consort: Radha and the goddesses of India*. Boston, MA: Beacon Press.
Hiltebeitel, A. (1994, November). Opening Remarks at Religion in S Asia Panel, "Is the Goddess a Feminist," AAR Annual Meeting, Chicago.
Hiltebeitel, A., & Erndl, K. M. (Eds.). (2000). *Is the goddess a feminist? The politics of south Asian goddesses*. New York: New York University Press.
Humes, C. (2000). Is the Devi-Mahatmya a feminist scripture? In A. Hiltebeitel & K. M. Erndl (Eds.), *Is the goddess a feminist? The politics of South Asian goddesses* (pp. 123–150). New York: New York University Press.
Ilaiah, K. (1996). *Why I am not a Hindu: A Sudra critique of Hindutva philosophy, culture and political economy*. Calcutta: Samya.
Jain, K. (2000). The efficacious image: Pictures and power in Indian mass culture. *Polygraph*, *12*, 159–185.
Kinsley, D. (1988). *Hindu goddesses: Visions of the divine feminine in the Hindu religious tradition*. Berkeley, CA: University of California Press.
Liddle, J., & Joshi, R. (1986). *Daughters of independence: Gender, caste and class in India*. London: Zed Books.

McDermott, R., & Kripal, J. J. (Eds.). (2003). *Encountering Kali: In the margins, at the center, in the west.* Berkeley, CA: University of California Press.

McLain, K. (2007). Who shot the Mahatma: Representing Gandhian politics in Indian comic books. *South Asia Research, 27*(1), 57–77.

McLain, K. (2008). A comic book interpretation of the Hindu Devi Mahatmya scripture (Scripture and Modernity: A Tribute to Professor John Wansbrough). *Bulletin of the School of Oriental and African Studies, 71*(2), 297–322.

Menon, R., & Bhasin, K. (1993). Recovery, rupture, resistance. Indian state and abduction of women during partition. *Economic and Political Weekly, 28*(17), 2–11.

Miller, B. S. (1982). The divine duality of Radha and Krishna. In J. S. Hawley and D. M. Wulff (Eds.), *The divine consort: Radha and the goddesses of India* (pp. 13–26). Boston, MA: Beacon Press.

O'Flaherty, W. D. (1982). The shifting balance of power in the marriage of Siva and Parvati. In J. S. Hawley and D. M. Wulff (Eds.), *The divine consort: Radha and the goddesses of India* (pp. 129–143). Boston, MA: Beacon Press.

Omvedt, G. (1993). *Reinventing revolution: New social movements and the socialist tradition in India.* New York and London: M. E. Sharpe.

Pintchman, T. (1993). The ambiguous female: The conception of female gender in the brahminical tradition and the roles of women in India. In N. Smart & S. Thakur (Eds.), *Ethical and political dilemmas of modern India* (pp. 144–159). London: Macmillan.

Pintchman, T. (1994). *The rise of the goddess in the Hindu tradition.* Albany, NY: State University of New York Press.

Richman, P. (Ed.). (1991). *Many Ramayanas: The diversity of a narrative tradition.* Berkeley, CA: University of California Press.

Richman, P. (Ed.). (2000). *Questioning Ramayanas: A South Asian tradition.* Berkeley, CA: University of California Press.

Sarkar, T. (1994). Imagining a Hindu nation: Hindu and Muslim in Bankimchandra's later writings. *Economic and Political Weekly, 29*(39).

Sarkar, T., & Butalia, U. (Eds.). (1995). *Women and the Hindu right: A collection of essays.* New Delhi: Kali for Women.

Sax, W. S. (1991). *Mountain goddess: Gender and politics in a Himalayan pilgrimage.* Oxford: Oxford University Press.

Sunder Rajan, R. (1993). *Real and imagined women: Gender, culture, postcolonialism.* London and New York: Routledge.

Sunder Rajan, R. (1998). Is the Hindu goddess a feminist? Review of women's studies. *Economic and Political Weekly, 33*(44).

Vaudeville, C. (1982). Krishna Gopala, Radha, and the great goddess. In J. S. Hawley and D. M. Wulff (Eds.), *The divine consort: Radha and the goddesses of India* (pp. 1–12). Boston, MA: Beacon Press.

Visweswaran, K. (1994). *Fictions of feminist ethnography.* Minneapolis, MN: University of Minnesota Press.

White, D. G. (2003). *The kiss of the Yogini: Tantrik sex in its South Asian context.* Chicago, IL: University of Chicago Press.

Wulff, D. M. (1982). A Sanskrit portrait: Radha in the plays of Rupa Gosvami. In J. S. Hawley and D. M. Wulff (Eds.), *The divine consort: Radha and the goddesses of India* (pp. 27–41). Boston, MA: Beacon Press.

# 10
## GENDER, WOMEN, AND ISLAM

In this chapter, we try to look beyond the stereotype of Islam as in opposition to gender equality. At the same time, the very real problems of women who are Muslims, as expressed both by themselves and by others concerned about them, need to be explored without reservations about the dangers of stereotyping. Maybe the trick is simply to go beyond the division into "good" and "bad" Muslims, the "progressive" and "regressive" camps, and beyond the impasse that you can be either an authentic Muslim or a modern person. Maybe we could find an innate feminism in an old religion with a complex history and a vast geographical spread. There are discursive spaces and cultural legitimations that could be read into the scriptures and the law, and there is historical evidence that could be produced to make a feminist case. As with Hinduism, we do not approach Islam in this book as a fixed entity with a categorisation that has only one possible meaning or interpretation. Islam, like Hinduism, is a fluid discourse, understood and interpreted by people according to their location and purpose, and is full of diversity and conflict.

Islam, when founded by Prophet Muhammad in Arabia in the seventh century CE, made actual contributions to women's rights, even if the term was not used then. It banned female infanticide, husbands and wives were seen as holding reciprocal rights over each other, divorce and remarriage became legal, and women's rights to inherit and administer property independently of men were recognised. Scholars suggest that certain practices, such as veiling, that seem to be inherent to Islam, were partly the practice only of elite families such as the Sayyids, as a mark of honour and not of repression. Partly they were the contribution of societies such as Iran's, once it was conquered. The high position of women in the early days of Islam is also documented. The earliest convert to Islam was Khadijah, the first wife of the Prophet, an independent trader in her own right.

DOI: 10.4324/9781003393252-11

Aisha, a later and younger wife of the Prophet, was a transmitter of oral tradition and is credited with composing or preserving over two thousand *hadith*, or the sayings and acts of the Prophet. It seems fair to say that an existing patriarchy was moderated with new considerations of a woman's potential, even while some old forms of patriarchy continued and new ones were formulated.

The fact that since those early days Islamic societies have displayed an unquestioned patriarchy where women are often actively repressed is explained by some scholars as a feature of two conflicting voices within Islam regarding gender. One consists of the hierarchical regulations for society and the other, an ethical vision of egalitarianism. There are verses in the Qur'an, such as Sura 2: 228: "men are above women;" sayings of the Prophet such as "wives should prostrate themselves before their husbands;" and plenty of other evidence from the early years of Islam that testify to inequality between the sexes. Often, this is seen as a difference in the message of the Qur'an from that of its interpreters and enforcers, who were typically more authoritarian in line with their political interests. Asghar Ali Engineer in his *Rights of Women in Islam* (Engineer, 1992) phrases the two voices as a normative versus a contextual exegesis. No doubt the text must be respected, but the text that is being normatively interpreted should also be seen as historically produced. Its sociological context then becomes relevant, as does that of the contemporary interpreter. Engineer goes to great pains to show that the line between a contextualised reading, or *tafsir bi'al rai*, and an exegesis that simply suits one's convenience is a thin one, and as the history of reform in Islam has shown, a fraught one. Whereas leaders such as Maulana Abul Kalam Azad (1888–1958) have held that a Qur'anic interpretation, like any other literary or cultural product, is also a product of a specific intellectual environment, therefore destined to vary with time, other, more orthodox, 'Ulama condemn any such idea and do not favour any changes in interpretation at all. Engineer takes up many excerpts from the Qur'an and Islamic literature to exemplify how the positions taken in these conflicts may be carried to extremes and the disagreements between them range from labelling the exact same position as divine revelation, or patriarchal prejudice. An example is the following picture of an ideal woman.

> An ideal woman . . . speaks and laughs rarely and never without a reason. She never leaves the house, even to see neighbours or her acquaintance. She has no woman friends, confides in nobody, and relies only on her husband. She accepts nothing from anyone, excepting her husband and her parents. If she sees relatives, she does not meddle in their affairs. She is not treacherous, and has no faults to hide, nor wrong reasons to proffer. She does not try to entice people. If her husband shows the intention of performing conjugal rites, she is agreeable to satisfy his desires and occasionally rouses them. She always assists him in his affairs. She does not complain much and sheds few tears. She does not laugh or rejoice when she sees her husband moody or sorrowful, but shares his troubles, and cheers him up,

till he is quite content again. She does not surrender herself to anybody but her husband, even if abstinence would kill her. . . . Such a woman is cherished by everyone.

*(Engineer, 1992, p. 57)*

This picture of an "ideal woman" is the picture of a nightmare for some. On the whole, however, the Qur'an, as Jane Smith argues, could successfully be interpreted as declaring the religious and spiritual equality of men and women, and the *hadith*, with the exception of some questionable verses with weak chains of authority, also sees women and men as equal partners directed to live lives of integrity and righteousness under the law of God (Smith, 1987).

We should address two separate parts to this debate: the everyday conditions of different classes of Muslim women, including the question of the more authoritarian practices of Islamic patriarchs being resisted or challenged throughout its history, and the fact of change in Islam, the question whether the Qur'anic and Prophetic injunctions were addressed to a particular society or intended to be permanently binding. Let us look at each of these points historically: change in Islam and change in the conditions of women. After the death of the Prophet, there were sectarian dissensions within his followers. When Islam reached South Asia, it was already divided into Sunnis and Shias, and within each of these, into other divisions. The "Muslims" of South Asia were originally the Arabs but were soon followed by Turks, Afghans, Central Asians, and Iranians, and alongside the immigrants were growing numbers of converts. The ideology, whatever further shape it takes, is based for all Muslims on two things: the *shariah*, or the combination of the Qur'an and Sunnah, the two pillars of Islam, and *fiqh*, or jurisprudence, which seeks through consensus and interpretation to present the rules of life. Interpretations were the realm of a class of literati, called the *ulama*, who were professional scholars. The *ulama* are seen from the outset as different to the *sufis*, mystics with a different understanding of the Qur'an and Islamic law. The sufis were not a sect, but through the schools developed by charismatic sufi teachers, came to be present in South Asia as four sects: the Ahmadis, Chishtis, Sirhawardis, and the Naqshabandis. To a large extent, the role of the ulama in state policies, and the role of the sufis on the ground, has been responsible for changes in South Asian daily life for both Muslim men and women, especially women.

The distinctively South Asian flavour of Islam in South Asia begs two of the most pressing questions in Indian history. What were the processes involved in the spread of Islam in the subcontinent? And what was the nature of Islam in South Asia as it spread, got established, and flourished? In both of these historiographical discussions, women's role is central, albeit under the surface and in need of teasing out. There are other related debates as well that impinge on the experience of women, such as about the homogeneity of Muslims in South Asia. We will discuss these questions subsequently as related questions. Ours will be an anthropological enquiry, placed in a historical context. As with Hinduism in the previous chapter, we will look at specific issues, in this case, of women's lives in the zenana and domestic sphere, their seclusion and veiling. There are other issues that are relegated to chapters on Sultanate, Mughal, and colonial history and Partition. Modern education and nineteenth- to twentieth-century reform are discussed both here and in Chapter 7.

The spread, or acceptance, of Islam in South Asia had much to do with Sufi mystics from the thirteenth century onwards. Islamic beliefs were much more accessible to Hindus of ordinary stature when brought to them through the Sufi messages of love and intercession, practical aid, and remedy. Smith argues that

> women, squeezed out of the more formal aspects of the Islamic faith, developed their own forms of religious response ... [they] often chose intermediary forms of religious response that were apparently more appropriate to their needs and conditioning.
>
> (Smith, 1987, p. 243)

Important here is that Sufis are already seen as non-conformists with many other alternative practices. They often challenged normative gender concepts in Islam, though there were also those Sufis who did not, and boasted an unqualified patriarchy. On the other side, there were women who were themselves Sufis.

According to Asani (1988): "the overwhelming evidence indicates that the Sufis, and not the *shariah*-bound theologians and religious-lawyers, were responsible for initially spreading the message of Islam, in particular mystical Islam" (83). We could argue that not only was perhaps Sufism more suited to the Indian environment for various reasons, it was more suited to the lives and mentalities of *women* in South Asia. Sufis composed poetry and sayings in the vernaculars, oriented towards lower class and peasant lifestyles and idioms, even using established folk genres, such as *doha, chaupai, barahmasa, chakki-nama*, and other popular song genres. Many of these were sung also by women, and some exclusively so. We could say that women were active agents in the spread of Islam by being primary converts to the message of Islam, and being mediators and transmitters of the message to their families and communities. Eaton suggests the same in his story of the spread of Islam in Bengal, and elsewhere (Eaton, 1996, 1974–5).

In her book-length study called *In Amma's Healing Room* (2006), Joyce Flueckiger describes a Sufi *piriyanama*, or the wife of a Sufi *pir* (teacher) today. This woman, a professional healer who cannot (she says) officially be a Sufi *pir* herself, has hundreds of clients of all backgrounds who come to her for physical and psychological succour. What she does today – or did, in the recent decades of Flueckiger's research, being now deceased – is a close version of the ways in which Sufis worked as spiritual and worldly mentors, guides, therapists, doctors and other kinds of advisers over the centuries. In many cases, women could be revered as Sufi saints themselves. A very early saint is Rabi'a al-Adawiyya, or Rabi'a of Basra, who could be said to have transformed a more sombre asceticism into love mysticism. A slave girl who was set free, Rabi'a is the subject of many legends, mostly about her miracles, her sayings re: the immanence of God, and her utter poverty and abstinence. The Indian Chishti *pir* Qutbuddin Bakhtiyar Kaki said about her in 1235,

> When afflicted with pain, she was happy and said: 'Today my Friend was thinking of me!,' and should she not receive such affliction on any given day, she wept and said: 'What have I done wrong, that He doesn't think of me?'
>
> *(Schimmel, 1997, p. 37)*

We know of women saints in South Asia, such as the disciples of Fariduddin Ganj-i Shakar (d. 1265 CE) and several women alluded to in various discussions of Sufis in Northwestern India. In Sind there is a lore of the religiosity of women and the tombs of female saints to whom one may turn to for succour. Related to these in spirituality are other women who were scholars in their own right. Bibi Rasti (d. c. 1620) from Burhanpur was a Persian expert. Fatima Jahanara, a daughter of Shah Jahan (r. 1628–58), was initiated into Sufism by Mian Mir, a saint from Lahore, whose own sister Bibi Jamal Khatun was a saint also. Jahanara wrote as well as ordered the writing, commentary, and translation of many works, keeping loyalty mostly to the Chishti order of the Sufis. Her two nieces Zen un-Nisa and Zinat un-Nisa were also mystics, poets, and patrons of mosques.

Sufism did remain an ascetic movement, challenging worldly power with spiritual power, but further adapted itself in South Asia towards love and mysticism in locally inflected ways. Poetry that addresses the Prophet Mohammad, or God, Allah, or imams, and other spiritual leaders, has been produced in various South Asian languages, including Hindi, Awadhi, Urdu, Dakhani, Gujarati, and Bengali. Scholars have shown several important features of local Islamic practices. One is how the symbolism of the woman devoted to and yearning for her beloved is used to stand for the soul searching for Allah, typically through a teacher. The *ginan* (song of *gyan*, or wisdom) and *git* (song of praise) sung by the Nizari Ismailis, composed from the fourteenth century to the present, reflect this, including the medieval Indian trope of the *virahini*, or abandoned lover, who expresses a painful longing, or *viraha*, for her beloved – that is, the soul addressing the imam. One composition goes:

> O friend, I have prepared for you a bed of incomparable beauty . . . .
> (Lying) next to the Beloved, overwhelmed by love,
> I forget all of my sorrows.
>
> *(Asani, 2009, p. 56)*

A category of folk song that is little known is the *chakki* (grindstone) and the *charka* (spinning wheel) song, both kinds of which, as the names suggest, were sung by women in the course of their work. These songs are Islamic in two ways.

First, they establish the same connection as do *gits* and *ginanas* between the singer and her teacher, the Prophet or Allah. Second, there is a conceptual connection between the work of grinding or spinning, and the creation of the world and God's presence in the world. Such a song goes:

> The *chakki*'s handles resembles *alif*, which means Allah
> And the axle is Muhammad.
> (Eaton, 2009, pp. 90–91)

The best known of the many regional genres of mystical poetry is the genre called *qawwali*, composed over the centuries in several North Indian languages sprinkled with Arabic and Persian, expressing love, praise, and longing, including in their verses excerpts from the Qur'an or *hadith* as well as more abstract concepts. The verse below has been discussed by Hyder and Pietevich as part of a qawwali that is representative of the genre in its form and ideas. The beloved is being addressed by a female lover who is confident that she has seen through all the tricks of the beloved (sex unspecified), while asking the difficult questions of what/who actually the beloved is, meaning who/what Allah or Mohammad is.

> I've come to know your every gesture . . .
> I've figured out your ways and means, haven't I, my dear?
> (Hyder & Petievich, 2009, p. 97)

The gendered nature of Sufi poetry is rather explicit. The soul is typically presented as a *virahini*, a female lover away from her beloved, perhaps a waiting bride. This is an echo of the folk poetry sung in the woman's voice of the village woman longing for her lover/husband's return. It is also an echo of the many renditions of the love of Radha and Krishna and of the Punjabi and Sindhi romances of Hir-Ranjha, Sohni-Mewar, and Sassui-Punhun. In each case, the woman becomes the seeking soul of Islam who must return "home," be true to the primordial covenant, and overcome lesser attractions and temptations to finally find peace. The physical attributes of the heroine and the external quest or longing for the lover become translated to a quest within the soul, all the time located in a familiar landscape of sand, sea, rivers, birds, flowers, and skies. As Asani puts it:

> By drawing extensively on metaphors and symbols connected with the experience of women, especially their experience of love, the Sufis could convey their idea of the soul's relationship to God in a manner which even the most illiterate segments of society could understand. In addition, they also had at their disposal the whole repertoire of inherited forms derived from the range of activities common in rural life – ploughing, sowing, hunting, milking, planting, and so on.
> *(Asani, 2009, p. 88)*

However, there are shifts within the heterosexual imagery of male–female love that is both spiritual and worldly. There is a prevalence of homoerotic poetry, music, and confessional writing in which the lover and the beloved are both male. When God is directly addressed by a male lover, he is pictured as an adorable boy. Apparently, the Prophet saw God as such, and this "picture of the beloved with his hair escaping from his headgear is one of the most popular images in Urdu and Persian poetry at least till the middle of the nineteenth century" (Vanita & Kidwai, 2008, p. 129). Salim Kidwai talks about this as a historical development starting in the thirteenth century with a masculine culture of the streets, and in the next century with a flourishing book trade that cut across classes. Men congregated at taverns, brothels, and shrines. The wine servers and singers were typically male and present-day images of the *saqi* (wine server) and entertainer as always a woman is wrong. The evidence of this homoerotic culture, male brothels, and prolific homoerotic poetry goes against the grain of the Qur'an and *hadith* that define homosexuality as a crime. Severe penalties were prescribed for offenders, including in the Hanafi School, which was the predominant Islamic legal school in India. These legal provisions, however, could rarely be implemented, and there was dispute throughout regarding the severity of the punishment needed. "Compared to Christian Europe, trials and punishments for homosexuality are rare in the history of Muslim peoples in medieval times" (Vanita & Kidwai, 2008, p. 129).

By making a human being's love of, and quest for, God equivalent to the yearning of a woman for her beloved, Sufi poets, just like some Hindu and bhakti peers, managed to make their religious preaching attractive and even hypnotic and irresistible. The core importance of gender in this strategy reflects the centrality of gender in all South Asian schemes of thought rather than the importance of actual, living women. More practically, the shrines of Sufi saints and teachers are beloved places of periodic pilgrimage. In a typical North Indian city, there would be scores of such shrines and on a designated day of the week, women gather there, sometimes with their families, to get peace and blessings, socialise, and pray. This saint veneration has been the target of criticism and reform by religious leaders for centuries and continues to be today. However, while some women, as well as men, do get converted through the preaching of religious leaders to a more formally pristine Islam, the vast majority of the Muslims of South Asia, and predominantly women, continue to exercise their choice of religious practice by seeking out and paying affectionate reverence to mediators such as Sufi saints.

Thus, the Sufi voice is predominantly feminine, and there are actual Sufi-esque female characters, such as Laila of the Laila-Majnun duo, or Hir of Hir-Ranjha fame, *and* there have been female Sufi teachers much admired by men acolytes. Performative genres, such as of qawwali, however, are male-dominated. The female version is described as *sufiana-kalam*, or the solo performance at shrines. Abbas (2002) describes her interview with Kubra, an established *sufiana-kalam* performer in Hyderabad, Pakistan, in which Kubra expresses reluctance to name herself a musician. While the concept of the female voice as the best approach to a mystical devotion is accepted by men, the actual performance of poetry and music in public space by women is not. Therefore, women might perform apologetically, and at any rate perform only in private and local contexts, while qawwali has become popular on the world stage by male performers. The notion of

> shame (izzat) is a concern for men, and they are silent about their womenfolk singing . . . this is evident . . . when she [Kubra] admits that she is ashamed to sing because her husband will not let her do it. Her husband has a visible public position at Sind University. Thus, if she sings for money as a professional musician, the couple's trades will not blend socially.
> *(Abbas, 2002, p. 51)*

Here we come back to the one axis of sexuality, which I argue lies at the heart of women's confinement in *parda*. For a woman to sing publicly, she would perforce be present before men, including unrelated males and strangers. This is precisely where the "shame" to the family or community comes in. We will see later in the chapter how qawwali, as well as other genres such as *marsiya*, or the songs of lamentation about the tragedy at Karbala, and *ghazal*s, or Urdu love and mystical poetry, were performed by courtesans. The performance in public, including the *presence* in public, is what marked the loose woman without shame. She was different from the pure, secluded woman respected by males by being without the protection of the men of her community. Courtesans, from what we know from fiction, film, and putative memoirs (Amrohi, 1972; Hadi, 1996), tried to improve their standing by privatising themselves. Interestingly, a woman may work in public if her husband, or other male protectors, gives her permission to do so. In Flueckiger's ethnography, the healer Amma, who earns over four times as much as her husband, who in fact does not know Arabic or her specific written healing practices, confirms again and again that she does what she does because her husband has permitted her to. Her own daughter is not thus permitted by her son-in-law and, therefore, both the men and women informants agree, there can be no question of her working as Amma does.

When men, and some women also, discuss why women may not be sufi *pirs* as men may, they cite biology as the reason. Women are polluted during the time of menstruation and childbirth: they may not conduct *namaz*, observe the Ramadan fast, go to shrines, or participate in various festival gatherings, such as at Gyarhawin Sharif. Many informants, as reported by Flueckiger, would say that gender is the most important difference in humans. "There are only two castes [jati]: men and women" (Flueckiger, 2006, p. 137). She adds that this is a statement made more often by women than by men. Her own primary informant, Amma, is quite clear about what characterises the jati of woman – and jati means "classification," rather than "caste," in the sense of the English word. It is trouble, pain, and suffering, things that men can turn away from and not be affected by. At the same time, Amma herself does "a man's work" and explains that it is *personality* and not biology that decides that. Her own daughters or daughters-in-law could not do it, but Indira Gandhi could. The picture suggested is of superior energy, planning and focus, where none of the housework or mothering is necessarily neglected, but the public work is done in an impressive way on top of it all. However, the reality is that the time for housework has to be reduced, and many women choose to remain busy at their women's work, and *cite* their being busy as the reason they are obliged to be different to men.

A second constraint, apart from menstruation, on the work of women is the *parda* or seclusion they must observe. Now, at first sight, this seems to be a restriction that exists across the board for Muslim women of all classes and communities. To some extent this is true. However, *because* "woman" is also a symbol of the community, when reform movements became popular in the nineteenth and twentieth centuries with both Muslim and Hindu groups, the upwardly mobile, modernising classes were keen to weaken *parda* bonds. Women of the new middle classes, *sharif* or *bhadra* women (cultured, gentlefolk), should now preferably have an education and be able to selectively appear in public. A new Muslim woman was imagined who was alive to the challenge to Islam from the West, from secularism and other religions, and from science and modernity, and engaged in a project of educational and reformist work chiefly through spiritual leadership. Hazrat Inayat Khan (1882–1927) formally initiated women as *murshid* or sufi guides. Khwaja Hasan Nizami (1878–1955) in his prolific writing addressed to women claimed that his wife Laila Banu was wiser and more spiritually adept than he was.

"Reform" in Islam has had a variety of meanings and consisted of both modernisation and reversal to a newly defined or objectified tradition. Together with opposing women's seclusion, there was a call for more advanced religiosity by Muslim women. The book of advice called *Bihishti Zewar*, or "The Jewellery of Paradise" by Maulana Ashraf Ali Thanawi (1863–1943), originally published in 1904 and many times since, was perhaps the most popular publication of its time. It advised its female readers in detail about how to conduct their lives, taking them step by step through the different pathways their lives in the zenana would follow. Addressed to middle- and upper-class women, it presumed that women had means, leisure, choice, and the consciousness to reflect on themselves as important and as subjects of change. Equally, it presumed that the world was dictated by men and that women were both protected and controlled by men. If looked at in a dichotomous way, the book is certainly conservative and would have no purchase with a truly modernising young woman of the twentieth century who did not wish to conform to the shackles of religion and custom. If looked at with more imagination regarding the subjecthood it presumes in its readers, and the coaching it gives them not only to develop a love and sensitivity towards themselves (both body and soul) but to think more intelligently and contextually about their Islamic identities, Thanavi's book comprises a step forwards in modernity: in subject-formation, rationality, and a certain scientism.

That some of this rationality and science may not agree with the Western version of rationality or science, is, as Francis Robinson (2008) in his discussion of South Asian reform points out, only to say that "modernity" may come in various guises.

More concretely, what exactly did different religious reformers of the nineteenth and twentieth centuries want for Muslim women? Colonial control and the loss of authority over their political, and gradually, their civic and social, power meant a stock-taking for Muslims in eighteenth- and early nineteenth-century India. In this, both the *ulama*, or religious leaders, and the Sufi *pirs*, or spiritual leaders, sought to set out new paths. The range of reform movements included those known as Barelwi, Deobandi, Firangi Mahelli, and Ahl-e-Hadith. Ahmad Raza Khan of Bareilly (1856–1921) founded the "Barelwi" sect, claiming it to be a reform towards individual decision making for an ethical life. That Barelwis believe in intercession, in the power of relics and saints, and in the live power of the graves of holy men makes them open to accusation by other sects of anti-reform and anti-Islam. In South Asian small towns and villages, Barelwis are in a majority. For many, this goes together with the poverty and illiteracy of the majority of Muslims. In all these characteristics, women share equally with men, and perhaps bear a larger brunt of the weight of poverty, illiteracy, "backwardness," and being harangued by strict ulama for their unreformed existence.

Maulana Muhammad Qasim Nanautawi (1833–1880) and Rashid Ahmad Gangohi (1829–1905) set up a seminary in 1867 in the town of Deoband, the graduates and ideology of which came to be known as "Deobandi." Deobandi stands for the reform of practices by Muslims that are understood as derived from the history and context of the Islamic presence in South Asia, such as the visit to shrines or the prayers for intercession at the graves of *pirs*. The Deoband seminary itself was modern in most respects, with a formal management, staff, curricula, examinations, publications, libraries, and awards. It was not against English and a modern education and presented itself as an alternative to that. It was vastly influential. Because of its stress on the undisturbed path of the Qur'an and hadith, however, it made less impact on Muslim women than on men. Insofar as all madrasas either were founded by one sect or another or came to affiliate themselves with one sect or another, girls' madrasas too, as they proliferated, belonged mostly to the Deobandi or the Barelwi sect.

The Firangi Mahal was an idea and a place dating from the end of the seventeenth century when a teacher's family was given a European's (or *firangi*, literally, foreigner's) house in Lucknow to live in. The family developed a new syllabus of study called the Dars-e-Naizamiyya, which came to be respected as a norm of modern Islamic studies, and used in many madrasas, including girls' ones. Its main characteristic was its high level of challenge and excellence. The fourth sect or *maslak*, Ahl-e-Hadith, or "people of the hadith," was founded by Syed Nazir Husain Dehlawi (1805–1902) and Siddiq Hasan Khan (1832–1890), among others. It put emphasis even more than the Deobandis on the primacy of the Qur'an and hadith and the non-tolerance of all interpretations, debates, and popular practices.

Although there were individual differences, the main Islamic reformers were anti-Sufi to different degrees. We have argued that Sufi approaches, broadly speaking, were compatible to women's socialisation and circumstances, and, accordingly, we find that the main reformers of nineteenth- to twentieth-century South Asia were not favourably inclined to women's culture. Either women's culture was coarse and in danger of adulteration, if not already adulterated, by Hindu practices, and needed to be guarded and purified. Or it was in danger of contamination from the West, and women needed to be kept closer to the patriarchal norms. There *were* other reformers, including women reformers, who could see beyond dichotomies and pay attention to the material reality of women's bodies, lives, and spaces. Rokeya Sakhawat Hossain (1880–1932) was one such. Known chiefly for her educational work, she wrote evocatively on the problem of *parda* and seclusion, and also advocated reform in ritual and religious practices. She was clear in her vision that the inequality of gender was caused by "excess," both an excess of ritualism as many reformers claimed and an excess of spiritual zeal among reformers, overwhelmingly male. She writes:

> My sisters, you see for yourself that these religious books are nothing but rules fabricated by men. The ancient sages have said all these things. Had there been a woman sage you might have seen the opposite. Some might say, "Why bring in religion when talking of social customs?" I would say, "It is 'religion' that has made the chains of our slavery stronger and stronger. Men are lording it over women in the name of 'religion.'" So I have been forced to bring religion in. Let the god-fearing and the pious forgive me.

Rokeya Hossain wanted to carve out a new, reformed practice of equality for women, where they could, within their own circumstances of home and kitchen, on the basis of their own questioning and intelligence, carve out a more religiously rigorous sphere of themselves. There is evidence that in her later years, Rokeya Hossain resigned herself to the admission that the majority of her female readers were comfortable with their housewifely existence and did not seek to go out of a narrow path towards more striving for equality with men. She now makes more conventional arguments about the value of education for girls, including for botany and chemistry, in making better housewives. She says openly:

> Anyway, if women do not understand my words about spiritual equality then let us not talk about high ambitions or any elevated things at all. I will ask today: 'What is your aim in life?' Probably you will reply in unison: 'To be a good housewife.'

The reform of women came to revolve mostly around education. We must be careful here to not repeat a linear story. According to this narrative, the poor, secluded women in both Hindu and Muslim communities were deprived of education and freedom, and it was the coming of colonial and missionary education that gave a leg up to their progressive freedom and enlightenment. Research shows that in the nineteenth century, several overt and hidden forms of patriarchy increased for women and subtle shifts took place in their situation that did not necessarily mean more power or freedom. Let us re-create the story of education for women.

In the early colonial period, women were, like most men, not formally educated. They married early and became part of the new household of their husbands and of a woman's world. In this world, senior women ruled, and their decisions influenced the lives of younger women as well as children and, to some extent, young men. Women were seen as exercising power. When widowed, and if propertied, they were expected to exercise financial control as well. The importance of the harem, zenana, or domestic space was not disputed, nor was a clear distinction drawn between the inside and outside, the domestic and public.

An important point is the role played by another kind of woman, the courtesan, who was important at life-cycle ceremonies as well as a paramour and teacher of aesthetics to the elite males of precolonial societies. Even as we know about their social presence, we have very few records of the experience of courtesans, isolated instances such as *Umrao Jan Ada* (Hadi, 1996) aside. Umrao Jan, who putatively dictated her memoirs to the author Mirza Mohammad Hadi Ruswa, was a courtesan of mid-nineteenth-century Lucknow. In the book she/Hadi describes her professionalism, her independence, but also her emotional fragility when she wants commitment from her lovers and is denied it, or tries to be accepted in her natal family and is refused. The historian Margrit Pernau explains evocatively how the question of this model of love is related to the question of the expression of love, as in the poetic form called the *ghazal*.

Love is an emotion hard to study or to analyse – at best, we could approach the expressions of love and restrict ourselves almost totally to a linguistic analysis. The ghazal was written most often in Urdu, and occasionally in *rekhti*, or a woman's version of Urdu (originally called *rekhta*). The ghazal is mired in a world of metaphors of figurative language, the absorption in which is largely the pleasure of composing and reciting this kind of poetry. The love is forever unrequited, and when reciprocal, ends in tragedy. Ghalib, one of the most famous poets of the time, explains, "The ideal of a lover is to match Majnun. His Laila died before him, and your mistress died before you; in fact you excel him." He is here addressing his friend Mihr whose lover had died (Pernau, 2013, p. 141). Indeed, often the subject being addressed as beloved was sex-neutral and deliberately kept ambiguous, perhaps to heighten the experience of desire.

As we have already seen in the case of vernacular poetry, the ghazal was also ambiguous in its levels of discourse, between the mystical, a soul addressing a Supreme Soul or God, and the worldly, a man and his beloved. Even here, the actual, living woman was unimportant. Some women did compose poetry, and courtesans all performed the poetry and were much celebrated, some reaching the heights of fame and autonomy, and in theory, at least, the poetry could be said to pay high compliments to women. However, women were not typically the *subject* of the poems. The male poet experiencing emotions, revelling in metaphors, suffering, living, and dying, was the subject. Ghazals were poetry composed by men for a male audience, in which women figured only as tropes, as objects of desire, and as the medium of expression of emotions.

Urdu, in the changing political scenario of the late nineteenth and early twentieth centuries, came to be seen as a coquettish female in its battle with a more robust Hindi. However, insofar as Urdu came to stand for Muslims, it is but a reflection of the tendency in patriarchal societies to always feminise the weaker party, or the party that is sought to be proved to be inferior.

In the absence of formal education, and in their confinement within the walls of the women's quarters, Muslim women, exactly like their Hindu counterparts, did not read or write as the males in upper-class families did. Their language has been described as *begmati zaban*, or women's speech, or the speech of the zenana. The *begam* refers to an *ashraf*, or cultured, upper-class woman. However, the language and accompanying beliefs were shared by upper- and lower-class women, the latter playing a direct role in the former's lives as providers of various services, from domestic work to supply of every kind of provision, including crafts to entertainment.

What took place in the second half of the nineteenth century has been described as an Islamicisation of everyday life and of women (Pernau, 2013, pp. 148–149). Women's culture, with its own spaces, speech, consumption, activities, leisure, and meanings, was now targeted as backward, ill-advised, and in need of reform. Exactly as we see women's magazines for Hindu women doing, the new publications for Muslim women harangued them to try to become a match for their educated, civilised menfolk. In particular, they had to become converted to more classical and rigid versions of Islam and shun any trace of "pollution," such as demonstrated in visits to shrines, supplications to saints, search for popular medical remedies, and an overall casualness towards the boundaries of Islam.

The historical literature on the subject is quite clear: these reformist moves that sought to re-make women in a new mould were not about elevating the position of women *qua* women. It was *men's* identities as normal, progressive, robustly masculine, virile, and a match for their colonial masters that were created through an insistence on the reform and improvement of women. The reform was brought about by Muslim men, in a total parallel to that being introduced by Hindu men in their own communities. Similarly, in both worlds, women themselves were complicit in the reform. None of them spoke up as far as we know, against the new disciplining of the household, of women's time, women's energies, women's ways, and women's choices. They were supposed to worship their husbands and to consider their man second only to God. Begam Shah Jahan (r. 1868–1901), the ruler of Bhopal, wrote about and publicly introduced the new reforms, and she was crystal clear that none of the common women's practices (saints, shrines, cures, etc.) was permissible. Only belief in the Qur'an and hadith was, followed by men and their rules.

An explanation, if one needs to be found, as to why women themselves did not want more autonomy and were complacent about their new makeover as *better* women than before, but clearly second and inferior to men, could be the following. In a situation of an iron-tight patriarchy, where the state, its different arms, its various voices, its personas, simply everything, supported each other in declaring the control and superiority of men to be inviolable, a woman might not have choices (apart from lunacy and suicide). She might then exercise choice, as she sees it, to opt for the "new" as against the "old" patriarchy. That she cannot quite see, in the blurred picture that history presents while one lives through it, that the "new," dominated by the husband and senior males, is partially at least more pernicious than the "old," dominated more by senior females and women's culture, is not surprising. That she could not deconstruct colonialism to be the pact that it was between ruling men and ruled men who themselves had limited choices is also not a surprise. What we might want to end with is the thought that the women *did* choose, and if they chose what in hindsight is still subservience, the feminist adage that choice is the point, not the correctness of the choice, should still stand. Insofar, as Pernau points out, citing Walsh, they learnt to read and write, certain gates were now thrown open to them that would lead them in new directions in the long run.

So much for the ashraf women or the *bhadramahila*. Women of the labouring classes, such as artisans, for instance, the silk weavers of Banaras, were not initially targeted by reformers in a similar way because such was not the community identity of the society they belonged to. But with time, and the growing influence of the seminaries at Deoband and Nadwa, they too adopted a posture in which women had to be recast and remade in a new image. As the whole community struggled for status and viability in a modernising state, women were explicitly the bearer of the community's burden. They were accused of backwardness; whenever false practices were mentioned, they were described as "women's foibles." Alongside, women's inferior status in terms of reproductive rights, inheritance, divorce, education, and professional work continued, ensuring a structural "backwardness" that was certainly not voluntarily constructed by them.

## Bibliography

Abbas, S. B. (2002). *The female voice in Sufi ritual: Devotional practices of Pakistan and India.* Austin: University of Texas Press.

Ahmad, A. (1964). *Studies in Islamic culture in the Indian environment.* London: Oxford University Press.

Ahmad, A. (1969). *An intellectual history of Islam in India.* Edinburgh: Edinburgh University Press.

Ahmad, I. (1966). The *ashraf-ajlaf* dichotomy in Muslim Social Structure in India. *IESHR, 3,* 268–278.

Ahmad, I. (1976). *Family, Kinship and marriage among Indian Muslims.* Delhi: Manohar.
Ahmad, I. (1978). *Caste and social stratification among Muslims in India.* Delhi: Manohar.
Ahmad, I. (1981). *Ritual and religion among Muslims in India.* Delhi: Manohar.
Ahmad, I. (1983). *Modernization and social change among Muslims in India.* Delhi: Manohar.
Ahmad, I. (2008). Cracks in the 'mightiest fortress': Jamaat-e-Islami's changing discourse on women author(s). *Modern Asian Studies, 42*(2/3), 549–575.
Alavi, S. (2008). *Islam and healing: Loss and recovery of an Indo-Muslim medical tradition, 1600–1900.* Bassington: Palgrave Macmillan.
Amin, S. N. (1997). The early Muslim Bhadramahila: The growth of learning and creativity, 1876 to 1939. In B. Ray (Ed.), *From the seams of history: Essays on Indian women* (pp. 107–148). Delhi: Oxford University Press.
Amin, S. N. (2000). *The world of Muslim women in colonial Bengal, 1876–1939. Social, economic and political studies of the middle East and Asia* (Vol. 55). Leiden: Brill.
Amrohi, K. (1972). Writer, director, producer, *Pakeezah.*
Asani, A. S. (1988). Sufi Poetry in the Folk tradition of Indo-Pakistan. *Religion & Literature, 20*(1), 81–94.
Asani, A. S. (1991). *The Buj Niranjan, an Ismaili Mystical Poem.* Cambridge, MA: Harvard Middle East Center.
Asani, A. S. (1993a). Bridal symbolism in the Ismaili *ginan* literature. In R. Herrera & R. L. Salinger (Eds.), *Mystics of the book: Themes, topics and typologies.* New York: Peter Lang.
Asani, A. S. (1993b). The Ismaili *ginans* as devotional literature. In S. Mcgregor (Ed.), *Devotional literature in South Asia.* Cambridge: Cambridge University Press.
Asani, A. S. (2009). Satpanthi Ismaili songs to Hazrat Ali and the Imams. In B. D. Metcalf (Ed.), *Islam in practice in South Asia* (pp. 48–62). Princeton, NJ: Princeton University Press.
Eaton, R. (1974–75). Sufi Folk literature and the expansion of Islam. *History of Religions, 14*(2), 115–127.
Eaton, R. (1978). *Sufis of Bijapur.* Princeton, NJ: Princeton University Press.
Eaton, R. (1996). *The rise of Islam and the Bengal frontier, 1204–1760.* Berkeley, CA: University of California Press.
Eaton, R. (2009). Women's grinding and spinning songs of devotion in the late medieval deccan. In B. D. Metcalf (Ed.), *Islam in practice in South Asia.* Princeton, NJ: Princeton University Press.
Engineer, A. A. (1992). *The rights of women in Islam.* New York: St Martin's Press.
Flueckiger, J. (2006). *In Amma's healing room: Gender and vernacular Islam in South India.* Bloomington, IN: Indiana University Press.
Friedmann, Y. (1986). Islamic thought in relation to the Indian context. *Purusartha, 9,* 79–91.
Hadi, M. M. R. (1996). *Umrao Jan Ada* (Trans. D. Mathews). Delhi: Rupa Publications.
Hossain, R. S. (1988). *Sultana's dream and selections from the secluded ones.* New York: The Feminist Press.
Hyder, S. A., & Petievich, C. (2009). Qawwali songs of praise. In B. D. Metcalf (Ed.), *Islam in South Asia in practice.* Berkeley: University of California Press.
Lawrence, B. (1984). Early Indo-Muslim saints and conversion. In Y. Friedmann (Ed.), *Islam in Asia* (2 vols). Jerusalem: Magnes.
Metcalf, B. D. (1992). *Perfecting women: Maulana Ashraf Ali Thanawi's Bihishti Zewar.* Delhi: Oxford University Press.

Metcalf, B. D. (2000). Review of Sonia Nishat Amin. *Pacific Affairs, 73*(3), 464–465.
Metcalf, B. D. (Ed.). (2009). *Islam in South Asia in practice.* Princeton, NJ: Princeton University Press.
Minault, G. (1983). Hali's Majlis-un-Nisa: Purdah and women power in nineteenth century. In M. Israel & N. K. Wagle (Eds.), *Islamic society and culture: Essays in honor of Prof Aziz Ahmad* (pp. 39–49). Delhi: Manohar.
Minault, G. (1986). *Voices of silence. Khwaja Altaf Husain Halis Majalis un Nissa and Chup ki Dad.* Delhi: Oxford University Press.
Minault, G. (1990). Sayyid Mumtaz Ali and 'Huquq un-Niswan': An advocate of women's rights in Islam in the late nineteenth century. *Modern Asian Studies, 24*(1), 147–172.
Minault, G. (1998). *Secluded scholars. Women's education and Muslim social reform in colonial India.* Delhi: Oxford University Press.
Naim, C. M. (2001). Transvestic words? The Rekhti in Urdu. *Annual of Urdu Studies, 16*(Pt. 1), 3–26.
Oesterheld, C. (2004). Islam in contemporary South Asia: Urdu and Muslim women. *Oriente Moderno, Nuova Serie. Anno, 23*(84, Nr 1), 217–243.
Osella, F., & Osella, C. (2008). Introduction: Islamic reformism in South Asia. *Modern Asian Studies, 42*(2/3), 247–257.
Pernau, M. (2013). *Ashraf into middle classes: Muslims in nineteenth-century Delhi.* Delhi: Oxford University Press.
Raman, V. (2010). *The warp and the weft: Community and gender identity among Banaras weavers.* New Delhi: Routledge.
Robinson, F. (2008). Islamic reform and modernities in South Asia. *Modern Asian Studies, 42*(2/3), 259–281.
Roy, A. (1983). *The Islamic syncretistic tradition in Bengal.* Princeton, NJ: Princeton University Press.
Ruswa, M. H. See Hadi, M. M. R.
Sangari, K. (1999). *Politics of the possible. Essays on gender, history, narratives, colonial English.* Delhi: Tulika.
Schimmel, A. (1975). *Mystical dimensions of Islam.* Chapel Hill, NC: University of North Carolina Press.
Schimmel, A. (1982). *As through a veil: Mystical poetry in Islam.* New York: Columbia University Press.
Schimmel, A. (1983). A nineteenth-century anthology of Urdu Poetesses. In *Islamic society and culture: Essays in honor of Aziz Ahmad.* Delhi: Oxford University Press.
Schimmel, A. (1985). *And Muhammad is his messenger: The veneration of the prophet in Islamic Piety.* Chapel Hill, NC: University of North Carolina Press.
Schimmel, A. (1997). *My soul is a woman: The feminine in Islam* (Trans. S. H. Ray). New York: Continuum.
Smith, J. I. (1987). Islam. In A. Sharma (Ed.), *Women in world religions* (pp. 235–250). Albany, NY: SUNY Press.
Vanita, R., & Kidwai, S. (Eds.). (2008). *Same-sex Love in India: A literary history.* Delhi: Penguin Books.

# 11
# SEXUALITY, FILMS, AND THE ARTS

At the heart of the conundrum of a woman's relative inferiority lies the problem of how to comprehend and thus control the dangers of her sexuality – and thus how to formulate its very discourse. It may not have been always so, but Sherry Ortner shows that since the emergence of settled societies and the emergence of states and social stratification, the control of women's sexuality becomes obsessive (Ortner, 1996: chapter 3). It has been so in every society, and it has been so in India as well. According to the high texts, the beginning of a woman's menstruation cycle (*ritu*, or appropriate season) indicates her sexual maturity. In the past, and to some extent even today, the parents' duty is to make marriage plans for their daughter before this point. The couple's sexual consummation, or at least co-habitation, can begin at this point. This cycle is understood to be not only physiological but also psychological. Women are supposed to be themselves desirous of love and sex upon sexually "maturing," which is how the onset of menses is looked upon. A deprecatory term is coined in the *Ramayana* for the man who will not go to his wife when she wants him, and folk songs by the scores sing of the sexually obsessed wife or lover waiting because presumably the "time" is right. On the other side, kings such as Yayati justify their sexual transgressions with the argument that the woman's invitation in her *ritu* period would have been a sin to refuse (Meyer, 1930/1953, pp. 220–222). Yayati's tale, originally told in the Bhagavat Puran, may also be regarded as a tale of a man's lust, rather than one of a woman's choice, and the spin about a woman's invitation as merely a man's excuse. At the same time, the tale also reveals women's agency in its frank discussion of competing ambitions between the king's wives.

The epics, *Mahabharata* and *Ramayana* both dated approximately around fourth century BCE to fourth century CE, have a complex discussion of sexuality. Two important stories in the *Mahabharata* are of Kunti and Satyavati. Kunti is given a

DOI: 10.4324/9781003393252-12

boon (because she is an excellent server to a *rishi*) that allows her to call down a god. Young and curious, she calls down Surya, the Sun-God. He comes in all his blazing glory and is ready to sleep with her, which is the meaning of the boon. She is afraid and asks him to go away. He convinces her, however, that she will remain a virgin and that he is not to be trifled with: once called, he must satisfy himself. So Kunti becomes the mother of his son. To get rid of the unwanted baby, she abandons him. Her maidenhead is restored, and her secret kept. The son, Karna, grows up adopted in a loving home and becomes a fabled warrior, but Kunti is denied the joys of motherhood towards this son.

Satyavati is an adopted daughter of a fisherman and smells of fish, even as she is irresistibly attractive. She is persuaded by a sage to have a quick, secret love-making session. She will remain a virgin, he promises, and, in addition, her wish of becoming sweet-smelling is granted. Satyavati, still a maiden, and now fragrant as well, has a son, Vyasa, whom she also abandons, like Kunti. She later attracts King Santanu, and becomes his Queen, with a promise that her own progenies will rule in future. Because her sons die childless, she invites Vyasa to father children with her daughters-in-law. Her ambition that her bloodline will rule is fulfilled. Satyavati is typically discussed as a "self-made" woman who knew her mind and could strategise to fulfil her desires. Both she and Kunti use their sexuality as weapons to strategise and respond, bearing children out of wedlock whom they leave,

Important to emphasise, however, is the weight put on virginity, the preservation of which is a condition in both the cases above when giving in to sexual advances – and this may be a later interpolation in the *Mahabharata*, meaning that the preoccupation with virginity grew as tribal states evolved into kingdoms. As we saw in Chapter 7, "caste" is also a name for bloodline, and the bloodline can only be claimed to be pure if the mother's sexuality is trustworthy. Even when the Epic and Purana heroines act with the volition of their own desire, they mention the control that they live within, such as of the father or husband. They are brave in bearing children extra-maritally but practical in keeping them secret – and in requesting boons of restored virginity. And yet, there is no "punishment" in the larger sense. The illegitimate son of Satyavati is Vyasa, the very author of the *Mahabharata*. The illegitimate son of Kunti is Karna, the most heroic of the heroes of the *Mahabharata*. Indeed, it is the ravishers of female chastity who are punished in both epics. Draupadi is sexually harassed in the *Mahabharata* and swears revenge on the Kauravas for doing so, which she gets. The whole battle of the *Ramayana* is the fruit of Ravana's kidnapping of Sita. In the *Mahabharata*, the faithful wives, Damayanti and Savitri are ideal types, but significantly, they are women who can use their wits to achieve their ends of a continuing consummated marriage. Other important stories include that of Rishiringya in the *Mahabharata*, a story of how sexuality may be discovered by a child brought up in the isolation of a forest, deliberately away from society, and how sexuality may then be performed, and cleverly domesticated.

With all the meandering stories and levels upon levels of meanings within mythology and the epics, scholars agree on a few broad implications of sex. One, that women desire it as much as men and are as importunate when they do. Two, nature plays a role: both flora and fauna are holistically expressive of sexual desires and responsive to them. Three, discipline is enjoined in several ways, including through marriage. Coveting another's wife, especially the teacher's, is never proposed. The *Kamasutra* of Vatsyayana is addressed to the young aristocratic urban man, but in the techniques it proposes for sexual satisfaction, the advice it gives, and the philosophy it rests on, it presumes equal sexual interest on the part of the woman. In their translation, Doniger and Kakar (2009) describe how women are attributed choice, will, and even a quirky personality by the author. Being didactic, the *Kamasutra* is difficult to read as true description, which is the case as well with the narrative and stories of the epics and Puranas. We can only read them as discourse, as articulations of power, and the cultural grammar of a society.

In order to understand the layers of complementary meaning of sexuality for men, we must take a step back into the two ontological realities of Hinduism. One is *purusha*, literally, man, which also has the meaning "spirit" or "consciousness," and *prakriti*, which is female, and means "matter" or "nature." Everything animate and inanimate that exists and is knowable to the senses is part of *prakriti*. Although this dualistic division is most characteristic of the philosophical schools called *Samkhya* and *Yoga*, the great *advaita*, or non-dualistic philosopher Shankara, is most closely associated with the division by succeeding in overcoming it. He personifies the triumph of the spirit that can transcend matter and its innumerable manifestations. Just as, being a celibate, the great Shankara is blind and deaf to the charms of women, so, as the great non-dualist, he does not succumb to the siren calls of the material world.

> After Sankara completed his studies and left the house of his guru he maintained his vow of chastity and thereby remained invulnerable to the *feminine* allure of the material world. As love weakens the male and gives the female strength, the chastity of the male weakens the female and empowers the male.
> (Siegel, 1983, p. 21; italics mine)

However, debates were the celebrated technique for proving one's intellectual acumen, and a moment of crisis arises when, in a debate with the householder priest Mandan Mishra, Shankara wins on all points but loses overall because he does not have knowledge of *kama*, or sexual pleasure, thus being stranded with incomplete knowledge. He takes a month off and entering the body of Amaru, a King, learns everything there is to know about courtly sexual pleasures. This is celebrated in the *Amarushataka*, which was composed by King Amaru or by Shankara or by both. Upon Shankara's return to his own body, he wins the debate, finally untouched by his sexual forays because of his previous all-important knowledge of the fallacy and illusiveness of all worldly appearances.

Throughout, we have a tussle in men between the roles of erotically aroused and ascetically withdrawn individuals. Shiva is a god who combines in his person the attributes of both. Human men find themselves in the pursuit of one or the other roles, or at least one at one time. The attractions of asceticism are spelt out in Sanskrit literature, and in brief, asceticism leads to the highest and purest forms of power, power that no earthly weapons or martial prowess can beat. The attractions of erotic love, on the other hand, are equally statuesque, and reams exist in praise of the erotic in all branches of literature and the arts. This is a man's pursuit, even though the *atman*, the soul or self, is gender-free, and asceticism and eroticism can both in principle be followed by women as well as men. It is a man's conceit, and it has masculine undertones and imagery. The god Shiva is directly the patron-deity of the balanced erotic-ascetic figure, and though Shiva is himself half male and half female, it is *he* who is so. He is first and primarily male and represented by his *lingam*, or sexual organ.

So, we have a division between the good wife and the free woman in the matter of female sexuality, and a division between the sexually active male and the ascetic in male sexuality. There have been clear ups and downs in the fates of both these divisions in both experience and representation over the centuries of Indian civilisation. For the last two hundred years, there is an interesting politics, with a resurgence of male–female difference, and male domination through legal and market changes, leading up in the last two decades to a resurgence of neo-liberalism. While present developments are too new for extensive academic comment, the process is well studied for the colonial period.

The editors of the two-volume *Women Writing in India* (1993), Tharu and Lalita, begin their second volume on the Modern period with the story of the eighteenth-century poet Muddupalani. Considered a great poet in her own Thanjavur period of Telugu literature, she had come to be marginalised and forgotten as an author, and was sought to be re-published by Nagaratnamma in 1910. Nagaratnamma was a scholar and connoisseur and spoke feelingly about the precise beauties of Muddupalani's poetry. The marginalisation of the book had been due to an imputed immorality in the verses, extended by association to the poet herself, accused of being an "adulteress." When Nagaratnamma had it published, the government censors seized and banned the book. She followed up with petitions and was supported by nationalists who were indignant at the government's interference in Telugu letters. The ban continued, however, through the colonial period, and was lifted only in 1947. *Radhika Santwanam*, the two-hundred-year-old text, may be read now with a recognition of how it provides us with an entry into the interwoven relationships of class, caste, gender, colonial politics, and the emerging nation.

The work was an epic poem in a well-established genre that retold the familiar story of Radha and Krishna, timeless lovers who are also metaphors for the individual and the cosmic soul. All artwork in India (of a Hindu provenance at least) rests for its success on the subtle and suitable evocation of *rasa*, the flavour of the work and the emotion it produces. There are nine *rasas* and the *sringar rasa*, or the mood of erotic pleasure, would be predominant in this genre. The poet, Muddupalani, was not only skilled in her craft, she turns around the depiction of sensuality to present Radha, the woman, as the subject. It is Radha's desire, initiative, and pleasure that is given centrality. It is woman's sexuality that Radha, in another section, instructs a niece about.

The banning of this work, centuries after its acceptance at court, tells us directly about the new norms for social respectability that emerged in the colonial period. The new norms were a product of economic, political, and ideological changes and were led by Indians who sought new definitions of "tradition" and the "classical." Educational changes, as we saw in Chapters 6 and 7, produced new fissures between upper and lower classes. Women's artistic expressions could be dismissed now as crude, and women of respectable families defined by their separation from hitherto acceptable cultural practices and performances. Whereas a newly canonised "tradition" had its uses, and a new, progressive "modernity" was embraced by many, this artificial-but-normalised dichotomy left out many actual practices and values. Included in those were the voices of poets, performers, and scholars like Muddupalani and Nagaratnamma.

The arts, such as of dance and music, are a good example of this. Somewhere at the end of the nineteenth and the beginning of the twentieth centuries began a campaign in most parts of India to reform certain cultural practices such as dancing in *kothas* (brothels), temples, processions, and festivals, and the ritual singing by women at weddings and other life-cycle ceremonies. Women were accused of being uneducated and coarse. In the case of temple dancing, such as by *devdasis* in the South, and *kotha* dancing by courtesans in the North, women were sought to be "rescued" from the grips of custom. As these reform movements became popular, almost all aspects of women's performative culture disappeared. Many of the avenues women had of economic independence (in the case of courtesans), the right to property (for *devdasis*), and power in the community terrain (for ordinary women in life-cycle rituals) vanished or were weakened. The gap between upper/middle and lower-class women widened. The spaces for a woman of privilege narrowed, even as education offered her a new mobility. She was now characteristically defined in opposition to the poor and vulgar woman. The weight of respectability created this new Indian upwardly mobile woman as a reflection of the Victorian gentle, protected, flower-like creature who ruled in the pure domestic realm but could have little hope of any freedom in public spaces. Public spaces, loud voices, expressive language, humour, satire, and a sense of reality were all now distinctive marks of the backward lower classes. Explanations for this lie in the history of colonialism and nationalism, and have been partly given in Chapters 6 and 7.

One of the best-recorded histories is that of the "temple-dancers," the *rudraganikas* (Siva's courtesans) or *devadasis* (Servants of the Lord) in South India and Sri Lanka (then Ceylon). Recorded in autobiographies such as *Siva's Courtesan* by Ancukam in 1911 and many others, the writings represent devadasis as part of the "golden age" narrative of Indian nationalist history. Calling herself part of the lineage of "those wise women who wore virtue as an ornament and grew prosperous on account of their piety," Ancukam includes discussions of philosophical schools, including Saiva Siddhanta, thus broaching on male Brahman territory. She describes legendary courtesans and addresses herself to her contemporary "sisters." The work of the devadasis is described as *civattontu* or "service to Siva." The exact nature of the dances performed in temples is less clear, and, according to the scholar Davesh Soneji, consisted of courtly dancing, or a mixture of Tanjavur-style and "Hindustani" dancing (Soneji, 2010a).

Since *nautch* in Northern India and temple dancing in South India and Ceylon were of interest to travellers, missionaries, imperialists, and ethnographers in the nineteenth century, there was already a representation of the art as a familiar intersection of sexuality, religion, and occupation. Christian missionary critiques of Hindu practices produced, as early as the nineteenth century, calls for reform. Arunuka Navalar (1822–1879) was one such reformer. Through publications and oratory, he denounced music and dance in temples and the "moral standards" of devadasis and their patrons. Reformers like him were not immediately effective although they contributed to building up a discourse for reform. In the 1920s, Gandhi echoed the same call and gave it a more holistic dimension through his overall opposition to sensuality. In 1927, he said in a talk at Jaffa Hindu College:

> A prostitute has as much right to go to a house of worship as a saint. But she exercises that right when she enters the temple to purify herself. But when the trustees of a temple admit a prostitute under cover of religion or under cover of embellishing the worship of God, then they convert a house of God into one of prostitution.
>
> *(Soneji, 2010a, p. 44)*

In autobiographies like Ancukam's, we see the conundrum of an avowal of relationships that are "honourable" even when non-marital, and simultaneously a disavowal of the moral degradation this is supposedly based on. The older "semantics of pleasure and morality" (Soneji, 2010a, p. 46) needed no legitimising of the devadasi community. At the same time, there were trenchant critiques of the greedy devadasi, from the perspective of the hero who was duped. It is with the advent of the reform movement that accompanied the nationalist movement in India as well as Ceylon that the calls for self-reform were focused on abolition or reform of the devadasi system. The calls come to a head in 1928 when S. Muthulakshmi Reddy introduced a Devadasi Abolition Bill in Madras Legislative Assembly.

Responses to this bill were diverse. *The Humble Memorial of Devadasis of the Madras Presidency* (1928) describes the religious basis of the institution, compares devadasis in their dedication to Siva to Buddhist or Catholic nuns, and pleads for education to dispel ignorance. By the 1970s, the revised dance form, now called *Bharatnatyam*, is compared to yoga and religious consecration. Its practitioners are given a space in the history of the nation and the globe. Its aesthetics and virtuosity are canonised into a "classical" form, indeed, India's premier classical dance form.

And what of the actual woman? Amrit Srinivasan (1985) gives an evocative description of the life of a devadasi, though the life is inextricably tied up with the value it has for the larger society. A young girl, perhaps 12, was consecrated to a temple deity before puberty in a public ritual with the agreement of her mother and grandmother. This ritual resembled a high-caste marriage and was under-written financially by a well-placed and high-caste "proper" patron, and socially by the temple and its devotees. The girl was now the equal of a married woman, expected to be economically and sexually active, a *sumangali* who would always have the protection of a husband, in her case, a god. Puberty ceremonies followed and were attended by elaborate ritual expenses and public appreciation of her dance training. While off bounds to other men, she was accessible to her patrons. The secular values embodied in her attractiveness were balanced with the sacred nature of her status. The temple itself, and society at large, could make the norms of conjugality coexist with extra-conjugality, the ethics of householders with those of devotees and artists, of marriage and money with the sacred. "As a picture of good luck, beauty and fame the *devadasi* was welcome in all rich men's homes on happy occasions of celebration and honor. Her strict professionalism made her an adjunct to conservative domestic society not its ravager" (Srinivasan, 1985, p. 1875). The Anti-Nautch campaign, started in 1892, gathering speed in the 1920s, sought to label *devadasis* as "prostitutes" and prohibit their performances. Within a generation, they were reduced to paupers without a means of economic sustenance and a legitimate social standing.

In Orissa, the parallel to devadasis was the *mahari* tradition of performing music in and around temples. Losing patronage in the colonial period, *maharis* almost disappeared in the twentieth century, only to be revived as Odisi dance, a "classical" form. Beginning from the end of the nineteenth century, as the nationalist movement grew, a consciousness also grew in India of the need to have a "classical" system of music that was on a par with the European system. A group of men in the North and the South began to construct a classical lineage for Hindustani and Karnatak music, respectively, that could demonstrate the pedigree, textual base, purity, and strict rigour and discipline of the two systems, respectively. Modern pedagogy, music notation, and connoisseurship of the audience were part of the requirements of classicism.

If we look at the question of music and its gendered history, the most persuasive scholarship is that which shows the transition between the court- and temple-based performance and that patronised by the democratic state and its institutions. Research, especially in South and Central India, tells us of how music was patronised by various courts and temples. We know less about its actual musical nature or content than about the politics of its transmission and professionalisation. Women had a role in performances; *devadasis*, for instance, were trained to sing as they were to dance. In the nineteenth century, a new imperative arose from the demands of the nationalist movement to present a tradition in all aspects of Indian history where it did not exist before. The term "classical" that had become applied to European music circa 1800 (Schoefield, 2010) now appeared as a challenge insofar as it signified, yet again, superiority and purity. This necessitated a new formal structure to be imposed on Indian music, a new lineage traced, and connections made between texts and performance, often leaving out strong oral traditions in favour of the written. Simultaneously with this ideological drive occurred economic and political changes that shifted power from landlords and older elites to the state, and, slowly, to a gradually emerging new educated class.

The processes were not smooth. The past had to be reimagined and the future negotiated. That performers in the past had low status and were often of low caste could be resolved by redefining the music as proper for higher-caste performers. That performers in the North had been, and were, mostly Muslim was sought to be resolved by marginalising them and emphasising the Hindu scriptural roots of the performing arts. That performers were often women who were then regarded as the opposite of the housewife model was restructured by domesticating the arts to be a proper subject or hobby for girls and women within the paternalistic family. An important part in this cultural change – called cultural production to emphasise that the creation is new and powerful – is played by the "voice." The ideal voice is a female voice singing the compositions of poet saints – the voice of divinity but also, as embodied in Subbulakshmi, of the sari-clad emblem of domestic virtue. This is a discourse that comes into being through politics and technology. The politics is that of a modernity that creates its tradition, along gendered lines. The technology is that of the violin, the microphone, the gramophone, and written notation, all of which not merely influence the voice but contribute to giving it its character. In South India, as the scholars Weidman (2006), Subramaniam (2006) and Niranjana (2006) have shown, there can be little understanding of the meaning of "classical music" outside historical and political configurations.

In North India, Bakhle (2006) argues that before the late colonial period there was no distinction between elite and non-elite, high and popular, music and that the chief patrons, the courts, did not even prize the music they patronised above other entertainments such as wrestling or pigeon-breeding. There was no consciousness of the importance of age, purity of lineage, or link to written philosophies, such as Bharata's. Music was not prestigious or symbolic of civilisational status. Court patronage, however, came to be replaced by a new market for music. Schools and colleges were established for the teaching of classical music to the laity. The music itself was systematised, especially by V. N. Bhatkhande. Its history was written to link it directly to ancient texts. Musicians were judged on their knowledge of and ability to include texts deemed ancient and authentic in their teaching. Systems of notation were experimented with. A new performance style and audience reception style was developed. The middle class, including girls from respectable families, now felt safe to study, practise, and perform classical music, which had hitherto been the domain strictly of *baijis* or *tawayafs*, that is, courtesans. This was done by sacralising the teaching and learning environment of music but also by simultaneously degrading courtesans as totally unacceptable role models. Bakhle traces the development of this sacralised teaching environment from the Hindu-leaning earlier schools and music appreciation societies such as the Poona Gayan Samaj and the Gayan Uttejak Mandali to the overtly religious milieu favoured in the Gandharva Mahavidyalayas that were established by Vishnu Digambar Paluskar and his disciples.

Many eminent musicians had been and were Muslims, and Abdul Karim Khan was one of them. His daughter, famous as Hirabai Barodekar, is an example for North India, as M. S. Subbulakshmi is for the South, of a female singer who breaks from the performance tradition in her family – with mothers and grandmothers as professional singers – to become an independent public performer who is considered neither a courtesan nor in any other sense less than respectable. This example of Hirabai Barodekar and M. S. Subbulakshmi was followed by many other women from performing families and marks a restricting in many ways of women's public sphere. Victorian mores and the prejudiced views of the Anti-Nautch campaign combined to show courtesans and devadasis in light darker than warranted. Women did not enter the public sphere with the acceptance of Indian classical music as "Indian" and "classical." Women were already in the public sphere as performers. These particular women – "hereditary matrilineal musicians" as Qureshi (2001, p. 98) calls them – were stigmatised and replaced by a new kind of performer who was acceptable to the upwardly mobile middle classes. This was on pain of a continuous occupation by her of the high altar of chastity and domesticity, from which there should be no slippage.

Moving on to films, a persuasive case has been made for how Indian films – and here we will restrict ourselves mostly to Hindi films with a few exceptions – may be read as "realistic" and also as "dreams" (Kakar, 1989). They are realistic in the sense that fantasy and fairy tales are realistic, expressive of psychological realities. Other scholars, such as Madhav Prasad (1998), have demonstrated that the film industry wields power through its economic and political muscle. If it favours patriarchy, then control of women's desire is what it teaches, including in the forbidding of the kiss, a declaration of autonomous desire. Yet others, such as Jyotika Virdi (2003), put emphasis on the nation-building work of the film industry, which includes a particular interpretation of the role of women. Tejaswini Ganti (2012) looks at the social presence of women in the industry and the discourse about their agency and victimhood. Ravi Vasudevan (2001) does a close reading of films; De (2011b, 2016) does the same through a singularly gendered lens. Dwyer takes a more general view that ties up many arguments together. Here, in following some of these scholars in reading particular films, our intention is to grasp the nature of gendered reality in social, economic, political, historical, and psychological terms. In doing so, we will be ranging between the propositions readily made and displayed by the culture, and the dream or fantasy that speaks of the "forbidden" and "invisible" – "the unlit stages of desire where so much of our inner theatre takes place" (Kakar, 1989, p. 41).

In Aparna Sen's Bengali film *Paramitar Ek Din* ("One Day in the Life of Paramita," given the English title of "House of Memories"), the protagonist Paramita visits her ex-husband's house for the death ritual of his mother, Sanaka. In the hours she sits at the ceremony her eight or ten years of life there are played out in her memory. She was married to an alcoholic and insensitive son of the house who showed little respect for her, especially when the child they had was diagnosed as suffering from cerebral palsy. The lack of sexual and personal bonding between husband and wife is never dwelt on. We know of its extent from a few passing scenes on which the camera does not linger, but mostly from Paramita's decision to divorce her husband, once her son dies and she has no ties at all left.

However, she does have ties with Sanaka, her mother-in-law, as the latter reminds her with tears when she announces her decision to leave her husband, and by extension, the house. "*Bari* (house)? Why do you keep telling me about the house?" demands Paramita, alert now to the need to further her own autonomy by escaping. Sanaka explains, pathetically, that the house is all she herself has, never having had a bond with her own husband, having a disabled child herself, and being confined to the house after marriage, without a job or independent life of her own. We are momentarily torn – how wonderful for Sanaka if she could in fact continue to have the companionship of Paramita as she so longs for. But how much more wonderful for Paramita to leave her present husband – and house – and build up a new life with a job and a man she loves. It is the new man she marries with whom we are shown the only intimate sexual moment in the film.

This movie exemplifies an important point about the depiction of sexuality in Indian cinema. Sexuality resides in the woman's body, and there are definitely two kinds of sexuality; not necessarily two kinds of women: one could display both types of sexuality in turn. One is the staid and proper one that emphasises procreation as the result. Paramita is shown as bringing, soon after her marriage, her baby proudly into the home. Women are socialised into being proud of motherhood and drawing boundaries around it. But it is, as many women soon realise, all for the preservation of the male line, and for the comfort and status of men. The other sexuality is the libertarian one, of courtesans and prostitutes, low-class women, or the occasional "fallen" or wayward woman. Women could be proud or defensive about it but are more often apologetic, and regard it as illicit, to be explained and regretted. Men are fine with it and regard such available sexuality as a compensation for male work and struggle, as an aesthetic pursuit, and as a justified facet of masculinity. However, Indian films do not draw black-and-white pictures, as a rule. They show with layers of meaning how a woman, such as the elite protagonist of *Sahib, Bibi aur Ghulam*, could be in a loveless marriage and torn by solitariness. Her husband spends time with courtesans. She is ready to cross the virtue-vice barrier and act like a courtesan herself, in order to win him over. She is ready to try charms and to drink – ending up as an alcoholic. In countless other films, including the classic many times made *Devdas*, the change is in the other direction, from vice to virtue: the courtesan is contrite about her profession and wishes to reform, to be worthy of the man she has fallen in love with. In Tagore's story the neglected wife turns to the stage and is celebrated as precisely the kind of hypnotising public woman that her husband used to neglect her for.

This is clearly a double burden for women. If they are disciplined in their sexuality, they are boring and undesirable. If they act as free agents, they are never quite pure or good enough for the men (the most pathetic statement of this is imputed to Raj Kapoor who was in love with his leading lady Nargis but would never have married her, because "Kapoor wives do not act"). The most distressing picture of such boring women is in U. R. Ananthamurthy's novel, also made into a film, *Samskara*, which depicts the good wives as dry, unattractive, and unimaginative. But if women are honest regarding their desires, they are seen to be of questionable character and become the butt of condemnation by society, likely to be abandoned by the one man they care for. The free woman in *Samskara* is the prostitute Chandra, a woman who men lust after but cannot respect. Conversely, if women are free in their sexuality *and* try to rule their own lives, they are doomed. The courtesans in *Umrao Jan* (1981), *Pakeezah* (1972), and many other Hindi films have no family any more. Their only community is the salon they belong to, and until they head their own, are captive within. When they try to escape, they are pushed back both by society and their own fears.

Of course, cinematic imagination extends to the beautiful, even luscious, but virtuous, woman who is monogamous *and* attractive, and keeps her man happy. She often comes to a bad end, however, becoming injured or dying. Sexuality when combined with virtue is seldom rewarded, and that only after a trial, but there is no controversy that the longing and the readiness for sex is a universal of womanhood.

In the 1950s and 1960s, when the Nehruvian project of building up the nation was fully supported by the Bombay film industry, films used direct narratives to exemplify how Indians could live together. Hindus, Muslims, and Christians come together in *Amar, Akbar, Anthony* (1977). Other films bridged the distance between rich and poor in complex ways, including by depicting the tribal, as in *Madhumati* and the peasant, as in *Naya Daur* (1957), while showing the old, feudal order fading, and the new capitalist one becoming reformed through proper ethical self-reflection. The films presented the lives of the rich to mass audiences in ways that could produce identification with the rich and the pleasure of hegemonic example. They presented the lives of the poor as simple and upright, worthy of pity and support, typically doomed to extinction before the onslaught of progress but worthy of being given credit. Most of all the threat to the nation, from regional, gender, class, or religious diversity was transcended through the device of constructing the nation as the family, and the family as the nation, and working out the conflicts at the level of the family to produce a doubly positive emotional response of rightness with both the family and the nation. Much of the conflict could be also resolved through love: romantic love, maternal love, family love, and love overall that proved itself as true by being prefaced by sacrifice. The nation was sometimes personified as a liberal, secular, balanced male who overcomes the forces of feudalism and authority, in turn personified as a female, as in *Aan* (1952). The authoritarian, feudal figure, Raj (literally, the Empire), is subdued by the gentle but powerful Jai (literally, Victory), a clear symbol of the progressive over the retrograde. The nation is also one populated by indigenous, subterranean cultures, personified by the female in *Madhumati* (1958) who both escapes and is re-united with the modern male hero after a strategic defeating of authoritarian power symbolising both feudalism and colonialism.

Then there is the famous story of the peasant woman Radha in the film *Mother India* (1957). Radha battles natural and social odds, including losing her harvest and her home, her husband and two sons, to emerge victorious as the mother of the village. The title of the film as applied to the village woman could not be more appropriate. Everyone, audience, critic, and biographer, agreed that the actress who played Radha, Nargis, had outdone herself. Nargis, as was not uncommon at the time in Bombay cinema, was of a performing family, and a Muslim. Her mother was a courtesan and she had herself been inducted into films – which few people of "good families" joined at the time – at a young age. She was the lover of another star (Raj Kapoor), who publicly stated that he would never marry her, meaning that she was not a respectable gentlewoman. Acting as "Mother India," critics such as Parama Roy (1988) argue, gave Nargis the legitimacy to claim genteel identity, indeed the identity of personifying India. It helped that just after the making of the film she married a lead actor of the same film (Sunil Dutta) and retired from the profession that had given her star status but denied her respectability. She could live out her life as the legend she had become while personally avoiding the twin stigmas of being the child of a dancer and a Muslim. We can be sure, as well, that while her personal history expresses the marginalisation of women's arts and careers in modern India, the modernity of India as male and "virtuous" was also re-emphasised by her own choices: playing roles of Hindu women and Hindu symbols, leaving her career for a domestic life, marrying a Hindu and minimalising, at least publicly, her Muslim-ness.

In the 1970s and 1980s, the state was under a cloud because of its failure in delivering public service across the board. Films depicted a new frustration with the nation, expressed through the new heroic figures of the angry young man, the bandit, the terrorist, the smuggler, and the criminal underworld mafia-leader. Many differences were shown to be reconcilable only after violence and victimhood, often of the woman. In *Roti, Kapda aur Makan* (1974), the working-class woman Tulsi stands for all the working class, raped by capitalists. In other movies, such as the Amitabh Bachchan starrers, women are in minor roles only and strictly the supportive girlfriends and wives of the heroic men. The separation of the woman into the two images of purity (the wife and mother) and vice (the cabaret dancer or prostitute) was continued through various reconceptualisations. Sometimes, the fall from the former to the latter, or the rise from the latter to the former, was through social forces, and sometimes it was through her own ingenuity and inward authenticity. Often a fallen woman, even when raised up by a man or her own inner drive, died because even reform could not purify her enough to be reintegrated into society.

In the same period occurred what has been described as "gentrification" (Ganti, 2012) – the effort to make Hindi films more respectable. This process includes a redefinition of the nation, the market, and the caste and class hierarchies, and also, crucially, gendered divisions into society. If we turn from the meanings that films convey and look at the film industry's workings, we find it to be an integral part of the cultural histories of modern India. As in the case of dance and music, acting was also both caste-defined and gendered. Performers belonged to lower castes. Even when they became successful, famous and rich, their caste origins would not be forgotten. If they were not from lower castes, they occupied a marginal status of some other kind, or were individually relegated to such a status. Because of the stigma attached to acting, and the fear of stigma, women's roles were initially played by men, as they were in the Parsee theatre. In 1930, Durga Khote, for instance, born and married into an upper caste, chose to act simply to earn better than her husband and she did. This choice, in 1930, perpetrated a big publicity effort by her producer to market Hindi films as now featuring respectable actors. It took some five decades more, however, for women to have the choice of acting and still be respectable.

Two films, *Teesri Kasam* (1966) and *Guide* (1965), revolve around the stigma of the female performer. In *Teesri Kasam*, a naive cart-driver begins to love and respect the *baiji* played by Waheeda Rehman only to have her abandon him because she does not want to have him learn the truth about her, namely that she is sexually available to the highest bidder. In *Guide*, the same actress plays the role of a married woman abused by her husband because of her love for dance inherited from her courtesan mother. In several other movies featuring courtesans or prostitutes, such as *Pakeezah*, *Umrao Jaan*, and *Devdas* (1955), the plot largely focuses on the internal pain of the female protagonist in bearing the burden of the stigma when it was a chance occurrence that gave her the professions thus stigmatised, and when she remains at heart simple, honest, suffering, therefore "pure."

The new distinction that had arisen in the late nineteenth century that set the emerging middle classes apart from others was largely based on education. "Respectability" meant, for the new middle classes, a comparatively upper-caste origin, economic stability in a new profession, higher education in English, and gendered norms of privacy and exclusivity. Film was an industry in which children of respectable families did not venture. Many processes, economic, political, and ideological, changed such gendered divisions (many others have not yet changed) and from the turn of the twenty-first century, repeated articulations by industry members themselves (Ganti, 2012) underscored that there was no more stigma attached to working in films for women. But it remains a work in progress. Until recently there is an ongoing discourse within and about the Bombay film industry that is starkly gendered. To get a break, men may roam around to make contacts and be seen; women should not. The sets and producers' studios, and Bombay city by association, are dangerous places where women should be careful of sexual predators. Women must be alert as to the nuances of the relationships they build and the interactions they have in their profession, including with cameramen and assistants. Men do not have to be. Acting is poised to be seen as the opposite of middle-classness, education, and respectability, and modern female members of the film industry, while feeling safer and freer than ever before, feel that they still have to fight both an experiential and a discursive battle.

At the same time, certain scholars downplay the divisions of gender and class and consider there to be a shared space and a common language in Indian culture. There are images, texts and styles that comprise popular/public culture that Christopher Pinney (Dwyer & Pinney, 2001) calls shared "desire" or "epistemological space." In doing so, Dwyer, Pinney, and other authors disregard the great dividing authority of colonialism as well as the tensions that accompany the hegemonic activity of the national state. The nation state's appropriation of culture is accompanied by the objectification of elite ("classical"), folk and mass cultural forms resulting in an ongoing tension between all of them. This contested cultural space is labelled "public culture" by Appadurai and Breckenridge (1988) because it goes beyond the older dichotomies of high–low, elite–popular, classical–folk, traditional–modern and so on, revealing new tensions and overlaps. Certainly, divisiveness characterises Indian society but is not necessarily visible in its cultural products.

One way out of the dichotomy of sexuality as both wonderful and despicable as commonly exercised in the Hindu traditions of philosophy and the arts is to consider all *passion* as one, whether passion of the ascetic in pursuit of liberation or passion of the lover pining for his beloved. Even when the imagery is elaborated erotically as far as one can go, at the bottom of it, it can still be about the one thing: the soul seeking liberation. In Sanskrit poetry and philosophy, and by extension, performance, and, to some extent, everyday life, the resolution can also be made through metaphor and imagery that sees a common outcome for both the renouncer and the pleasure-seeker. Both, the ascetic in his penance and the lover after his beloved, will know in turn: seduction and resistance, faith and abandonment, argument and reconciliation, anger and love, separateness and union, maya and reality, desire and oblivion, life and death. The poetry of pre-modern India, from the Gupta to the colonial periods, is full of these complexities. Poetry of the Sufi schools that sings of the human/divine love afire in the seeker's breast has been studied extensively and a wonderful collection of research accompanied by primary materials is available in Metcalf 2009. Poetry that centres around Radha and Krishna is arguably the most erotic of all, while all the time being about the human soul's quest for the Supreme Being. This poetry can be enjoyed and understood in works by Hawley (1981) and Coleman (2010), among others.

There are interesting spaces where love, both romantic and erotic, and sexuality play roles in India. One is that of the Bengali temple of the seventeenth–eighteenth centuries, as studied by Pika Ghosh. She gives us an inscription from a temple at Vishnupur in Bankura District in Bengal that says: "For the pleasure of Sri Radhika and Krishna a new bejewelled temple was given by Maharaja Sri Raghunatha Singh, son of Sri Vir Hambir, the king in the Malla Saka year 949 [1643]." She explains that, apart from the political and technological reasons for the building of new-style temples,

> The inscription cited above also points to the reconceptualization of temples as the pleasure grounds of the gods, where Krishna and his beloved Radha could rekindle their passion. Krishna is the focus of Gaudiya Vaishnavism, the *bhakti* (devotional) movement led by the Bengali saint Chaitanya (1486–1533) that swept up Bengal and Vrindavan in north India in a frenzy of ecstatic devotion and passionate song and dance over the sixteenth and seventeenth centuries. Chaitanya advocated a deeply emotional and intensely personal engagement with Krishna, modeled on Radha's single-minded dedication. The inscriptions' deployment of terms such as *mudita* (pleasure, happiness, delight) and *rasa* (taste, deliciousness), given specific connotation in a century of literary texts, leaves no doubt that the monuments were dedicated for the expression of this intensely passionate love shared by Radha and Krishna.
>
> *(Ghosh, 2005, p. 17)*

This extract is a fairly auspicious and piquant way to conclude a chapter on "Sexuality and the Arts." It is one more stopping place, if we like, on a seemingly non-ending, difficult, and challenging journey into a philosophical and practical territory, where we could linger forever. As the *Kamasutra* says: "Not only in erotics but in all fields, few know the theoretical aspects. Theory is fundamental, even if divorced from practice" (*Kamasutra* 1.3.5–6, quoted in Kakar, 2000).

## Bibliography

*Aan.* (1952). Produced and Directed by Mehboob Khan.
*Amar, Akbar, Anthony.* (1977). Produced and Directed by Manmohan Desai.
Ananthamurty, U. R. (1965). *Samskara: A rite for a dead man*. Delhi: Penguin.
Appadurai, A. (1988). How to make a national cuisine: Cookbooks in contemporary India. *Comparative Studies in Society and History*, 30(1), 3–24.

Appadurai, A. (1990). Disjuncture and difference in the global cultural economy. *Public Culture, 2*(2), 1–24.

Appadurai, A. (1991). Global ethnoscapes: Notes & queries for a transnational anthropology. In R. G. Fox (Ed.), *Re-capturing anthropology*. Santa Fe, NM: School of American Research Press.

Appadurai, A., & Breckenridge, C. A. (1988). Why public culture? *Public Culture, 1*(1), 5–10.

Arundale, R. D. (1979). Spiritual background. In S. Kothari (Ed.), *Bharat Natyam: Indian classical dance art* (p. 16). Delhi: Marg Publications.

Bakhle, J. (2006). *Two men and music: Nationalism in the making of an Indian classical tradition*. New Delhi: Permanent Black.

Bhattacharya, P. (2004). Of Kunti and Satyawati: Sexually assertive women of the Mahabharata. *Manushi, 142*, 21–25.

Brown, K. B. (2006). If music be the food of love: Masculinity and eroticism in the Mughal Mehfil. In F. Orsini (Ed.), *Love in South Asia: A cultural history* (pp. 61–83). Cambridge: Cambridge University Press.

Coleman, T. (2010). Viraha-bhakti and stridharma: Re-reading the story of Krishna and the Gopis in the *Harivamsa* and the *Bhagavata Purana*. *Journal of the American Oriental Society, 130*(3), 385–412.

Das Gupta, C. (1980). *Talking about films*. New Delhi: Orient Longman.

De, E. N. (2011a). 'Choice' and Feminist praxis in neoliberal times: Autonomous women in a postcolonial visual culture. *Feminist Media Studies, 12*(1), 17–34.

De, E. N. (2011b). *Empire, media, and the autonomous woman: A feminist critique of postcolonial thought*. New York: Oxford University Press.

De, E. N. (2016). Kinship drives, friendly affect: Difference and dissidence in the new Indian border cinema. In E. H. Chowdhury & L. Philipose (Eds.), *Feminism, imperialism and transnational solidarity?* (pp. 143–159). Champaign, IL: University of Illinois Press.

de Certeau, M. (1984). *The practice of everyday life* (Trans. S. Rendell). Berkeley, CA: University of California Press.

Deleuze, G., & Guattari, F. (1987). *A thousand plateaus: Capitalism and schizophrenia* (Trans. B. Massumi). Minneapolis, MN: University of Minnesota Press.

*Devdas*. (1955). Produced and Directed by Bimal Roy.

Doniger, W., & Kakar, S. (Trans.). (2009). *Kamasutra by Vatsyayana*. Delhi: Oxford University Press.

Dwyer, R. (2000). *All you want is money, all you need is love: Sex and romance in modern India*. London: Continuum.

Dwyer, R., & Pinney, C. (2001). *Pleasure and the nation: The history, politics and consumption of public culture in India*. London: SOAS Studies in South Asia.

Ganti, T. (2012). *Producing Bollywood: Inside the contemporary Hindi film industry*. Durham, NC: Duke University Press.

Ghosh, P. (2005). *Temple to love: Architecture and devotion in seventeenth-century Bengal*. Bloomington, IN: Indiana University Press.

Gopal, S. (2011). *Conjugations: Marriage and form in new Bollywood cinema*. Chicago, IL: University of Chicago Press.

Gopinath, G. (2005). *Impossible desires: Queer diasporas and South Asian public cultures*. Durham, NC and London: Duke University Press.

*Guide*. (1965). Directed and Produced by Vijaya Anand.

Haggard, S. (1989). Mass media and the visual arts in twentieth-century South Asia: Indian film posters 1947-present. *South Asia Research, 8*(1), 71–88.

Hawley, J. S. (1981). *At play with Krishna: Pilgrimage dramas from Brindavan.* Princeton, NJ: Princeton University Press.
Kakar, S. (1989). *Intimate relations: Exploring Indian sexuality.* Delhi: Viking.
Kakar, S. (2000). *The ascetic of desire: A novel of the Kama Sutra.* New York: Woodstock.
Kapur, G. (1991). Place of the modern in Indian cultural practice. *Economic and Political Weekly, 26*, 2803–2806.
Katrak, K. (1992). Indian nationalism, Gandhian 'Satyagraha,' and representations of female sexuality. In A. Parker et al. (Eds.), *Nationalisms and sexualities* (pp. 395–406). New York: Routledge.
Katz, J. (Ed.). (1992). *The traditional Indian theory and practice of music and dance.* Leiden: E. J. Brill.
Kersenboom, S. C. (1987). *Nityasumangali: Devadasi tradition in South India.* Delhi: Motilal Banarasidass.
Kumar, N. (1988). *The artisans of Banaras: Popular culture and identity 1880–1984.* Princeton, NJ: Princeton University Press.
Kumar, N. (2004). Do real men cry? Love, gender and seasonality in songs from India. In N. Krishna & M. Krishna (Ed.), *The Ananda-Vana of Indian art: Dr Anand Krishna felicitation volume Varanasi* (pp. 595–606). Varanasi: Indica Books.
Lal, V. (2000). Nakedness, nonviolence, and brahmacharya: Gandhi's experiments in celibate sexuality. *Journal of the History of Sexuality, 9*(1–2), 105–136.
Lutgendorf, P. (1990). Ramayan: The video. *Drama Review, 34*(2), 127–176.
*Madhumati.* (1958). Directed and Produced by Bimal Roy.
Mankekar, P. (1993). Television tales and a woman's rage: A nationalist recasting of Draupadi's disrobing. *Public Cultures, 5*(3), 469–491.
Manuel, P. (1993). *Popular music and cassette culture in North India.* Chicago, IL: University of Chicago Press.
Mazumdar, R. (1991). Dialectic of public and private: Representation of women in *Bhoomika* and *Mirch Masala*. *Economic and Political Weekly, 26*(43), WS81–WS84.
Meduri, A. (Ed.). (2005). *Rukmini Devi Arundale (1904–1986).* Delhi: Motilal Banarsidass.
Meyer, J. J. (1953). *Sexual life in ancient India: A study in the comparative history of Indian culture.* London: Routledge and Kegan Paul. (Original work published 1930)
*Mother India.* (1957). Produced and Directed by Mehboob Khan.
*Naya Daur.* (1957). Directed and Produced by B. R. Chopra.
Neuman, D. M. (1990). *The life of music in North India: The organization of an artistic tradition.* Chicago, IL: University of Chicago Press. (Original work published 1980)
Niranjana, T. (1991). Cinema, femininity and economy of consumption. *Economic and Political Weekly, 26*(43), WS85–WS86.
Niranjana, T. (2006). *Mobilising India: Women, music and migration between India and Trinidad.* Durham, NC: Duke University Press.
Niranjana, T., Dhareshwar, V., & Sudhi, P. (Eds.). (1993). *Interrogating modernity: Culture and colonialism in India.* Calcutta: Seagull.
Oldenburg, V. (1993). Lifestyle as resistance: The courtesans of Lucknow. In D. Haynes & G. Prakash (Eds.), *Contesting power: Resistance and everyday social relations in South Asia.* Berkeley: University of California Press.
Orr, L. C. (2000). *Donors, devotees, and daughters of god: Temple women in medieval Tamilnadu.* New York: Oxford University Press.
Ortner, S. (1996). *Making gender: The politics and erotics of culture.* Boston, MA: Beacon Press.

O'Shea, J. (2006). From temple to battlefield: Dance in Sri Lanka. *Pulse, 13*, 33–35.
O'Shea, J. (2007). *At home in the worlds: Bharat Natyam on the global stage.* Middletown: Wesleyan University Press.
*Pakeezah.* (1972). Directed and Produced by Kamal Amrohi.
*Paromitar Ek Din/House of Memories.* (2000). Directed by Aparna Sen. Kolkata: Rajesh Agarwal Productions.
Prasad, M. M. (1998). *Ideology of the Hindi film: A historical construction.* New Delhi: Oxford University Press.
Qureshi, R. B. (2001). In search of Begum Akhtar: Patriarchy, poetry and twentieth century Indian music. *The World of Music, 43*(1), 97–137.
Reddy, G. (2005). *With respect to sex: Negotiating hijra identity in South India.* Chicago, IL: University of Chicago Press.
*Roti, Kapda aur Makan.* (1974). Directed and Produced by Manoj Kumar.
Roy, P. (1998). *Indian traffic: Identities in question in colonial and postcolonial India.* New Delhi: Vistaar Publications.
*Sahib Bibi aur Ghulam.* (1962). Directed by Abrar Alvi, Produced by Guru Dutt.
Schoefield, K. B. (2010). Reviving the golden age again: "Classicization," Hindustani music, and the Mughals. *Ethnomusicology, 54*(3), 484–517.
Siegel, L. (1983). *Fires of love, waters of peace.* Honolulu, HI: University of Hawaii Press.
Soneji, D. (2010a). Siva's courtesans: Religion, rhetoric, and self-representation in early twentieth-century writing by Davadasis. *International Journal of Hindu Studies, 14*(1), 31–70.
Soneji, D. (2010b). *Unfinished gestures: Devadasis, memory and modernity in South India.* Chicago, IL: University of Chicago Press.
Spivak, G. C. (2002). Ethics and politics in Tagore, Coetzee, and certain scenes of teaching. *Diacritics, 32*(3/4), 17–31.
Srinivasan, A. (1985). Reform and revival: The Devdasi and her dance. *Economic and Political Weekly, 20*(44), 1869–1876.
Sriram, V. (2007). *The Devadasi and the Saint: The life and times of Bangalore Nagarathnamma.* Chennai: East-est Books (Madras).
Subrahmanyam, P. (1979). *Bharata's art: Then and now.* Madras: Nrithodaya.
Subramaniam, L. (2006). *From the Tanjore court to the madras music academy.* New Delhi: Oxford University Press.
*Teesri Kasam.* (1966). Directed by Basu Bhattacharya, Produced by Shailendra.
Tharu, S., & Lalita, K. (Eds.). (1993). *Women writing in India: 600 B.C, to the present. Two volumes.* New York: The Feminist Press at The City University of New York.
*Umrao Jaan.* (1981). Directed and Produced by Muzaffar Ali.
Vanita, R., & Kidwai, S. (Eds.). (2000). *Same-sex love in India.* New York: Palgrave Macmillan.
Vasudevan, R. S. (Ed.). (2001). *Making meaning in Indian cinema.* New Delhi: Oxford University Press.
Virdi, J. (2003). *The cinematic imagination: Social history through Indian popular films, 1947–2000.* New Brunswick, NJ: Rutgers University Press.
Weidman, A. (2006). *Singing the classical, voicing the modern: The postcolonial politics of music in South India.* Durham, NC: Duke University Press.
*Veer Zaara.* (2004). Directed by Yash Chopra. Mumbai: Yash Raj Films.

# INDEX

*Aan* 187, 190
Abul Fazl 66–69
Abul Kalam Azad, Maulana 161
acting: in films 188–89; *see also* films, courtesans
*adab* 65
Aditi 34, 147, 150
Adolescence/puberty 111, 182
*agha* 67
agriculture 85–86
Ahalya 37
Ahl-e-hadith 169–70
*Ahval-i Humayun Badshah* 64
Aisha 161
Akbar 4, 60, 63–64, 66–67, 71
Akka Mahadevi 73
Allender, Tim 97, 104
*Amar Chitra Katha* 156
*Amar Jiban* 95
Amba 38
Anandibai 102
*Anandmath* 136–37, 141, 153
Anandmayi Ma 153
Ancuman 181
Andal 72
androgynes/androgyny 17, 34–35
Appadurai, Arjun 189, 191
Arabic 99, 167
*Ardhangini* 40, 53
*Arthashastra* 48, 57
Arya Mahila College 102

Arya Samaj 101
Aryan(s) 13, 27, 31, 55
Asani, A.S. 163–5, 174
asceticism: and Buddhism 46, 50, 53–54; and Hindu nationalism 153; and passion 189, 192; and power 38, 50, 179; and Siva 22, 179; and solidarity 57; and Tantrism 153; as penurious 66; as *purusa* 19; as self-discipline 7, 114, 179; Sayanand Saraswato's 101; Sebendranath's 79; in Ramayana 4, 36; in Vedic period 4, 440; Sufis' 163–64; yogis' 39
Asher, Katherine 59, 70–71, 73–74
Ashoka 48, 54–55
*ashraf* 94–95, 173
*Ashrafisation* 82
Aurangzeb 60, 63, 67–68
Awadhi 71
Azizunissa Begum 93–95

Babar 63–64, 67–68
*BabarNama* 63
Bakhale, Janaki 183–84, 191
*Bamabodhini Patrika* 130
*Bande Matram* 137
*Bandit Queen* 108
Banerjee, Nirmala 85, 90
Banerjee, Sumanta 85, 90
Barelwi 169
Barodkar, Hirabai 184

## Index

Basham, A.L. 42, 47
Basu, Chandramukhi 100
Basu, Kadimbini 78, 100
Bayly, Christopher 79, 90
Bentinck, Lord William 115, 129
Bernier, Francois 67–68
Berreman, Gerald 122, 124
Besant, Annie 100–101, 131–32
*bhadra, bhadralok* 85–86, 88, 168, 173
bhakti/Bhakti movement 4, 71–72, 190
Bharati, Dharmvir 111, 125
Bharatnatyam 182
Bhasin, Kamala 139–141, 155, 159
Bhatkhande, V.N. 183
BJP (Bharatiya Janata Party) 32, 157
Bibi Rasti 164
*Bihishti Zewar* 168
Bose, Netaji Subhash Chandra 6, 136
Bose, Sugata 83, 90
Brahma 147, 151
Brahmans 47, 54, 56, 95, 101, 148–49, 181; Brahmanical 114, 150
Brahmo Samaj 78, 80, 97, 100–101
Breckenridge, Carol 189
Burton, Antoinette 15
*Bustan* 94
Butalia, Urvashi 22–23, 139–142, 157, 159

Carey, William 97
caste 55–56
Central Hindu School 100
Chaitanya Mahaprabhu 72
Chakrabarty, Dipesh 9, 15, 22, 90, 116–17, 125, 142
Chakravarti, Uma 3, 7, 26–28, 33, 42
Chanakya (Kautilya) 48, 54
Charter Act 1813 99
Chatterjee (Chattopadhyay), Bankimchandra 89, 136–37, 141, 153
Chatterjee, Indrani 14–15, 22, 76, 80, 87, 90, 125
Chatterjee, Partho 3, 8, 22, 90, 105, 121, 124–25, 141
Chattopadhyay, Kamaladevi 134, 137
child/children 120
Chinnadevi 70
Chowdhury, Prem 121–22
Christianity 96, 101
Chugtai, Ismat 123–24
Classical: languages 5; music 183–85; period 47, 54
Colebrook, Henry Thomas 26

Coleman, Tracy 190–91
Colonial: constructions 107, 180; discourse 121; education 130; period/state 5, 14, 16, 26, 54, 117–18, 128, 173, 183; law 6; prejudice 46;
Concubines/courtesans 70, 98, 167, 171–72, 180–81; and music 184; and sexuality 185; in films 186, 188; *see also* devdasis

*dai* 88
Dalit 32, 87–88
Dalrymple, William 76
Damayanti 6, 113, 132, 153, 157, 177
Dancers: bar 88; *see also devdasis*
Dars e-Nizamiyya 169
daughters 34, 49–50, 59, 68–69, 94, 158
Debi Chaudhurani 136
Dehejia, Vidya 151, 158
de-industrialisation 84
Deobandi 169
*Devdas* 186, 188, 191
*devdasis* 49, 78, 133, 180–84
Devi Mahatmya 144, 151, 154
*dharma* 89, 110, 113, 155
*Dharmashastra*s 6, 113
Dhola: person, with Maru 70; epic 113
Digambari Debi 79
divorce 59, 160
Doniger, Wendy 17–18, 25, 33, 159, 191
dowry 87, 157
Draupadi 21, 39, 56, 122, 132, 153–157
Durga 6, 136–37, 147, 151, 154, 156–57

East India Company 5, 14, 26, 75–79, 80, 96, 115, 128
Eaton, Richard 163, 174
education 5, 13, 35, 40, 77–78, 92, 169–72; and class difference 179–80; English 86, 117; of music 183–84; plural 103; vocational 96
Elizabeth I, Queen 76
Elphinstone, Mountstuart 66
Engineer, Asghar Ali 161–62, 174
English 77, 99
Enlightenment/enlightenment 16, 92, 98
Epics 4, 7
Erndl, Kathleen 17–18, 22–23, 43, 158

female infanticide 87, 117, 160
Feminism 26, 154, 157, 160, 173: liberal 1–2; radical 2; postmodern 3–4; socialist 2

films 184–88
Flueckiger, Joyce 163, 167–68
Forbes, Geraldine 78, 85, 100, 134–35, 141
friendship 57

*gali* 109
Gandhi, Indira 168
Gandhi, Mahatma 6, 54, 102–103, 132–36, 140; and prostitutes 181
Ganesh 29
Ganga
Ganguly, Kadambini 130
*garbhadan* 119
Gargi 41–42, 54
Geertz, Clifford 35
Ghalib, Mirza 171
ghazal 171–72
Ghosh, Pika 190–91
*Godan* 86–87
Goddess (Devi) 20, 143–56; Mother Goddess 28
goddesses 6, 143–56; the Great Goddess 18, and rivers 18; and mountains 18; village 150; *see* individual goddesses, Radha, Sita etc
Gokhale, Avantikabai 134
Gold, Ann 112–113, 126
Golden Age 54
Greenough, Paul 83
*Guide* 188
Gulbadan Banu Begum 64
*Gulistan* 94

*hadith* 59, 161–62, 170, 173
Hali, Khwaja Altaf Husain 82
Hallstrom, Lisa 153, 158
Hamidah Banu 67, 71
haram 65–69
Hare, David 97
Harlan, Lindsey 108, 114–15, 154
Hawley, John S. 72–73, 156, 158, 190, 192
Heer-Ranjha/Hir-Ranjha 70, 165–66
Hegel 10
Hiltebeitel, Alf 18, 21–23, 28, 36, 39, 43, 56–57, 154–55, 158
Hinduism 6, 7, 26, 28–29
homoeroticism 61, 166
homosocialty/homosexuality 61, 64, 166
Hosain, Rokeya Sakhawat 78, 95, 103, 122, 170, 174
Humayun 63, 65
Humes, Cynthia 155, 158

Hyder, S.A. 165, 174
hypergamy 122

Ibrahim Adil Shah II 71
Iltutmish 60–63
Inden, Ronald 10, 23
INA (Indian National Army)
INC (Indian National Congress) 78, 130–31, 134
Indo European 26
Indus Valley Civilisation 4, 20, 28–30, 143, 150
ILO (International Labour Organisation) 84
Islam 6, 7, 121, 124, 160–75, 183, 187

Jainism 47
Jalal, Ayesha 138, 141
Jahanara, Fatima 66–67, 164
Jahangir 63–64, 67, 69
Jamal Khatun, Bibi 164
Jamison, Stephanie 34, 43
Jayasi, Malik Muhammad 70–71
Jeffery, Patricia 89–90
Jiji Anaga 67
Jinnah. Mohammad Ali 138
Jogmaya Devi 79
Jones, William 26
Joshi, Anandabai 78
Juergensmeyer, Mark 72–74
Juzjani 62–63

Kakar 2
Kali 6, 18, 29, 51, 144, 147, 150–56
Kalidasa 55
*kama* 57
*Kamasutra* 54–56, 190
Kapadia, Karine 90, 110, 123, 125
*karewa* 76
Karve, Dhonu Keshav 102
Kautilya *see* Chanakya
Khadija 160
*Khamosh Pani* 139
Khote, Durga 188
Kidwai, Salim 61, 166, 175
Kishwar, Madhu 101, 105
Khalji 60
Khan, Syed Ahmad 138
Kosambi, D.D. 27, 44
Kosambi, Meera vii–viii, 111, 121, 125
Kriplani, Sucheta 133
Krishna 71–73, 108, 145–46, 155–56, 165, 179, 190
Krishnadeva Raya 70

*kuldevi* 154
Kumar, Kapil 86–87, 90
Kumar, Sunil 60–62, 74
Kunti 37–38, 176–77

Lahiri, Jhumpa 89–91
Laila-Majnu 70, 166, 171
Lakshmi 6, 20, 36, 136–37, 147, 151
Lal, Ruby 62–63, 65–66, 68–69, 74
Lalita, K. 73, 95, 98, 111, 179
Lane-Poole, Stanley 66
law 117–120, 129
Levirate 86
Liberalism 2; liberal 27–28
Lodi 60
Lorik-Chandni 70

Macaulay/Macaulay's Minute 99–100, 115
McLain, Karline 156, 159
*Madhumalati* 71
*Madhumati* 186–87, 191
*Mahabharata* 4, 21, 37–38, 113, 122, 154, 176–79
Mahamaya 51
Mahashweta Devi 89, 155
Maitreyi 41–42
Man Singh Tomar, Raja 69
*Manavdharmashastra* see *Manusmriti*
Mandodari 37
Mani, Lata 115
Manthra 36–37
Manto, Saadat Hasan 139, 141
*Manusmriti* 40, 54
Mariam Makhani 67
Mariam al-Zaman 67
marriage: age of 7, 33, 87, 107–08, 110–11, 116–18, 124, 128; and Hinduism 143, 159; and Islam 59, 174; and Partition 139–40; as dharma 113, 177; as life stage 40, 110; ceremony 107–08; devdasis' 182; experience of 5–6, 109, 111; in colonial period 76–78; in Delhi Sultanate 61–63; in Epics 38; in films 109, 185–86, 191; in Mauryan-Gupta period 48, 49; in Mughal period 65–67; in Vedic period 35; in Vijaynagara period 70; lawsuits 118–123; reforms in 81; sexuality and 176, 178; *see also* widows, *sati*
Marxism 2; Marxist 27–28
matriarchy 150
matrilateral/matrifocal 110, 122
Mazumdar, Shudha 103
medicine 77–78

*meher* 59
Meluha 29
Menon, Lakshmi 84
Menon, Ritu 139–42, 155, 159
menstruation 176
merchants 79–81
Metcalf, Barbara 71, 107, 174–75, 190
middle classes 80, 86, 88, 121, 128–29, 136, 168; and bhakti 189; and respectability 180, 188; *see also bhadralok*
Mill, James 10, 25–26, 33, 66, 97
Minault, Gail 94, 175
Mira 72–73, 108
missionaries 5, 96, 100
modernity/modernization 82–84
Mohammad, Prophet 59, 160, 164–66
Mother/mothers 16–18, 67, 89, 95–96, 103, 130, 147, 151–53, 177
Mother India 136, 153
*Mother India* (film) 192
Mukhia, Harbans 60, 65–67, 74
Mamluk see Slave Dynasty
Muhammad Quli Qutub Shah 71
Muller, Max 26, 33
Mumtaz Mahal 66
music 180, 182–84; *see also* songs, courtesans, *devdasis*
Muslim League (All India Muslim League) 138
Muslims see Islam

Naidu, Sarojini 78
Nair, Janaki 12, 23, 126
Nala 113
Nandadevi 148–49
Nandy, Ashish 2, 8
Nargis 188
Nationalism/nation 6, 153; and culture 189; and films 186–87; Hindu 33, 155–57
Nationalist Movement 6; and prostitutes 181
nationalists 5, 14, 75, 121
non-violence 54
nuns 51
Nur Jahan 69

O'Flaherty, Wendy *see* Doniger, Wendy
O'Hanlon, Rosalind 23, 68, 74, 98, 105
Oldenburg, Veena 87, 192
Olivelle, Patrick 41–42, 44, 53, 57–58
Orientalism 1, 13, 26, 33, 55; *Orientalism* 11
Ortner, Sherry 176, 192
Oudh 86–87

## Index

*Padmavat* 70–71
*Pakeezah* 186, 188, 193
Pande, Ishita 8, 120, 126
*parda* 69–70, 107, 121–24, 167–68, 170
*Paromitar ek din* 186, 193
Parsees 98
Partition of Bengal 130
Parvati 6, 20, 136, 144, 146–47, 151, 153, 157
*pativrata* 113–14, 154
Patton, Laurie 34, 44
periodisation 46
Permanent Settlement 77, 80
Pernau, Margit 81, 171–73, 175
Persian 99
Petievich, Carla 165, 174
Phule, Jyotiba 98
Phulmoni 6, 117, 119
*Pinjar* 139–40
polyandry 122
polygamy 122, 157
*prakriti* 18, 21, 145, 155–56
Premchand 86
princesses 54, 67, 73
Prophet, *see* Mohammad
puberty 182
Public culture 189
*purusa* 18.21, 145, 155–56

qawwali 165–67
Qubbat al-Islam 60
Qur'an 59, 93–94, 161–62, 165, 170, 173
Qureshi, Regula 184, 193
Qutab al din 60–62
Qutab Minar 60

Rabi'a al-Avadiyya (Rabi'a of Basra) 163–64
race 31–32
Radha (in mytholody) 6, 72, 145–46, 165, 179–80, 190
Radha (film character) 187
Raheja, Gloria 109, 112–13, 123, 126
Rajput 68–69, 115, 121–22, 132
Ram/Rama 36–37, 56, 71, 146
Ram Mohan Roy/Rammohan Roy, Raja 80, 95, 97, 115, 129
Ramabai, Pandita 101
Ramakrishna 152
*Ramayana* 4, 146, 176–77
Ramprasad 152
Rana Kumbha 69
Rani of Jhansi 136

rape 139–140, 155
*rasa* 70–71
Rashsundari Debi 95
RSS (Rashtriya Swayamsewak Sangh) 32, 134, 157
Ravana 36
Razia Sultana 62–63
Reddy, Muthulakshmi 78, 132, 181
Rehman, Waheeda 188
Richman, Paula 36–37, 44, 159
Rishiringya 177
rituals 33, 40
*Roti, kapada aur makan* 187–88
Roy, Kumkum 26–28, 42
Roy, Parama 187, 193
Roy, Tirthankar 75–76, 91
Rukhmabai 6, 117–18
Rupa Goswami 145

*Sahib, Bibi aur Ghulam* 77, 186, 193
Said, Edward 11
Sa'idi 94
saints 4; *see also* Bhakti
Saivism *see* Siva 151
Sakti/ism/Shakti 6–7, 18, 146–56
*Samkhya* 18, 21
*Samskara* 186
Sangari, Kumkum 7–8, 12, 22–23, 42, 90–91, 105, 125, 141–42, 175
Samkhya 154
Sanskrit 7, 26, 29–31, 36, 54, 78–79, 99, 115, 129, 148, 150; sources 179
Sanskritisation 79, 82
*sapinda* 113
*saqi* 166
Saraswati 73, 137, 151
Saraswati, Dayanand 101
Sarkar, Sumit 119–20, 142
Sarkar, Tanika 96, 126, 142, 157, 159
Sarla Debi 130, 136
Sarojini Devi 102
Sati 114–17, 129, 143; *mata* 115; *daha* 6, 49, 55, 107
*satyagraha* 133–34
Satyavati 38, 177–78
Savarkar, V.D. 53–54
Savitri 111–12, 177
Savitribai 98
Sax, William 148–49, 159
Sayyid 60, 160
Sayyid Ahmad Khan 94
Schimmel, Annemarie 164, 175
Sen, Amartya 80, 83, 91

Sen, Aparna 185, 193
Sen, Keshub Chandra 100
servants 88; *see devdasis*
Shabri 37
Shah Jahan (Emperor) 63, 66–67
Shah Jahan, Begum 172–73
*Sharia* 59
*sharif* 88, 168; *see also ashraf*
Shiva, Vandana 2, 20
*shramans* 47
Sita 6, 36, 56, 112, 133, 146–47, 153, 155, 157
Sitala 20
Siva/Shiva 144, 148, 151, 153; and androgynity 179, 181
*Skanda Purana* 20
Slave Dynasty 4, 60–63
slaves 60–62
Sleeman, Major General 87, 122
Smith, Vincent 10
SNDT (Smt Nathubai Damodar Thackersay) University 102
Soneji, Davesh 181, 193
songs 4, 113, 163–67, 171–72
Spivak, Gayatri 193
Sri/Shri 147; *see also* Devi, Sakti
*sringar* 70, 180
Srinivas, M.N. 79
Srinivasan, Amrit 182, 193
Subbulakshmi 183
Subra
Sultanate period 4
Sufis 4, 7, 71, 162–66, 169–70, 189–90
*Sultana's Dream* 78, 103, 122
Sur Das 72
Surya 34
*swadeshi* 130–31, 133
*swaraj* 134
Swarnakumari Debi 89, 130

Tagore, Debendranath 79
Tagore, Dwarkanath 79–80
Tagore, Rabindranath 76, 96, 124, 137, 142
Talbot, Cynthia 28, 45, 59, 70–71, 73–74
Taluqdari Revenue Settlement 86
Tarini Devi 80, 95
*Tazkirah-i- Humayun va Akbar* 65
*Teesri Kasam* 188, 193
temples 190; and dance 180–81, 191–93; and music 181–82; and nationalism 132; and Tantrism 151, 158; destruction of 60; devadasis in 49, 180–82; Devi (goddess) 150, 155; Tarini Devi in 80; royal patronage of 70;
Thapar, Romila 13–14, 24, 27–30, 32, 47–48, 58
Tharu, Susie 73, 95, 98, 111, 179, 193
terrorists 6
Theosophical Society 100
Trautman, Thomas 28, 30–31, 45
Tripathi, Amish 29
Tripura Sundari 79
Tughlaq 60
Turkhad, Anapurna 98
Turks 60–62
*Tutunama* 71

*Ulama* 161
Umrao Jan Ada 169, 171, 186–88, 193
Upanishads 35, 41–42
Urdu 172
Ushas 34

Vaid, Sudesh 7–8, 12, 22–23, 42, 90–91, 105, 125, 141–42
Vaishnavism 190; *see also* Visnu
Vanita, Ruth 61, 166, 175
Vatuk, Sylvia 112
Vaudeville, Charlotte 45, 70, 74, 145, 159
Vedantic 4
Vedas 17, 35, 101, 132:
Vedic: period 4, 13, 27, 29–30, 33, 40, 150
*Veer Zara* 193
veiling 86, 160; *see also parda*
VHP (Vishwa Hindu Parishad) 157
Victoria, Queen 75
Vidya Bai 102,
*viraha* 70
*virangana* 157
Virdi, Jyotika 184, 193
virilocal 109, 112
Visnu/Vishnu 36, 72, 144, 148, 151
Visweswaran, Kamala 135, 142, 159
virilocality 6
VHP (Vishwa Hindu Parishad) 32

Wadley, Susan 112–13, 127
Weidman, Amanda 183, 193
Weinberger-Thomas, C. 114–15, 127
widows 49, 69, 88, 101–3, 116–17, 120, 139, 171
wives 59–62, 66–69, 81, 96, 103, 121, 130, 151, 153, 171

Wilson, Horace Hyman 26
Wulff, Donna 141, 158–59

Yashodhara (wife of Sidhartha Gautam) 50
Yashodhara (foster mother of Krshna)
Yogini 151

Yudhishtir 56, 155
yogi 18

Zen un-Nissa 164
zenana 15, 163, 171–72
Zinat un-Nisa 164

Printed in the United States
by Baker & Taylor Publisher Services